Magic Mistress

A 30-year affair with Reuters

Doon Campbell

TAGMAN

The Tagman Press
London, Sydney, Los Angeles
www.tagman-press.com

First published in the year 2000 by The Tagman Press

An imprint of Tagman Worldwide Limited

Internet: www.tagman-press.com e-mail: editorial@tagman-press.com

Registered office: Falcon House, City Road, Norwich NR1 2HG, England

Also at: 1888 Century Park East, Suite 1900, Los Angeles, CA, USA 90067-1702

and 31 Denham Street, Bondi, NSW 2026, Australia

ISBN 0-9530921-2-7 (hardback) 0-9530921-3-5 (paperback)

A CIP catalogue record for this book is available from the British Library

Edited by Bridget Bagshaw

Designed by Dick Malt

Printed in the United Kingdom by MFP Design and Print

Longford Trading Estate, Thomas Street, Stretford, Manchester M32 0JT

Contents

Dedicated to the cherished memory of Mary, without whose love, patience and tolerance this memoir might never have been drafted; and to our children – Kate, Archie and Andy

Dedicated also to Pat, with love and gratitude

Introduction

The title of this personal memoir of 30 years at Reuters was inspired by a letter to *The Times* in 1968 in which Lady Jones, better known as the author and playwright Enid Bagnold, said of her late husband, Sir Roderick Jones, 'Reuters was his magic and his mistress.'

Sir Roderick was head of Reuters for 26 years. Compared with that I was a very junior officer: war or foreign correspondent 1943–52, then deputy chief news editor, news manager, deputy general manager, editor and European manager until 1973, although I didn't retire until 1975. But, like Sir Roderick, I was besotted with Reuters. It set high professional standards and practised competent clean journalism. You felt proud to be in news. It taught you to approach issues without prejudice, with detachment and with proper scepticism; to check and challenge information; to quote named sources; to make sure of facts. Accuracy and speed, in that order, became a passion as well as a discipline.

What magic, just belonging to this Everest of the news world, and to work with totally supportive colleagues – correspondents, sub-editors and technicians – of unsurpassed excellence. Magical highlights for me included covering the 1944 assault on Monte Cassino, the Italian fortress monastery towering over Allied troops and blocking their advance on Rome; being on the Normandy beaches on D-Day;

crossing the Rhine in a jeep inside a glider with the American air-borne forces; the liberation of Brussels, the capture of Hamburg, and the German surrender to Field-Marshal Montgomery; being the man from Reuters in China, getting to know men like General George Marshall during Generalissimo Chiang Kai-shek's abortive peace talks with Mao Tse-tung and Chou En-lai; covering India dur-ing the transfer of power by the last Viceroy, Earl Mountbatten of Burma, and the assassination of Mahatma (Great Soul) Gandhi; interviewing rulers and statesmen of rare stature, including Nehru, Jinnah, the Shah of Persia, Ho Chi Minh, Norodom Sihanouk, King Hussein and his grandfather, Emir Abdullah. Even my most magic encounter, meeting my wife Mary, I owed to Reuters.

And my mistress? Well, I often slept with Reuters at 85 Fleet Street all week, going home only at weekends. While I was a bachelor, Reuters was my whole life, as well as my work. Reuters could be pos-sessive, demanding, seductive, provocative, kind and cruel, madly exciting, rarely mean, often generous, tolerant, understanding and forgiving. These moods more often heightened than diminished my affection.

In the early days, it sometimes surprised me that nobody chal-lenged Reuters' claim to be 'the world's leading news agency'. It was not financially great. By the late 1990s, Reuters' annual revenue was more than £3 billion, with a profit of nearly £600 million before tax, but when I joined the total global revenue was just £580,408. The largest contribution, of £178,399, came from Asia, mainly India, which paid almost £10,000 more than Reuters' owners, the News-paper Proprietors' Association (NPA) and the Press Association (PA).

Five years later, with ownership extended to the Australian Associated Press and New Zealand Press Association, gross revenue more than doubled, to £1,370,953, but that still compared poorly with the $21,000,000 revenue of our main competitor, Associated Press of America.

In this financial climate the constant injunctions to correspondents, so often addressed to me in the 1940s, were 'watch wordage' or 'cut wordage'. That applied especially to centres which filed by cable. In the 1950s for a considerable period one of my daily chores at Head Office was to make a detailed breakdown of the incoming daily news file from cable centres. Anything over £100 a day, to cover the whole world, was excessive, and called for appropriate 'hold-down' action.

Apart from the need for economy, Reuters' administration generally showed wonderful understanding of local difficulties encountered in the field, such as censorship and the perils of autocratic bullying regimes like that of Idi Amin. Tolerance had limits, of course. Early in my career I openly challenged the wisdom of switching me from Burma to China. At the time I had a fixation that I could be with the first troops at the recovery of Singapore. Reuters ended the exchange with a peremptory cable, 'Campbell, your instructions are to go to China. Advise soonest when on the way.'

After a year or so in Chungking, I was finding life tiresome, and invited the verbal Exocet from London, 'ProCampbell. You showing unfortunate prima donnaish tendencies . . .'

From the day I started scribbling for a Scottish weekly newspaper in 1938, I became a compulsive note-taker and hoarder of information. Sixty years on it's all there: volumes of cuttings, letters, diary pages, programmes, itineraries, messages, accounts, bouquets and rockets (Reuterspeak for complimentary and critical cables).

My guru, mentor and friend, on whom this memoir largely focuses, was Walton (Tony) Cole. We went to the same school in Edinburgh, George Watson's College, and Cole preceded me on the *Evening Dispatch*, but we did not meet until he recruited me to Reuters in 1943. He became editor of Reuters in 1945, general manager (chief executive) in 1959, and he died in his office in 1963.

In the intervening 20 years, he taught me the news agency business, and ruled my life with a stream of letters, notes, cables and

telegrams, often filled with praise which seemed of an almost mawk-
ish effusiveness, but which I early became aware was just his style,
and not to be taken literally.

No doubt other Reuter colleagues had similar notes. Cole also mys-
teriously varied the mode of address in his letters. One would begin,
'My dear Doon' and end, 'Sincerely WAC', while the next was, 'Dear
Mr Campbell' and signed, 'Yours sincerely, Walton A. Cole'. In my
first few years I used to mull over every letter, wondering what these
variations meant, and whether there was more between the lines.

He, and Reuters as a whole, showed great tolerance and understanding, especially with my wordiness. Many of my bylines were
earned because the London desk improved my copy. That's why I
asked Nick Carter, one of that elite corps of rewrite men on Reuters'
central desk who so often got my despatches into print, to reduce my
memoirs to manageable size. I am most grateful to him for his skilled
surgery, then and now.

My thanks also go to Joy Law, who patiently and skilfully put
together the manuscript in its first book format with my son Andy's
supervisory guidance. The final text was judiciously edited by Bridget
Bagshaw, daughter of the late Stanley Bagshaw, editor of the *Eastern
Daily Press*, who fed Reuters a succession of distinguished journalists.

1
Born in a Manse

My life began at 5 am on 11 March 1920 in Erskine manse, Annan, a small Borders town. My father, the Reverend Archibald Angus Campbell, was then minister of the United Free Church there. My mother, Jemima (Urquhart) Campbell, died there from cholecystitis, aged only 34, when I was two and, within two months of her death, my father received a 'call' from Craigmailen United Free Church in Linlithgow, a county town between Edinburgh and Glasgow.

For the next 17 years, Craigmailen manse was my home and, like most Scottish manses, this solid square stone house was undistinguished for architecture or comfort. We were a household of four: Dad; Urquhart, my elder brother; Maggie, the housekeeper; and me. Maggie did the shopping, cooked meals, mended clothes, scrubbed floors, polished furniture, took messages at the door and quietly and efficiently managed the manse. Daughter of a gamekeeper, Maggie was brought up on hard work, had been with my grandfather for several years and had known my mother and her sister, my Aunt Nell.

If he had not been a minister, I think Dad would have been happy and successful as a farmer or factor – something involving outdoor activity. He loved country life and his main recreational interest, indeed about his only enthusiasm outside work, was fishing, particularly fly-fishing for trout. As a boy he had spent every spare hour fishing Loch Doon, hence my middle name. I never asked him if he had become a minister by choice or custom, because of an impression that he never really had a choice, and it might have troubled him to give me an honest answer. The church, after all, was not just another job; it was special, a 'calling'.

My father's stipend as a Scottish church minister never exceeded £400 a year, but on that we could keep a car and enjoy month-long holidays. He never had much money, but he always had enough for all our needs. And a little bit more. We certainly never felt poor or deprived and, in any case, materialism in Scotland in those days mattered less than education and Sunday was the most important day of the week, with two church services, Sunday school or bible class, prayers before bed, and no newspapers.

At the local school we wore jerseys that might be darned at the elbow, patched trousers and tackity boots, but that was no hardship. Darns and patches, if well done, were no badge of poverty nor anything to be ashamed of, far from it – my father was a minister (*the* minister in my eyes) and we lived at the manse. If the occasion required, I could be superior, even snobbish, about family status.

We were proud of our father – he was big and strong, always fair-minded, a man's man and a sport, respected throughout the community. Although weighing up to 16 stone (100 kg), he was well built, muscular and carried himself well. Most mornings he exercised in the bathroom with weights and dumb-bells. He lived a lot of the time alone in his study, remote from us, yet always approachable, always reassuringly there if needed.

He seldom showed emotion, yet I could feel his pleasure when I chose to give the gang a miss and accompany him on his almost ritual 3-mile walk on Saturday afternoons up the hill towards Beecraigs reservoir, where he loved a day's fishing, or Cockleroi, our local 950-ft (300 m) 'mountain', offering a panoramic sweep of the Forth valley. Sometimes we took a billy-can, lit a fire at some scenic spot and had a picnic. Sometimes we would share a turnip, which he took from a field and peeled with a penknife. Sometimes he would offer me his hand for companionship. I remember a walk on which he told me Urquhart would be taking his first job as a clerk in the Linlithgow branch of the British Linen Bank – Mr Tulloch, the manager, was an elder of Craigmailen Church.

Urquhart and I always looked forward impatiently to school holidays, which we spent with Grandfather Urquhart and Aunt Nell at Skiddaw, their home near Annan. Grandfather, described on registration papers as a 'landed proprietor', made a positive impression. Elderly with white whiskers, forceful and kind, he enjoyed spoiling us.

Aunt Nell looked after him to the end and became a surrogate mother to us. We went picnicking and swam in the Solway, fed the chickens, surreptitiously smoked cigarettes while cleaning the henhouse, helped farmers with the hay and the harvest, rode bareback on Clydesdales, walked the dogs, painted the sheds.

Aunt Nell bought us each a leather golf-bag, and a new Raleigh bicycle for £4 19s 6d (£4.97½), and heaven could never be better than cycling off for a day's golf on the championship course at Powfoot, 3 miles away. By late afternoon we were pedalling back to the house for the further treat of a cream tea, then a film at one of Annan's two cinemas and finally, in the dark, a poke of chips to eat on the walk back to Skiddaw.

I never realised how possessive Urquhart and I felt about our father until he told us one day that he would be marrying again. Although never very close, we were usually mutually protective over things that mattered and this announcement left us stunned and hostile. We saw it as an encroachment and resented the idea of sharing our cosy Craigmailen manse set-up with anyone.

Our intolerant and unreasonable initial reaction soon changed, resistance crumbled and, in the event, it was the best thing that could have happened. We realised how very lonely Dad must have been, spending hours on his own in that big gas- and candle-lit study; visiting the sick and elderly, and appearing on ceremonial platforms, always alone; slipping off to Falkirk to watch a football match, then maybe taking in a cinema; holidaying apart from us.

His marriage in 1932 to Jean Cunningham, a school-teacher from Dumfries, was good for all of us and for the church. 'Jan' transformed the manse into a home, and gave Dad the love and companionship he had missed for so many years. She made a marvellous minister's wife and stepmother.

I went to three schools: Linlithgow Academy (private), Linlithgow Public (state); and George Watson's College in Edinburgh (fee-paying), but never shone, in class or on the playing fields. It was not until at Linlithgow Public School before the 11-plus, or 'qualifying' as the exam was then known, that I became aware I was somewhat unusual in that I had only one hand. Nothing had changed. Since birth I had always had a half-empty left sleeve, but that had never mattered or had never seemed to matter. Certainly not to me. I washed and dressed myself, cut my own nails, coped adequately at table, and got Dad or Maggie to tie my bootlaces. No one ever talked about it or seemed to think it was something that needed to be talked about. It was of no consequence, almost an irrelevance.

Then suddenly at school it seemed to make a difference. When classmates tried to be nasty, they called me 'broken-arm Campbell'. I could always give as good as I got. On reflection, however, I thought how ignorant, how stupid can they be? I had never broken my arm. (Not then, anyway; during the war when my jeep catapulted off a German bridge into a river, I cabled Reuters, 'Jeep probably write-off and arm – happily left – smashed two places.')

Anyway there, aged about nine or ten, in the rough and tumble of school playground scrimmage, in which I was invariably an active and leading participant, I had a moment of truth. But it was so unimportant I didn't even mention it to Dad or Maggie.

I was never considered for rugby or cricket and my enthusiasm for golf exceeded my prowess, but being keenly bid for in swimming team races made up for a lot. My scholastic record was unimpressive. My Highers examination results in 1938 included passes in English and history, with lower grades in Latin and French. The head's academic assessment: 'Not exactly setting the heather on fire.'

Golf had become an obsession and every evening, dodging a garden draft as often as possible, I would be playing Linlithgow's nine-hole course. The club had a wide and active membership, and it tickled me to have my name on the board as Honorary Secretary.

There was no ultimatum to leave the manse, nothing like that, not even any question of a time-scale to find work. But something urgent would have to be done, if only to get access to a little money.

One day I was told that Mr K was coming to supper at the manse on Sunday and I should be there. Mr K came to church and had business interests in Edinburgh. Alarm bells rang. I'd better move fast to ensure independence. I had no idea what I wanted to do, or could do. War seemed only months away and time was running out.

Unlike colleagues who joined newspapers with a sense of vocation, who sought excitement and adventure, who stumbled in or were pushed, I escaped into journalism. I had no ambition or motivation to do anything, lacked aptitude and qualification, but the prospect of being fitted into a safe slot pen-pushing by day and swotting at night to climb an insurance ladder was an anathema.

I applied for several jobs advertised in Edinburgh papers, lined up interviews; then realised my half-empty sleeve was causing blockage. Time and again prospective employers took a quick look, saw a hand missing and fumbled for a formula to get off the hook. Not one would come clean and just say straight, 'Sorry, we didn't realise – afraid you're not suitable.' Instead they would waffle on about prospects, the firm's potential, anything to suggest genuine interest before the inevitable bottom line, 'We'll let you know.' They never did.

So I went along the High Street to the *Linlithgowshire Gazette* and asked Willie Raitt, the local reporter, if he could use an assistant. Willie had a flair for news, was invariably bubbling to impart it, always in a hurry, always on the way to or from 'a good story'.

Within a week, I became an active contributor with a feature article on the history of fox-hunting in Linlithgow. Within a year I had launched a weekly golf column, modestly signed 'Albatross' (three under par), found I had no writing style but could get things into the papers, built up lineage (news items sold to other papers and paid on a basis of lines published) and had the occasional scoop. I revelled in it.

In September 1939, just after Britain declared war on Nazi Germany, I was poached by the rival weekly, the *West Lothian Courier*, and appointed their representative in Broxburn, a town ringed by copper-coloured shale bings, unsightly memorials to Scotland's first oil age, once known as 'Shaleopolis'.

The pay was £2 a week, and the 'office' was not much more than a hole in the wall, with a counter on which to lean while counting words to work out the cost of birth, death and marriage notices.

With the office came Pegs and her bicycle. Pegs scrubbed the floor, cleaned and dusted the office every morning, cycled home for 'denner' at midday, and reappeared in a crisp clean frock as the office secretary/clerical assistant/messenger/adverts rep/general factotum. She was paid 15s (75p) a week which, like my pay, came out of the till, providing it contained enough money.

My job meant writing three to five broadsheet columns of news weekly, chasing display ads for the *Courier*, and organising the weekly sale of 80 to 100 dozen copies of the paper.

I was also responsible for South Queensferry, a sprawl of grey pebble-dash houses hugging the hillside down to the river at the south end of the Forth railway bridge, 3 miles from Broxburn. I went there twice a week by bus, or on Pegs's bike (saving twopence on the bus).

A month after the war began, I had my baptism of war reporting in my own backyard. It taught me a lesson that later proved valuable time and again in Europe, the Middle East and Asia: take a calculated risk on timing but always be sure of your communications. On 20 October the mid-morning hum of Broxburn main street was broken by air raid sirens at the 'Ferry. German aircraft were reported over the Forth Bridge and the nearby naval dockyard at Rosyth.

Speed was of the essence. Pegs said I could have her cycle and, with no traffic to choke the narrow lanes, I made good time through Kirkliston, a halfway village which had a public telephone, and acknowledged the bike's defective brakes by getting off at the top of The Loan, a wickedly steep brae running down through South Queensferry to the water's edge.

On the way, the locals said, 'Aye, ther's bin a raid on the bridge awright.' No, they hadn't seen German aircraft but someone they knew had spotted them. Later the first citizen, Provost Peter Walker, told me he had heard shots; another man had seen a swastika on the tail of a plane being pursued by three Spitfires.

I headed for the Hawes Inn, a historic watering-hole almost directly under the bridge where Robert Louis Stevenson drafted *Kidnapped*. Outside, heavy-coated reporters, who had raced there from Edinburgh and Glasgow, were downing pints, scanning the sky with field-glasses or scribbling in notebooks as I approached. They looked such seasoned news-hounds, so professional, that I kept a respectful distance. In fact they were stymied.

In those early days of the war, the authorities pre-empted the use of public telephones in the immediate area of an alert. So these big byliners could not contact or be contacted by their offices and were reluctant to leave in case the raiders returned. Suppose a dive-bomber scored a direct hit on that immense structure of steel girders and cantilevers soaring 350 ft (100 m) above the water? They just could not afford to miss that story, that picture.

I had no such qualms. A deadline didn't arise. I decided to risk missing any later developments and head back to Kirkliston. There the public telephone was working normally. One after another I called the Edinburgh and Glasgow papers.

'Campbell of the *West Lothian Courier* calling from Kirkliston. I've just come from the Forth Bridge, do you want any copy?'

The response was always the same, 'We have our own reporters there but nothing's come in yet . . . let's have what you've got.' So I made a month's money in an afternoon, doubled the rate to Pegs for borrowing her bike, saw my first live war coverage in the daily papers and, more important, strengthened my contact with those other papers, especially the Edinburgh *Evening Dispatch*.

By 1941, despite a ten-shillings-a-week (50p) pay rise, I had two targets: to try wearing an artificial arm and to move on from the *Courier*. I had mixed feelings about the former – you don't miss something you've never had – but for cosmetic reasons I paid out the large sum of £21 and acquired 'George'. It took a bit of getting used to; I'd wear it for a couple of days, then revert to the more comfortable empty sleeve.

So in June that year I wore it to call on D. L. Glen, chief reporter at the *Evening Dispatch*, in *The Scotsman* building, dominating North Bridge, Edinburgh. The interview went well, and I was offered a reporting staff job at a salary of £180 a year plus a war bonus of £15. The follow-up letter added, 'It is understood that the appointment is temporary in the sense that it terminates when our permanent staff return from the war.'

The *Dispatch* had authority and fire, and a breezy content. Its newsroom was about as good a nursery for crash courses in journalism as Scotland could offer. It had several crackerjack newsmen. The best reporter was Bobby Leishman, whose beat was the top serials (continuing stories) including the City Chambers. A competent hardworking no-nonsense reporter, he could turn his hand to anything and dictate ready-to-print copy, with the right lead and a masterly condensation of essential points, direct from his shorthand notes. He was strong on discipline and morality and I could not have had a better mentor.

Out of the same mould was the chief sub-editor, Don Elliot, a bustling bundle of demonic energy. Outside the office, Leishman and Elliot were good colleagues, caring and considerate. Elliot represented the National Union of Journalists at its best, concerned about standards and principles no less than wages; and under his guidance I was for two years roped in as Edinburgh branch secretary of the NUJ. Initiative and enterprise were encouraged – and rewarded.

A character trait which persisted throughout my life surfaced about this time: a crippling social shyness and awkwardness became transformed on duty into an assertive, even pushy manner. The bigger the man, or the name, the more eager I was to find out what he was really like. I got interviews with Ivor Novello, the perfumed darling of the British theatre, when he was playing the lead in his hit musical, *The Dancing Years*, and with the American Ambassador John D. Winant when he came to collect an honorary degree.

I was doing well, and loved it. I liked to be first in and last out of the office; to surprise the doorman by turning up on a Saturday or Sunday; to volunteer for extra, or what are now called anti-social hours. I was ready for the next step.

Everyone at the *Dispatch* knew or had heard the folklore about Tony Cole, who had gone from the *Dispatch* to Fleet Street and later taken another colleague, Jim (Haig) Nicholson, to join him at Reuters. I did not then know how important Cole was to be in my life, but regarded him as a precursor to be emulated.

Tony Cole had also gone to George Watson's College, but had left at 15, his imagination fired with the desire to be a reporter. He had already learned some shorthand and had submitted occasional sports reports to the Edinburgh papers, so he got hired as a copy-boy, was promoted to telephone copy-taker, and was soon noted for his genuinely sceptical intelligence, his nose for news and his keenness to beat the rival *Evening News*.

Impatient for greater experience, in 1929 he moved 20 miles to Falkirk for a job as a reporter on the weekly *Falkirk Herald*, where he was regarded as 'an animated question-mark', according to his colleague Brendan Kemmett, later news editor of the *Daily Express*. Cole regarded his six years there as among the most formative and rewarding of his career. Falkirk was also the place where he met Janet Clingan, later to become his wife. By the time he was 23, Cole was confident enough to head for Fleet Street and take up a precarious life as a freelance, selling news items mostly to the domestic news agency, the Press Association (PA).

Soon after he arrived, he was among reporters trying to get an interview with Ramsay MacDonald, as the old Scottish politician was about to catch a train, at the time of his Labour Government's collapse in the 1931 economic crisis. Impatiently, the Prime Minister waved the reporters away. They all went, except Cole, who blurted out, 'Mr MacDonald, I'm a young Scot just arrived in London, and you know how important it is to do well at the start.'

'I'm a tired man,' MacDonald replied.

That was his only statement, but Cole built it up into a story that implied what was in fact true: that Ramsay MacDonald, politically, was played out.

He followed this up with a beat on the first non-stop run of the Flying Scotsman, by getting his story out before the train even arrived at its destination. There was a tunnel that enabled engine drivers to walk through the tender to take control of the train. Cole went through, picked up a piece of coal, wrapped his news-story around it, with a message asking the finder to phone it to the PA, and threw it on a station platform as the express thundered through. It was found and phoned in.

Soon Cole joined the PA staff at 85 Fleet Street as a reporter. Two years later he was deputy news editor, then day supervising editor, then night editor with executive responsibility for maintaining the news service through the blitz. At this time he was poached to head Reuters' editorial by Reuters' general manager (chief executive), Christopher Chancellor, who boasted to a Royal Commission on the Press, 'In its worldwide operations, Reuters has taken a leading place in promoting the concepts of truth in news, the independence and integrity of news services and freedom of news distribution in the international field.'

In 1943 I knew only as much about Reuters as the average reader of any newspaper publishing foreign news: it was the label at the end of an overseas news item. It must be big, important, prestigious, for no one ever seemed to challenge the accuracy of news from that source. But that was about it.

Nevertheless, I used to imagine meeting Cole, rehearsing the impression I'd convey, the sort of conversation we might have. It would of course be a brief encounter because I was only a junior reporter. I might say, 'Heard a lot about you, sir.' No, not 'sir' – too sycophantic, brown tongued. Just say, 'Mr Cole.' Keep George out of sight.

One afternoon early in 1943 it happened, almost as I had imagined it. I was short of time to get a story into the last edition and had to check a detail with Don Elliot. I barged into the subs' room and there, sitting next to Don, his bulk spilling over a typist's swivel chair, was a massive man with rimless glasses and a moustache. In sheer size and facial appearance he could have been King Farouk.

'Doon, meet Mr Cole of Reuters,' said Don.

Cole heaved himself up and held out his hand. It felt soft and pudgy.

'I've heard a lot about you, Mr Cole.'

'And I've heard a bit about you,' said Cole. He mentioned a story in the previous day's *Dispatch*. 'You did that – didn't you? I liked it.'

'Sorry,' I heard the idiot in me saying, 'I've only a couple of minutes to catch the paper. Please excuse me. Nice to meet you.'

Cole said he understood. I just made the last edition. Then it dawned; I had blown it. After my studious rehearsals, I had fluffed the heaven-sent opportunity to meet and chat and maybe even register with the big man from Fleet Street for the sake of one totally inconsequential news item. That night I scoured the shelves of the Edinburgh libraries for anything on Reuters. There wasn't much, but it was enough to torture me for having missed the boat.

Next day Don Elliot asked if I'd ever thought of trying for Reuters. But what could I offer such an organisation? I was tolerably well regarded by *The Scotsman* Publications, but wasn't that just because the war had stripped out its editorial core? Was I really any good?

An objective stocktaking: I was 22, with no knowledge of life outside Scotland, no university or school of journalism training, no languages, imperfect shorthand. I never regarded myself as a writer. I'd have given anything to possess the talent of James Cameron of the *News Chronicle*, and dismissed it as guff when David Glen, who handled my copy for two years, said I had 'an attractive literary style'.

But I could get copy into print. Success in that direction came easily. I knew what papers wanted. I had immense enthusiasm, an obsessive interest in newspapers and magazines, a gut sense of news. Over the telephone I could dictate instant leads from press conferences, political meetings, courts. I felt sure of myself on practically any story – after a fiasco on an earlier story I had enrolled myself for night classes in the Isaac Pitman shorthand class – and knew I could beat most of the local competition with hard news.

I told Don I was definitely interested. He suggested that I write at once to Cole. On 9 March I wrote, 'I offer myself for an editorial appointment with Reuters . . . I am totally exempt from call-up [the services did not want me], have no domestic ties, am prepared to tackle any job, go anywhere.'

On 11 March Cole replied, offering me a job:

It is for you to decide whether the potential opportunity it offers to someone like yourself who 'is prepared to tackle any job and go anywhere' exceeds the current security and comfortable remuneration of Edinburgh . . . Salary £350 a year, one month's notice on either side. I have no doubt that . . . you will make a career for yourself in Reuters and become one of the first-flight men in the team . . .

My immediate reaction to his repetition of my 'go anywhere' offer was that I must have all my teeth out. I was supposed to have 'chalky' as distinct from 'bony' teeth, and though the disintegration at the back of my mouth had not yet spread to the front, I had suffered toothache all my life. Imagine that happening when I was out of reach of a good Edinburgh dentist! I asked for a total extraction with immediate replacement by dentures.

I had arranged the extraction for a Thursday afternoon, after work, and the following Monday was an off-day. On Tuesday I was back in the office with a mouthful of new teeth. The problem was keeping them in. No chemist then seemed to have heard of fixatives, so for a day or two I feigned mouth infection and as far as possible avoided conversation. My landlady knew the truth, but the exercise in concealment extended throughout the *Dispatch*.

Such was the robust structure of these teeth that they saw me through war in Europe, Burma, India and China. There were a few embarrassing moments; when they bounced off the platform at New Delhi railway station; broke one morning when I was flying to Madrid to lunch with the Spanish political firebrand Manuel Fraga Iribarne; and again in a San Francisco hotel lavatory, when I could see the upper denture, in two pieces, resting between the splayed boots of a man enthroned in the next cubicle. But that dental decision, taken impulsively, spared me many hours of pain and sleeplessness.

I was now equipped to 'go anywhere', if only for a start, to London.

2
London – and Reuters

I was told to report for duty at Reuters at 4.30 pm on Monday 3 May 'for evening duty under Mr S. Mason, the night editor'. Cole's letter surprisingly added, 'Let me know your plans that day – we might have lunch together.'

The evening before, after arriving in London, I paced up and down Fleet Street, past *The Daily Telegraph* and *Daily Express*, staring at the big Portland stone building which housed Reuters. Under cover of darkness, almost afraid of detection, I lingered outside the swing doors, watching men and women going in and out. It was disappointing, a let-down, to see they looked so normal.

Over lunch at the Reform Club next day I accepted Cole's job description, 'trainee sub-editor to qualify as war correspondent', though I loathed subbing and wondered why he kept on about it taking two years on the desk in London to pick up the Reuter technique. I had never known exactly what a sub is meant to do, beyond checking and challenging – names, sources, spelling and grammar; cutting copy to size and putting headlines and captions on it.

At Reuters I was to learn that a sub could turn a staccato, cryptic cable or pedantic recital of facts into a readable, even rivetting news splash, or a copybook agency despatch into purple prose fit only for strident tabloids. For ten years as a Reuter correspondent I was blessed with rewriting by such craftsmen as Hubert Nicholson, who looked like Pan, wrote well received poetry and novels, but for five days a week produced the roundups and leads of Reuters' top stories.

Besides masterminding the news service, Cole was a one-man staff department. He directed me to Gowing's Private Hotel, at 24 Coram Street – 'comfortable and conveniently near the office' – which charged an affordable £5 a week for bed and breakfast (served in the basement below the pavement, where guests also assembled when bombs fell).

Tucked into one of the small rather seedy Bloomsbury streets behind the grander Russell Hotel, Gowing's was respectable. Impropriety, if it happened, was discreet. But Soho had nothing on the peep shows behind the uncurtained windows of a hostelry across the street. American and other servicemen came by taxi, or with tarts picked up from Southampton Row, and exhibited their virility in a manner foreign to the standards of the Linlithgow manse.

Accompanying Cole into the Reuter newsroom that first day, I was sweating with nervousness. From the moment I entered the building I was impressed by everything – the marble reception hall, the lifts, the machines, the personalities and, most of all, just the standing and prestige of Reuters and belonging, actually being a part of the 'world's leading news agency'.

At the heart of the operation was the general desk, a row of tables slotted together in a line, with a dozen sub-editors facing inwards along each side. At its head sat the night editor, Sidney J. Mason, the operational boss from 4.30 pm till after midnight. On his left was the 'copytaster', Muriel Penn, who made the selection from incoming news copy and handed stories out for editing.

'Sit down, cock,' said Mason, indicating an upturned wastepaper bin at his side. It was my seat for the next three days.

I had never met anyone like Mason, known to everyone as 'Sid'. A tough explosive little cor blimey cockney, he wore belt and braces and worked in shirt-sleeves rolled up to the elbow. He talked fast, liberally lacing his colourful language with unprintable words. I couldn't understand half of what he said, but he had a magical charm, and a reputation as master of his craft.

He gulped facts at a glance and gutted long communiqués while dictating direct to a teleprinter operator, thereby saving seconds if not minutes on the time to get the story round the world. At any moment he would be guiding one sub on how to handle the latest copy from a Pacific or European war-zone, bawling out another for missing the lead point in a yard-long despatch, pencil-subbing a third story himself, shouting for library background to flesh out a 'flash' or 'snap'. His telephones never stopped ringing, and he never stopped bobbing up and down. It was a virtuoso performance.

Next to Sid, a hard-driving hard-swearing self-taught human dynamo, sat Muriel Penn, a bespectacled lady who spoke quietly, in a sort of cultured drawl. She was university-educated, a linguist, a woman of formidable intellect and physique, and fearsomely professional. Between them was a touching bond, based on mutual trust and commitment to news.

The furious pace at which they worked spilled over with diminishing intensity down the desk. In reserved seats within easy reach and chatting distance was a small coterie of senior men, Glaswegians Charlie Wighton and Willie Stein among them, then the other subs distanced down the desk according to merit or favour, with the rookies and trainees jostling for places at the bottom.

Sid Mason must have thought Reuters was scraping the bottom of the barrel when he was lumbered with me. From my privileged seat next to him, where I had not really a clue what was going on, I was soon relegated to the bottom of the desk, there to experience the discipline, drudgery and frustration felt by every trainee sub.

Activity reflected desk positioning: fast lane at one end, pedestrian crawl at the other. Sitting largely ignored, reading and re-reading the clipboard files of copy issued in the previous news cycle, one felt psychologically unnerved by inaction amid such frantic activity.

The dribble of messages that eventually percolated down seemed a mockery of effort for an eight-hour shift. Each had to be processed and retyped, even if it meant altering only a few words, such as making the verb active instead of passive. Then the finished product was discarded on the spike more often than sent out on the teleprinter to subscribers.

One night Muriel Penn called, 'Campbell!'

'Recognition at last,' I thought, rushing to her side.

'A paragraph on that,' she said dismissively. 'That' was 300 words announcing the death of President Lin Sen, head of the Chinese National Government. One paragraph – maybe 50 words – for Reuters on the death of such a man could be written only one way: straight, without bias or slant, without looking for angles that did not exist in the original cable. I took only a few minutes to produce my version and put it in Muriel's tray:

President Lin Sen, head of the Chinese National Government, died here today, aged 81. Born in Foochow and educated in the United States, Lin Sen joined Dr Sun Yat-sen soon after the 1911 revolution, held several high Kuomintang offices and became President in 1932. Generalissimo Chiang Kai-shek has been appointed Acting President.

After 20 minutes, the summons was peremptory, 'Campbell!' She thrust my story back.

'Do it again – turn it round.'

I retreated, uncertain, on a slow boil. No good belting it out straight away – that would look too cavalier, lacking serious purpose. It was 15 minutes before I took the slightly recast version back to her in-tray.

Another half-hour, then again, even louder, more strident and

21

impatient, '*Campbell!*' By this time the desk was becoming aware of my movements, curious to know what it was all about. Was this gauche Scot about to be stripped of his last vestige of professional dignity? From her seat of power Muriel raised weary eyes to me, standing over her, 'Campbell, did anyone ever teach you anything about journalism?'

'Yes, Miss Penn.'

'Well, take it away, you can do better than that.'

The third version was without one substantive change from the first, but it got through and President Lin Sen's death went out in the Reuter service, almost two hours after the news came in. I felt sick. Speed, we were forever being reminded, was second only to accuracy in handling Reuter news.

What was this all about? It was not an isolated episode. Sure, I was still very much an apprentice or trainee on the Reuter desk with a lot to learn. But had I not been earning a living for five years on reputable Scottish newspapers, handling anything and everything, seeing my stories in print, winning bonuses for features and story ideas? Yet here I was being made to look like an idiot, incompetent and utterly inept.

I came very close to chucking the copy at Muriel, shouting, 'Stuff it!' and storming out. Instead I curbed my feelings and accepted Cole's invitation to lunch.

Tony Cole was used to bleats. I saw that as soon as I started my moan. 'Sure,' he said, I was right to react, but Muriel was a first-class desk editor and you had to weigh a lapse, especially a very occasional lapse, against overall performance.

'I told you it would be hell,' said Cole. 'Stick it, your chance will come.'

So it was back to the desk chores: reading-in on the last news cycle, decoding or unscrambling cables. Correspondents in those days of financial tightness had to save words by using 'cablese', which meant omitting 'the', 'a', and prepositions, and creating single words by such devices as turning 'keep up' into 'upkeep' and 'hold down' into 'downhold', or writing 'Londonwarded' instead of 'left for London'. Too often these economies were taken to excess; some reporters were so creative they were incomprehensible. Subs had also to cope with the imperfect English of some 'stringers', the part-time correspondents in less important news centres.

The nightly routine was relieved only by stained mugs of pencil-stirred tea or coffee, and Mary Coules's cookies and cakes. Mary was a senior sub, one of a handful of committed women at Reuters. Apart from her and Muriel, there was Joy Millner, who could hold her own with any man on the desk and went on to the *Christian Science Monitor*, and Olga Bolz, a Russian expert who brought a touch of glamour, with exotic earrings and a long cigarette holder. Olga worked on the desk 12 hours a day from D-Day up to the seventh month of her pregnancy, and called the baby Timothy, after General Semyon Timoshenko, commander in one of the Russians' first major victories. Sadly Olga died from tuberculosis shortly after giving birth.

Another Olga and another kindred spirit in those days was Olga Franklin, later to become a well known author and Fleet Street journalist, who at that time divided her journalistic efforts between 85 Fleet Street and the Reuter radio-monitoring station in two attic rooms of a coachhouse in the London suburb of Barnet. By 1943 some 800,000 words a day were being appraised by up to 29 Barnet listeners, and an average of 10,000 to 12,000 found their way into the outgoing news report. With the end of the war, voicecast listening was cut drastically, and in 1953 was transferred to Green End in Hertfordshire, 30 miles north of London.

I felt Cole's idea of giving me a gradual indoctrination was a negative exercise. And then I botched the death of Dr Dafoe, the Canadian who brought the Dionne quintuplets into the world in 1938. Instead of leading with that phrase, I chose a dreary recital about his place of birth, age and biographical detail – material that belonged down column. Next day, came Cole's inevitable inquest: why was Reuter late? Who had made a hash of the lead? Cole never missed a trick.

One night Sid yelled, 'Campbell! Tee-dome background – fast.'

What did he say? What was he talking about? What was Tee-dome? I had never heard of it. The library downstairs would know, but the chief librarian, Clodagh O'Grady, was another *femme formidable* who, with a scathing word, could shrink to wimp size the toughest trainee or posturing writer who went to the library uncertain of what he wanted.

I hadn't a clue what I wanted, but I heard a sub mention oil and, adopting the only possible tactics for such a confrontation, I barged into the library and shouted, 'Tee-dome oil, at once!' Within seconds, Clodagh handed over a bulky file on the 1922 American Teapot Dome oil scandal, which involved bribery, criminal conspiracy, and the imprisonment of a US Interior Secretary for improperly and secretly granting exclusive rights to the Wyoming oil reserves. I rushed the file to Sid, having successfully concealed my ignorance.

His own previous acquaintance with the story may have come from a stint on the *Financial Times* earlier in his 43 years in Fleet Street. He had an encyclopaedic memory and, though his knowledge was often superficial, its range was wide. He did, however, claim to speak with some authority on archaeology, weaponry and chess, as well as on news itself.

Cole was the only administrative boss to appear regularly within the orbit of the night desk. Eyes followed him intently as he hove to. Who would be the victim? I was twice.

The first time he came up and leant over, arm on my shoulder, 'How's your shorthand?'

'Rusty,' I said. A hundred words a minute was hardly something to shout about.

24

'OK, fine, come with me,' said Cole, and led me to his distant and carpeted corner.

'What's happening?' I asked.

'Churchill's broadcasting from Canada on the anniversary of the Home Guard and I want you to take the check note.'

It seemed an awesome responsibility. My confidence was not boosted by the appearance of four sober-suited men from our House of Commons shorthand reporting team, led by one in a black jacket.

'They'll do the takes [spells of three to four minutes each] to get Churchill on the wire while he's still speaking,' said Cole. 'You do the full text.'

Churchill was not a fast speaker. I might manage a near-verbatim note of a short speech. But radio reception that night was awful – the voice roared, faded, garbled. I kept scribbling. When the broadcast was over, black jacket sought confirmation of two or three faint passages. I had them.

'Well done, son,' said Cole. 'Great help.'

The second time Cole's shadow enveloped me was one Friday afternoon, when two accumulated days off meant the pleasant prospect of a break until Wednesday. The build-up was carbon-copy: the big man in the zip-fronted golfing blouson walking purposefully down the length of the newsroom, everyone watching his approach. The arm came over my shoulder. 'Know anything about science, old boy?'

'Nothing. Failed it in Highers.'

'Okay, old boy. Fine. Like you to become our science correspondent. Need 1,000 words by Wednesday.'

Science was the umbrella heading for chemistry and physics at George Watson's College. I couldn't stand it, much less understand it. But now I was Reuters' science correspondent. Where to start?

On Saturday morning, I was at W. H. Smith's for an armful of popular science magazines and some more learned journals. Hours were spent fruitlessly scanning this pile without the emergence of anything remotely likely to provide a meaningful lead. I spent more hours in local libraries. Then on Saturday evening, looking through a telephone directory, I saw an Agricultural Research Station outside London. With simulated authority, I phoned and asked for the director.

'My name is Campbell,' I said. 'I am Reuters' science correspondent and I would like an update on your latest activities.'

The director, clearly gratified that his work was claiming the attention of the worldwide Reuters, invited me to lunch next day. He met me at the station in his car and for two hours we traipsed round pigsties, sheep-pens and byres, while he took me through a series of incomprehensible experiments and tests concerning swine fever, bovine tuberculosis and a host of other even less familiar diseases.

I filled two notebooks with hieroglyphics – inventing shorthand outlines when necessary – while mouthing appropriate remarks, 'How very interesting . . . Now, is this innovative for your establishment? . . . And what about funds – are you adequately covered for such an impressive catalogue of activities?' We shook hands, exchanged cards, agreed to keep in touch. The director seemed anxious to keep open this important channel for disseminating information.

Back in the hotel at Coram Street, I turned the pages of my notebooks: utterly useless, a wasted day. The deadline – tyranny of the hack, deep psychological need of the successful journalist – was approaching. Should I come clean, tell Cole I had failed? Had he not heard when I said I knew nothing about science? Was he deaf?

Cole had heard all right, but to him any reporter worth the name was capable of any assignment. 'Impossible' did not exist in his journalistic vocabulary.

Next morning, Monday, miserable from inability to find a lead line for my debut as Reuters' science correspondent, I saw in an early edition of the *Evening Standard* a diary brief about a 'miracle healer' on the Sicilian battlefield. I tracked the source, a government ministry, and telephoned its press department.

A woman answered, 'Is that Doon Campbell?'

She had been a good news contact at St Andrew's House, the Scottish Office in Edinburgh. This item in the *Standard* was the only publication the handout had had.

'Come round and I'll give you a load of copy,' she said.

The story began:

The distillate of a deadly fungus is a miracle healer of the Sicilian battlefields. The wonder drug is penicillin, an extract from penicillium mould. A team of British specialists recently flew to Sicily to experiment with the drug in forward positions and at base hospitals. It has now returned with glowing reports of its curative properties. American doctors are also reporting remarkable successes . . .

So, four months after joining Reuters, I had my first byline: by Doon Campbell, Reuters' science correspondent. Cole, who made it his business to read every new service, scrawled, 'Damned interesting article. Thanks. You're on right lines.' From that moment, I had to supply British, North and South American markets with a weekly science feature. Cole's weekly appraisal, critical or complimentary, meant far more to me than money. But the continuing drudgery of normal subbing duties on the night desk, still confined to fillers and hardly nibbling big stories, made change imperative. I got it by volunteering for the 'death watch' from about 11 pm until 7.30 or 8 am.

Although Reuters handles news round the clock, in London the pressure eased overnight. A B-team of three or at most four subs, including the editor-in-charge, took over the desk. The editor then was often Michael Fry, a stylish and donnish young American with a deceptively casual attitude to work, and a laconic way of speaking.

At about midnight, after a prolonged 'read-in' on the news clips, Michael allotted the main continuing stories among his staff, then swivelled his chair round and joined one or two teleprinter operators in a relaxed game of chess. This meant that sub-editors like myself, instead of handling squibs or tiddlers, could get their teeth into the big running serial stories.

I always bid for the Russian front, finding it somehow tidier and less diffuse than the Pacific and more exciting than Europe. Writing these roundups involved poring over maps, plotting positions and digesting copy from several sources: our Moscow correspondent Harold King, the Soviet news agency Tass, the Foreign Office (discreetly), the BBC's radio listening service at Caversham and our own monitoring sources listening to Moscow Radio, and a score of national news agencies – Finnish, Polish, etc. – which tried to keep close to Soviet affairs.

I particularly recall the Russians thrusting towards the River Dniester, which involved us in close study of the maps in the editorial, as we received successive reports of the Russians 'approaching' the river, 'nearing' it, 'within heavy artillery range' of it, 'overlooking' it, then, memorably, a despatch from King describing 'brave Cossack cavalrymen watering their horses in the Dniester'. We drained our stained tea-mugs in salute to a classic piece of reporting, its eloquence of expression and elegance of subterfuge in getting a significant if not historic military gain through the Soviet censor.

Harold King wrote later:

The censor, a very sympathetic lady, did not spot the implication but wide-awake sub-editors in London did. Hundreds of newspapers in Europe and the Middle East changed their front-page headlines to 'Red Army in Poland', and Reuters had a big success.

Vishinsky, evil star of the purge trials in 1935/37, was then number two to Foreign Minister Molotov. He had intended, we learned, to hold a special press conference, making it clear no doubt that the territory the Red Army was now advancing across was part of the Soviet Union and not part of the future Poland. But he never held the planned press conference. Reuters had stolen his thunder. He wasn't at all pleased.

Now, gradually I began to adjust to the Reuter editorial mould, to feel a rapport with desk colleagues and seniors. Outside the news-room, in the old Press Club or the Punch or Old Bell, Sid and Muriel became human. I respected and admired them both. Even that elu-sive 'Reuter technique', which Tony Cole kept reminding me I would need at least two years to master, lost its mystery. Recognition of 'lead' news became instinctive, a habit.

Reuters stood above all else for accuracy, then speed in handling and distributing news. It needed clear crisp unambiguous writing, and sources for facts and statements. Who said that? Where, when, in what circumstances? In a speech? Answering a question? What was the question? Who asked it? Content was important. So was balance. We knew that.

What was not always apparent on the desk was the financial strait-jacket imposed by having gross revenue of only £580,000. It was probably most visible in the unremitting vigilance over cable costs. Word-counting once again became part of my routine.

Another symptom was the sparing, even hesitant way in which cor-respondents were sent overseas. It was brought home to me as much as anything by Cole's reply when I asked if we were really getting rid of a certain European correspondent.

'Yes, the man's not up to it,' he said, 'and besides, he's costing us over £900 p.a.'

3
'What about another chukka?'

Italy's surrender was announced on 8 September 1943, as Allied troops invaded the south of the mainland at Salerno and Taranto. On 28 September, a shell fired from a German half-track at Scafati near Salerno killed three British war correspondents, Stewart Sale of Reuters among them.

Cole sent for me. He was about to work the Reuter magic on me. Reuters, he said, had decided to take a chance and send me to Italy as war correspondent. My name had already been passed to the War Office for acceptance and accreditation. I would have to submit to a 'tough' War Office medical examination.

'You will be in Italy until the end of the campaign,' said Cole. 'We don't expect much from you, but try to be competitive with communiqués and briefings. Remember home-towners and good eyewitness stuff from the front. Watch McMillan. We expect the main action – the big news – soon to be elsewhere.'

He meant the Italian campaign was going down-page, and the news spotlight would switch to the Second Front in France, still eight months away, but much in the minds of editorial planners. Although not fully trained, I was felt to be adequate for the declining story in Italy.

By 'home-towners' he meant quotes from servicemen, together with their full names and street addresses. Local and regional papers always used these, with the all-important Reuter credit. The 'McMillan' to whom he referred was Richard McMillan, star war correspondent of United Press and its British subsidiary BUP, whose copy frequently appeared in British papers in preference to Reuters.

My salary, Cole added, would go up from £350 to £500 plus 30s (£1.50) a day living allowance. I had a £75 kit allowance, which went a long way at Moss Bros towards a tailored gaberdine uniform with green cloth shoulder-tabs bearing the words 'WAR CORRESPON-DENT' in gold letters. The label, abbreviated to 'WC', was also worn as a badge on caps and berets.

A colleague told me there was a store in the Reuter basement where I could lay my hands on supplemental kit, free. Sure enough, there I found a sleeping-bag and a brand new 'British warm' great-coat. The coat had been bought by a prospective war correspondent who for some reason never got his British war correspondent's licence. Worn through several wars and insurrections, and used as a blanket in Kashmir and Jerusalem, that British warm still retained its shape and usefulness half a century later.

My war correspondent's licence came through by mid-November, certifying among other things that I was 'authorised to follow the Armed Forces of the Crown, and . . . entitled in the event of capture by the enemy to be treated as a Prisoner of War under the provisions of Article 81 of the International Convention relative to the treat-ment of Prisoners of War. For the purposes of such treatment this sta-tus is equivalent to that of an officer in the British Army with the rank of Captain.'

'What a break,' I thought. 'What a God-given break!' The magic of Reuters and Cole filled my head, as is clear from a letter home, written on 18 November 1943:

For your private information the sked [schedule] *is that I'm leaving by air for Lisbon Saturday or Sunday. I may be there for one day or seven, then on to AFHQ at Algiers for short spell before a hop to Italy. I'll be with the American Fifth Army* *– taking the place of Stewart Sale, Reuter correspondent, killed along with a couple of other good blokes a few weeks back. It's a terrific break. Most anxious moment was the War Office medical. But the quack hardly seemed to notice* George *– just asked if I could swim and type. Against 'distinctive marks' in my licence 'nil' has been entered. Great stuff. One great advantage – I'm going with Sid Mason's blessing. 'You're* OK,' *Sid said the other day, 'you've come through the right school and your assignment has my complete approval.' Sid is a little Cockney senior editor, one of the hardest boiled newsmen in Fleet Street. Wighton also assured me: 'We'll look after your copy.'*

Tony Cole is terrific. Don't be surprised (confidential this) if you hear within the next few years I am studying at Yale or Harvard. It is part of a proposed new policy. Cole – ruthless result-getter that he can be – is a professional. And an idealist. That may seem funny, but he is. David Blair [my form master at George Watson's] *was the first to mention that and I pooh-poohed it as bunk. But he is. I see it more forcibly every day.*

He now virtually controls a great world organisation with roots in India, Australia, South Africa, America and Europe. He has given himself ten years to build up Reuters to an unrivalled peak in the wire service business. One thing disturbs – he's rather a fanatic about it all. He's got tremendous resources of physical energy and mental resilience and he throws them full blast all the time at this news agency child he is nursing. I spent last Sunday at his home in Beckenham. He is 31, incredibly young for his position. His wife, Janet, charming in cord slacks, is absolutely without pretension.

My salary is now £500 p.a. – draw on it ad lib. I leave you an entirely free hand . . . Don't know how long I will be away – maybe three months, maybe three years. My trunk and case from London will arrive shortly. Please ask Mum [my stepmother] *to unpack these.*

If anything happens to me please burn box of letters marked 'private'. My love letters! [These were from my fiancée Pat Cameron.] *My luggage is restricted to 44 lbs. I must travel in mufti for obvious reasons – my first port of call, Lisbon. Don't know what the future holds – I've been chosen against Fleet*

Street competition for this assignment and I'll do my best. I am proud to belong to Reuters . . . I have confidence in your judgment and happily leave my affairs in your hands . . .

On 24 November I flew to Lisbon, for an overnight stop, and on the next day to Algiers, in transit for Italy. Algiers airport was chaos, with long queues everywhere. The Reuter correspondents usually worked at the Agriculture Building 20 miles away in Algiers, where briefings were held, but nobody at the airport had heard of it.

The bus to Algiers was already 90 minutes late. Eventually an RAF officer took me in a jeep with three Shell officials. All the way to town, cafés, houses and other buildings bore the slogan, *'un seul but – victoire'*. The driver, a blunt flat-nosed American called Butch, dropped me three streets from the Agriculture Building. I had made it.

Next day, I filed my first despatch as a Reuter war correspondent, the story of a Nazi massacre in Italy:

Allied HQ, Algiers, Thursday – The men and boys of Bellona village in the Province of Naples (54 of them) lie buried in a common grave – the bottom of a stone quarry . . .

The story came from an official press release and, wrongly, I left this source to the last paragraph of my story. It should have been in the first sentence. The importance of the source – allowing readers to evaluate the credibility or strength of news – cannot be exaggerated.

However, next day I received a cable, 'ProCampbell congratulations maiden effort your air roundup Italian Lidice both scored.' It was signed not by Cole but by Christopher Chancellor. I was deeply impressed that the head of Reuters did not find himself too over-whelmed by global considerations to miss such detail.

Allied Forces HQ was providing services for 125 media representa-tives, the majority American. Most of their news copy was being transmitted by fixed-time radio voicecast, that is, read over the air and recorded at the destination. More than 10,000 words a day were being moved in this way, two-thirds of them going to New York.

Most correspondents tried to get into the Aletti Hotel which, though crowded and run down, was still the up-market place to be. I was at the Regina, where my breakfast that first day was, for a ration-conscious Briton, a feast of tangerines, semolina, bacon and eggs. There was an abundant choice of fairly good food in Algiers and the living was cheap. We had mess facilities and access to the American PX; 20 Three Castles cigarettes cost 10 francs and there were 200 francs to £1.

At lunch and other times I tried to meet as many colleagues and service sources as possible. Pre-lunch drinks at the Aletti with Philip Ure of *The Times*, and a pre-dinner session at Le Bosphore with Robert Dunnet of the BBC or Cyril Bewley of the *Daily Sketch* became a pleasant routine. Alice Delysia, French actress, singer and one-time toast of the Moulin Rouge, might join us sometimes.

Philip Ure seemed to know or be known by everyone. He was a tall imposing man, a shade gruff on first acquaintance, who was rumoured to have been a cowboy and a farmer in Canada before joining *The Scotsman* in the early 1920s. Philip was the first war correspondent I got to know, and a good colleague.

Drinks twice a day were out of my experience, but the wine and cognac were so ridiculously cheap I was consuming them with somewhat unusual, indeed reckless abandon. I soon miscalculated my capacity, and at about midnight one night I just made it to my room at the Regina, to be violently sick in the bidet. Since that crowning glory of French plumbing was hardly a standard fitting in pre-war Scottish manses, I did not know what the thing was really for.

Such was the force and volume of my input that I blocked the bidet drain, then I fell asleep, leaving both taps on. Water gushed over the bidet, flooding carpet and corridor and dripping into the room below. Mercifully I was roused – in a pool of water – by a young warrant officer banging on the door. He fixed everything, at nominal cost and without any repercussions, but it was a chastening experience.

After two weeks in Algiers, it was time to join the 5th Army in Italy. On 8 December I flew to Tunis with a group of American correspondents to cover a visit by General Henry (Hap) Arnold, the US Army Air Force commander. The group, led by Major Max Boyd, included Sammy Goldstein of *Life* and Wes Gallagher, who eventually became chief executive of the leading American news agency, Associated Press.

Unable to land at Tunis's main airfield because President Roosevelt was due, we came down at a small airfield built and abandoned by the Germans, and after supper bedded down three to a room at a nearby station. Next morning we flew on, over Sicily and then the smoking volcano of Vesuvius, to the big American air base at Foggia.

Foggia town was the most appalling sight I'd ever seen. The scale of destruction was terrifying. The marshalling yards were a heap of twisted steel, wrecked wagons and engines. Women and children were lying on the streets, looking too ill, hungry, dirty or cold to move. Others wandered about aimlessly, in awful apathy. Their lives had been shattered. It was a town of death – of the soul as well as the body.

We found the former residence of an Italian Admiral which now housed General Carl Spaatz, commanding General of the US Strategic Air Forces, helped ourselves at his bar and smoked his cigars until he arrived with a clutch of American top brass, including Generals Hap Arnold and James Doolittle. We all lunched together on Spam and pears.

General Arnold agreed to brief us that night. He told me, off the record, that two days earlier the Germans had for the first time made use of a radio-operated bomb. He said that in the previous month the US had delivered 460 heavy bombers, and calculated that 75 per cent of German ball-bearing output had now been crippled.

Major Boyd said we should give him our copy and he would look after its transmission. Several, including myself, did so. I noticed Wes Gallagher had disappeared. Next day London cabled, 'Thanks Arnold. You just pipped by Associated.' Gallagher had slipped away and personally steered his copy through the censor, ensuring fast clearance. Major Boyd, I discovered, was a former AP staff man. I learned another lesson: never entrust your copy to anyone else if you can possibly handle it yourself.

We dined that night with field officers in the former Fascist HQ in Foggia. Hundreds of starving Italians huddled outside, a few yards away, offering their bodies for a few crumbs of bread. We had a six-course meal and slept in a palace.

The next night I was also sumptuously housed, this time in Naples. It was a suite once occupied by a Fascist professor who must have been a keen Rotarian. The cupboards were stuffed with Rotarian literature, his will was tucked behind the bathroom pipes, and personal papers were scattered about.

There I was telephoned by Haig Nicholson, formerly of the Edinburgh *Dispatch* and now Reuter correspondent based with the 5th Army, who arranged to pick me up next day, and soon I was settled with other correspondents in a hilltop villa where the food was even better.

Major Nigel Dugdale ran this five-star super mess with two Viennese cooks whose profusion of delicious food was so rich that a cold table of plain beef and ham was kept for those with simpler tastes. Mess secretary David Heneker, a gourmet as well as a composer of popular songs, would sing and play the piano after dinner. I wrote home on 15 December:

I'm typing this looking across the calm blue Bay of Naples to Vesuvius. The old man puts up an awful lot of smoke and flame. I'm staying in a villa high on a hill where wealthy Neapolitans used to live, about two miles from the centre of the city. It belonged to an Italian Count: now it accommodates War Correspondents accredited to the American 5th Army. It is a well built and charmingly situated residence set in several acres of wooded grounds with little bridges, rustic seats, the lot.

Most delightful of all is the view: away from the slums, Naples looks an exquisite city. And the food. The Italians must be among the world's best cooks. Advance word of the quality of the villa's meals had spread to Algiers.

Breakfast: pure fruit juice, porridge and cream, bacon, eggs and tomatoes, coffee, toast and marmalade. Dinner – four or five courses of delicious food, tastefully prepared and served.

I share a bedroom with Christopher Lumby of The Times. *My desk at the moment is loaded with figs, almonds, apples, oranges (you can stretch out of the window and pick them) and a free issue of cigarettes.*

Shops carry extraordinary stocks of everything – silk stockings of a fashion and elegance you've not seen in Britain for years. Very soon I'm moving on. A change of plan means I'm going to Monty's 8th Army front.

I hear correspondents there pig it in abominable conditions. I hear too that Reuters correspondent there, dead tired after four months on the job, has just packed it in and is returning to his native South Africa. I like the sound of the setup, more realistic than here, and at last I may get a chance to do some real war reporting.

I'm writing as much as any correspondent and it seems by warco standards we've been busy. After what I've been used to I'd hardly call it busy, indeed it's difficult to know why we are being paid – not paying – to live like this and do this so-called work.

I'm not sending anything home 'cos it seems things go astray rather often. And bargain house though Naples is, prices have peaked within the last few weeks. The time for real bargains is just after occupation (Naples was entered on 2 October) – wait till Rome!

Other correspondents here include Alan Moorehead of the Daily Express, *Alex Clifford of* Daily Mail, *Basil Gingell of* Extel, *H. R. Knickerbocker of* Chicago Sun, *Frank Gillard of* BBC. *As at Algiers they are a great lot, good company.*

Have not had a line from you or anyone else yet – imagine you'd cable if anything serious.

Remember if any emergency and you want to contact me, just call Reuters – they'll reach me faster than anyone else . . .

The luxury was short-lived. Within a few days I crossed Italy from Naples to 'Dysentery Hall' in Vasto, a bleak square toiletless house on the edge of the Adriatic, where the remnants of correspondents accredited to Montgomery's 8th Army lodged in overcrowded and sometimes slum conditions.

The Officer Commanding was Captain Sir Gerald Fortescue Boles of the 17th/21st Lancers, a product of Eton and Sandhurst and onetime ADC to the Governor of Bermuda, who listed his recreations in *Who's Who* as hunting, shooting and fishing. He slept in a tidy little caravan parked alongside Dysentery Hall.

Hermione Baddeley, entertaining the troops in the area, gave us a flavour of her own intimate revue over supper, and after, one drunken night in the mess.

We correspondents slept several to a room in small beds. Next to me was Christopher Buckley of *The Daily Telegraph*, schoolmasterish but not stuffy, and known among us as 'the General', because he could be counted on for a weighty contribution to any discussion on tactics or strategy.

Other correspondents still at the Hall, tired and impatiently awaiting the call to come home, included Clifford Webb (*Daily Herald*), Cyril Bewley (*Daily Sketch*), Richard McMillan (British United Press) and Ted Gilling (Exchange Telegraph). Alan Moorehead, Alex Clifford and quite a few others who had been with Monty since the battle of Alamein were already on their way home, some summoned after telling their editors, 'Monty hopes to see me with him on the next party.'

As Cole had foreseen, by this time the Italian war was not making headlines. The weather had turned much of the terrain into a quagmire and swollen rivers slowed the 8th Army on the Adriatic, while the Benedictine Abbey of Monte Cassino, a natural fortress for the entrenched Germans, blocked the 5th Army's advance to Rome.

My youth, artificial arm, total inexperience and keenness to see action caused a degree of bemused cynicism among my companions. That suited me; I had the front largely to myself.

I established an early rapport with the youngest conducting officer, Lieutenant Ken Best, a dashing devil-may-care young man, eager for action. Dispensing with a driver, and with Ken at the wheel, we would set off 'to see the war, where there was some fighting'. That usually took us towards Ortona or Orsogna along the main road, unless megajams of trucks, tanks, ambulances, jeeps and armoured cars made movement impossible.

Then we might turn down a secondary road, to find a peaceful country scene with clear blue sky and bees buzzing, like Surrey in spring – but the Germans might be just beyond the bottom of the next field, unseen.

On one such glorious December day we were meandering along a quiet trail when I saw a British military policeman at a crossroads a short distance ahead, lazily directing the occasional vehicle. Our jeep was about 20 yards (20 m) and a few seconds away, when a low whistle broke the silence and the policeman's face was simply sliced off his head. Blood spouted from the neck before the body fell. By this stage I had seen bodies, German and Canadian, in various death postures and agonies, but this was the first time I had witnessed a man actually *being* killed.

Two days later, on 28 December, we heard that the Canadians had finally cleared Ortona, a small town on a lofty promontory 200 ft (60 m) above the sea. They had first attacked a week earlier with Sherman tanks and it had become a vicious and bloody operation to flush the town out building by building.

We had been on the outskirts of Ortona several times before, usually leaving Dysentery Hall before 9 am because the road was so often jammed. It was now 1.30 pm and I had planned to go to the afternoon briefing at 4 pm.

'What about Ortona?' I said.

'I'm game,' said Ken. Ken was game for anything that smacked of adventure. It was 25 miles, with rain threatening, but he was a good driver, fast without taking risks. At Canadian Divisional HQ outside Ortona a logbook recorded, 'Noon – Seaforths report town of Ortona definitely clear.' And two hours later, 'Ortona is now clear of the enemy but it is full of booby traps and mines.' A day or two earlier a Canadian platoon commander had established headquarters in an Ortona townhouse. It blew up, killing 18 of the 32 men.

Every vehicle was checked before passing into the town by the newly opened coastal road. We drove slowly over pot-holed streets to the main square. It was menacingly quiet. We parked the jeep and strolled around.

Suddenly an explosion nearly blew us off our feet. The few soldiers and civilians disappeared. Then four more explosions, too close for comfort.

'Better go inside,' said Ken, standing close and cool. We dived under a crumbling archway into what had been a bank, and crouched behind a counter.

'How long does this last?'

'All depends whether it's harassing fire or a barrage,' said Ken. Then we heard a missile coming. Had this one got our name on it? The explosion threw us back. 'Christ!'

'Sorry for bringing you into this,' said Ken, ignoring the fact that it had been at my suggestion that we left the jeep and landed ourselves in this predicament.

'I'll see how it looks,' he said, taking a couple of paces to the door. He had counted 20 shells.

'Let's make a run for it – reckon they'll be reloading now.'

Stepping over several wounded and dead, we saw a hole right on the spot where we had been standing. Miraculously the jeep was intact. By the time the second barrage began we were out of Ortona and going like fury.

I began to shake. Suddenly I'd become scared.

I was shaken, too, to have such a reaction. For two days I brooded. Could I go on? Could there be any future in this dashing to the front, dodging death? No, I couldn't take it. I was frightened. What had been stimulating, exciting, something that turned me on, that really got the adrenalin going, had suddenly become a sick nightmare.

I had thrown myself rashly into reporting a battle. London was calling for more 'action copy'. What could I do; what could I say?

As far as possible I kept to myself, but my colleagues saw and recognised the symptoms; in varying degree some of them had had similar experiences. It took just under a week to jerk myself out of that black despondent mood and adjust to a more rational approach.

War correspondents have their own dilemmas of conscience about 'going forward', seeing action, getting the feel of the front, or staying close to headquarters and covering the war mainly by relaying what official spokesmen say.

Sometimes, of course, the correspondent has no choice. For a news agency like Reuters, on which thousands of papers and broadcasting outlets rely, it is essential to have a twice daily update on how the war is going – something that can only be obtained from an official briefing, really a perfunctory reporting chore, miles from shot and shell.

Here with the 8th Army on the Adriatic coast, 'going forward' often meant exposure, however briefly, to danger. Having gained a little maturity about deliberately risking danger (as distinct from the unexpected mine or booby trap), some sense about measuring the degree of risk against the importance of the news to be obtained, I still felt admiration for others who seemed to know no fear, or certainly never showed it.

Having come to terms, I liked being a war correspondent again. I wrote to Cole:

I'm not filing today . . . It's New Year's Day at Dysentery Hall. Cliff Webb's voice penetrates the reek – 'I'm talking about the annihilation of thousands of Germans.' The General, alias Christopher Buckley, disputes Cliff's strategy. Now the voice of experience, the 'old hand' Ted Gilling. Ted is always ready to contribute – usually sensibly – to any debate.

This is all going on in the common-room of the Hall – a smaller room than your lounge. Here we eat, argue, roister, type copy (when Hermione Baddeley, cigar in one hand, glass in the other, or some other guest is not flopping over the table). A dull, dirty orderly brings in tea. It's petrol-flavoured in handleless mugs. The Adriatic is stormy, splashing the back door. From the front window just about everything seems to be floating.

This place has no toilets, which makes going to the lavatory in these conditions a wet and miserable exercise. My arm (the right one) fell out of the bed clothes into something wet and cold at 3 am. It was rain driven in by the gale – most windows have no glass. The Hall seems ready to topple over at any moment. Shutters banged and the warcos swore as they hammered them shut. Pools of water in every bedroom, where we slept at least four to a room. In every bedroom irate figures in pyjamas cursing, blaspheming.

Most of them drank the Old Year out and the New Year in – with good margins each end! I tried to sleep through the orgies. The roast lamb of the old year's dinner contained too much veteran mutton for my digestive organs. The sheep had been picked up outside Ortona this week. The conducting officer noticed it frolicking near a minefield and brought it back alive in the jeep. A variation in diet here is always welcome. The sheep, with a long lead, enjoyed freedom to fatten itself for two days, then we saw it starkers in the kitchen. The dirty young orderly grinned from ear to ear as he stood over the carcass clutching the bloody knife. He was in his element . . .

I now realised all things are relative. Dysentery Hall with its stone floor, sagging sofa, lamps and rationed water for washing could seem a heavenly haven of comfort after conditions at the front. As for the Germans, the discomfort in the enemy lines was clear from this translated extract from a typical letter found on a captured soldier:

If I am still alive today it's a miracle. The water in the dug-out rose and rose . . . We kept emptying it with our mess tins but it was just a waste of time. It rose knee-high . . . [we were] almost weeping with misery and cold. Early morning the enemy shot up our position with the English 'Stalingrad barrel-organ' − the shells travel as fast as machine-gun bullets. Food is very bad. We get one hot meal a day at two in the morning. During the day we get a small piece of sausage or cheese, a little margarine and three cigarettes. Can it be any worse in Russia?

But I found Italy enchanting: the little sun-drenched (or more often rain-lashed or even snow-bound) villages, set high on the hill-tops; the olive groves on the hill-slopes; the terraced vineyards and square farmhouses; the people, friendly and tolerant, seeming almost impervious to the mayhem.

Moreover, Reuter correspondents were the envy of other media representatives for the regular 'feedback' we received from London, marvellous for morale. Such service messages from London might start 'FYI' (for your information) and indicate the degree of prominence that stories had achieved, mention a fact or quote exclusive to or missing from the Reuter story, or give comparative timings on significant news breaks: Reuter 16.14; Associated 16.19 (Associated Press, sometimes abbreviated to Primary, a code that fooled no one); United 16.22 (United Press, sometimes coded as Secondary). They also might suggest that certain secondary items were 'dispensable cablewise' but okay for radio voicecast or airmailed 'situationers' (i.e. not worth cable tolls but fine if transmitted free). I attracted a lot of these suggestions.

Ten days after writing my letter to Cole, I watched General Montgomery, a slight figure in battledress and black beret, say 'good-bye' to the 8th Army he had led to victory in North Africa. It was a real family farewell. Two thousand 'Desert Rats', from generals to privates, crowded into the battered little opera house in Vasto, as moved by the occasion as Monty himself.

Four times he repeated, 'The end of the war is definitely in sight.' The 8th Army loved it as he described the occasion as a farewell to his staff, 'and when I speak about staff I mean every single person in it – lance-corporals, clerks, orderlies and everybody down to the cooks in the cookhouse. If you were to say to me what is the first essential for success in war, I would say "the human factor". It is not tank and armoured car or battleship that is going to win this war. It is the men inside them . . . Everything hinges on the human factor.'

They gave him three cheers and as he left the theatre shouted, 'Good old Monty.' 'Cheerio, boys,' he said. Afterwards he spoke to a few of us from the steps of his caravan. He thanked war correspondents for their 'help and kindness and patience' throughout the 8th Army's campaign. We were an integral part of the Army. He had taken us into his confidence whenever possible and never once had we let him down. He hoped to meet us in a new theatre.

This was an easy and successful story for Reuters because with shorthand I had an edge. I took Monty's farewell address almost ver-batim and saw it widely published. The services newspaper *Union Jack* carried it across four columns under my byline.

The new 8th Army commander, Lieutenant-General Sir Oliver Leese, also had something to say to and about the war correspondents. He made headlines right away by telling us he did not want 'any bombastic advertisement'. It was 'unnecessary in the British Army', though he appreciated it was necessary to appear a certain amount in the public eye so that 8th Army men and their relatives might have confidence in their leaders.

He went on:

I think you can do a tremendous amount of good in the home countries by letting them know what their husbands, sons and relatives are doing, and the conditions and climate in which they are living. Any time you see my car stopped on the road and you want to know anything about how the battles are going, come up and ask me and I shall be delighted to give you anything I can.

It turned out that when he eventually did, the censors prevented me from reporting it. I was not, however, to spend much longer with the 8th Army. At midnight on 22 January, British and American troops landed at the small port and seaside resort of Anzio, 100 miles north of Naples, in an attempt to bypass Cassino. Haig Nicholson was with them, covering the attack for Reuters.

In the first week of February, I had a cable from my immediate boss, Reuters' American bureau chief in Algiers, David Brown:

Nicholson being moved home from beachhead soonest possible etwant [and want] *you unhesitate move to 5th Army front if action there interestinger as it seems be now. Permission been granted you cover both fronts.*

With Montgomery gone and the 8th Army crawling up the Adriatic coast with no big prize in sight, Cassino seemed a more exciting news prospect. I set out on the 100-mile drive over the Apennines, often nudging along serpentine roads, and reached the house where British war correspondents were billeted at the little town of Sessa Aurunca, near Highway 6 and a safe distance from the front line.

Here I made another greenhorn's error. Having had several cables direct from Cole and Mason, when I found a message about Nicholson's condition was waiting, instead of cabling via Brown in Algiers I shot off a message direct to London:

ProCole. Nicholson ordered parspecialist [by specialist] *undergo special treatment Algiers medical report following. Whats my position? Regard this front* [Cassino] *importantern* [more important than] *beachhead* [Anzio] *presently – view confirmed parmilitary – etsuggest eye stay here. Unpersonal desire proceed beachhead.*

This brought a swift rebuke:

ForCampbell from Brown: Cole received yours re Nicholson leaves decision your move to me. Basis your plea tis okay you stay Fifth Army. Nick can get his treatment Cairo and arrangements his move there already underway. Outpoint youve consistently violated orders both exhere [from here] *etlondon to address your services to me. This is your bureau headquarters and you should never bypass.*

Yet another lesson learned, but at least I was not sent to the Anzio beachhead; that job fell to Henry Buckley, older than myself and a first-class newsman. I was left to cover the American, British, Canadian, French, Indian, New Zealand, Polish and other troops who fought under the 1,700-ft (520 m) mountain summit dominated since AD 529 by the Benedictine monastery. To them the abbey itself had in a sense become the enemy, as it towered over the battlefield.

I went up Highway 6 to Cassino most days – there was no other way to reach the various Brigade headquarters for information – and on 12 February was cheered by a message from Algiers:

'Tell Campbell his coverage now excellent. His voicecasts today examples, wells [as well as] *overnighters about Garibaldis greatgrandaughter typical stories we like see – Sid Mason'. Attaboy Yours Dave.*

My first big story from the Cassino front was on Valentine's Day, 14 February, about Allied guns being deliberately trained on the monastery for the first time, firing canisters with hundreds of warning leaflets that fell within the outer walls, behind which German troops were sheltering. They said in Italian:

Italian friends. Beware. We have until now been especially careful to avoid shelling Monte Cassino Monastery. The Germans know how to benefit from this. But now fighting has swept closer and closer to its sacred precincts. The time has come when we must train our guns on the monastery itself. We give you warning that you may save yourselves. We warn you urgently – leave the monastery. Leave it at once. Respect this warning, It is for your benefit. Fifth Army.

Next day was crisp and sunny as I watched the abbey from an observation post less than 2 miles away. At 9.20 am the first wave of 30 heavy bombers appeared at a height of 20,000 ft (6,000 m), looking like half-inch black smudges. Their 1,000-pound (450 kg) bombs seemed to creep through the sky towards the monastery. The first hit the corner of the abbey with an explosion that rocked our lookout. It was the start of one of the most intensified 20-minute periods of aerial attack against a pinpoint target in the Italian campaign. Stick after stick of bombs rained down from two more waves of heavy bombers, followed in the afternoon by three waves of medium bombers.

It was terrifying, spectacular, dramatic. Monte Cassino, widely considered the most perfect natural defensive position in Europe, was being subjected to its greatest destruction ever.

'Dispatches topflight impressive likewise your fine work and enthusiasm good luck,' cabled Cole, and Sid Mason came in with, 'If ever get chance reach monastery outfind what happened Benedictine. Your coverage well played here.'

I took that chance when it came, and scored world headlines with a description of the abbey having become 'a mass tomb of Italian men, women and children, victims of one of the worst acts of barbarity yet seen on the Italian front'. It won me a byline in the American newspaper *PM* and Francis X. Dealy wrote from New York:

This is the first Reuter war correspondent's story that has been credited in a long while. This is a good story and it is the kind of stuff that people want to read in this country.

In a letter home, written on 26 February and received in Linlithgow two days later unaltered by the censor, I told the background to filing that despatch:

I had a world beat on the Abbey survivors. It was the first interview with Italian survivors who lived through the air bombardment of the Abbey. I took my copy to Army Group for censorship. It caused a minor sensation and was almost referred to General Alexander himself.

A Major looked at it and passed it on to a Colonel. The Colonel looked at it and passed it on to a Brigadier. The Brigadier called in another Brigadier. Then they called me in to tell them – Army Group – the story I'd left untold in my story.

They were going to stop it altogether, but I argued and argued and argued until they agreed to let it through, provided I wrote it more in accord with British propaganda.

The 15 February attack was far from finishing off Cassino. Later that month Field-Marshal Kesselring, the German C-in-C, relieved the 15th Panzer Grenadiers at Cassino by sending in the 1st Parachute Division, who were among the most redoubtable of all German formations in Italy – highly trained, resourceful, fanatical fighters. The 1944 battles for Monte Cassino were among the most bitter of the two world wars, likened to Verdun or Stalingrad. Almost 105,000 Allied troops were killed or wounded as well as at least 80,000 Germans.

Amidst all this, the 'home-towners' Cole had demanded were available galore. I recall an 18-year-old Somerset-born youth, taken to Italy when he was four, escaping from the Germans in Cassino by hiding in the surrounding hills.

48

There was Sergeant M. Massie, a big sandy-haired chuckling Scot from Castle Douglas, who had led 20 men in storming a hill. I met him in a cowshed by the side of Highway 6. He had just come out of Cassino and incongruously was listening on his radio to the strains of the 'Blue Danube' from London.

The civilians fleeing the debris and death of Cassino included women with faded red bundles balanced on their heads and babies in dirty shawls. There was a gnarled old man with two teeth and dust caked in lines on his face, declaring he had not slept on a bed, taken off his clothes or washed for five months. It was easy to believe that.

War is a nasty, brutalising business, but war correspondents are not continuously in the firing line, or obliged to endure the discomfort of kipping down in hastily dug foxholes, or worse, or trying to live on emergency packaged food rations and stale water. It is part of the job to know about these things and to be able to put up with them and suffer privation and hunger and the rest in extreme conditions in certain situations. But after work, when things were organised as they were by those looking after the Cassino war correspondents, material comforts were enjoyed at no mean standard.

The house in Sessa Aurunca had plenty of good food and wine, dry beds or sleeping-bags, adequate washing and laundry facilities. With characteristic generosity the Americans extended PX facilities, apple pie and other homespun goodies. I never missed a chance of going to their HQ for briefings, lingering always to savour the American way of life.

Newspaper correspondents, as most were, seldom tried to write more than one main story a day. They knew it had only to be in London, New York, Chicago, Melbourne or Wellington by a certain hour to be in time for the following day's paper, or at least its main edition. But Reuters demanded immediate cover on newsbreaks, updates on the 'trunk', or continuing story, for morning and evening news cycles, an unending supply of 'sidebars' and 'target' pieces for some country or region, human interest items, situationers and off-beat angles, like the food standards laid down for army mules.

I was bashing away at the typewriter first thing every morning and, when others had packed it in for the night, I would engage any officer who happened to be about for a detail to act as the peg on which to hang a forward-throwing 'freshener' for the next news cycle.

Messages of praise kept my motivation high for this endless task. My letter home of 26 February showed I realised this:

I've been here with 5th Army nearly three weeks . . . getting messages almost daily. One from Cole the other day read: 'Your initiative in monastery survivors particularly appreciated. Glad you settled down and doing excellent job work.' The messages I'm getting show the psychologist as well as the newsman in Cole. He's tops. I don't give a damn about bylines as long as I'm giving London, giving Reuters, what it wants. I've been out here three months and am still waiting for a rocket about something.

Had new room mate the other night – Captain the Hon. Seymour Berry, son of Lord Camrose. He's a good bloke. But he keeps his long pants on in bed! Shows keen interest in London's reaction to my copy. Thinking of asking him to suggest to Tony Cole (he's going home shortly for Second Front) that they recall me for Second Front.

I go out quite a lot with Norman Smart of the Express *and Chris Buckley of the* Telegraph. *I'm years younger than these characters yet often feel I've an edge in handling copy, certainly quicker in getting it down and away . . .*

P.S. Letter from Sid Mason just in – 'Your copy getting excellent showing . . . I trust your judgment and will back you to hilt . . . keep your Highland temper down a bit . . . don't be bloody fool and keep poking your nose into firing line . . . everybody here thinks you're doing extremely well.'

On 15 March, in the words I used at the time, 'Cassino disappeared under the greatest front-line air blitz in history.' At 8.30 am that day, though already full of ruins and rubble, the monastery lay

quiet in the spring sunshine. By noon it had been ground into dust by
an avalanche of bomb clusters, falling in an almost unbroken hail for
more than three hours.

Hollywood never produced such drama as the Allied Air Force put
on. At one time several hundred planes were counted in the air –
massed formations of Liberators, Flying Fortresses, Mitchells and
Marauders, with up to 72 heavy bombers unloading their bays simultaneously, until Cassino was a second Pompeii, but uglier and more
grotesque.

Since early morning most of the Allied top brass had congregated
for a ringside view. They included the tall and ruthless 5th Army
Commander, General Mark Clark, and Lieutenant-General Sir
Bernard Freyberg, surveying the annihilation of the town in what one
writer described as a 'picnic atmosphere'. I watched from an olive
grove. Sir Oliver Leese came by. 'What about another chukka?' he
said with a laugh. The censors cut that line from my despatch.

Remembering how as a cub I won an edge over other reporters
during the supposed German raid on the Forth Bridge, I decided
after the first waves of bombers that I had seen everything. Huge
clouds of dust, punctuated by sheets of flame, were going to be
repeated as long as the onslaught lasted. So, quietly and discreetly, I
slipped away and drove open throttle to Caserta, the vast marble
palace 25 miles away where the censors operated. My copy then went
to Naples and London. The ploy paid off. Dave Brown wrote that
evening from Naples:

*Your Cassino bombing story got here in excellent time around 3.30 – just after
we'd flashed the HQ version about the size of the raid, number and variety planes
etc. etc. Your four-part eye-witnesser was good, I thought, and went off at once by
cable. (Incidentally, just at that time Cable & Wireless went off the air – a lorry
backed into and smashed their antenna.) We routed your copy via New York.*

I felt five stories was altogether too voluminous. Remember the size of the papers, after all, and a considerable amount of your background stuff was decidedly of a secondary nature which London would doubtless have been very sore about paying cable tolls on. I think it would certainly have bounced back on your head if we hadn't taken steps with it here.

From one of your other four stories we lifted about one-third, some good paragraphs about fighters weaving in and out among the bombers, no enemy fighters etc., etc. and sent it off as an add to your eye-witnesser.

Your other three stories describing the correspondents' arrangements, bomb saturation technique and scenery, we rewrote and put on the voicecast . . . London can use it if they see fit but won't have the feeling you are sending luxuries.

Leese unfortunately was cut from your eye-witnesser. I argued it for a long time but the 'cut' orders were very strict and I could make no headway.

Later Cole cabled, 'Congratulations superlative Cassino descriptive splashed morningers.' A few days later, while the New Zealanders were still struggling for control of Cassino, Cole was handing me the plaudits again, 'Campbell's "bloodiest square mile of history" despatch winner.'

This despatch, dated 19 March, read:

Cassino will live in history as the bloodiest square mile in the Italian campaign. The defence has been fanatical. Young Nazi disciples have obeyed their Führer's instructions to hold on until death. They resist to their last breath – and their last bullet. They know Cassino is blocking our drive to Rome.

They are street fighting specialists – the same breed the Canadians came up against in Ortona. They will demolish whole blocks of buildings and use the rubble as pillboxes.

One unit, buried in a cellar on the day of the aerial bombardment, took four days to claw their way out. Instead of withdrawing, exhausted, they set about building a strongpoint from which to carry on the fight.

You smell death without always seeing the dead in Cassino. The German parachutist's conceit is colossal – even after being taken prisoner.

Most of the prisoners are about 20 years old, some younger. They still plug the old theme – Germany will win; Hitler is the Almighty.

They cannot tell you how Germany will win, nor can they rationally explain deification of the Führer. But so sure are they, that they are prepared to die for Hitler in the interrogation office as well as in the front line.

The situation in Cassino is deadlock; very largely a battle of endurance, slugging it out, with infantry on both sides having a very tough time.

My next lucky success came partly because the 5th Army commander, General Mark Clark, an American, knew the value of publicity and told me one day that, if ever I wanted a look at the Cassino battlefield from the air, I should feel free to use a Piper Cub, the small aircraft used for artillery spotting. I recalled this offer when Vesuvius started to spout molten lava, and discussed it with Reginald Beckwith, a BBC correspondent and the author of *A Soldier Home for Christmas.*

'What about flying over Cassino and Vesuvius?' I said. 'Mark Clark has made his Pipers available.'

Within an hour we were airborne. It was exciting, dangerous and made a good story: Cassino a man-made volcano; Vesuvius hugely more impressive. We landed at Naples, went to the Allied Forces Headquarters, wrote and sent our stories.

Next day Cole cabled, 'Vesuvius flight enterprisingest grand descriptive great work. You shortly homecoming for new assignment.' Dave Brown's relay added, 'Congratulations.' So a hunch, a stunt, or at best a gimmicky sort of story had projected me forward for a prize posting.

Less than four months after being assigned to Italy 'until the end of the campaign', I had my marching orders. By the time Cassino finally fell on 18 May, I was back in England, preparing for the Normandy beaches.

4

D-minus plus

When I reached London, Tony Cole's greeting was effusive, his briefing sparse, 'You are getting one of the top assignments Reuters can offer a correspondent – with the British on the Second Front. But no front-line nonsense this time. You've had enough shot and shell for a bit – you'll go in after the beachhead's established.'

New colleagues appeared in the editorial. Reuters had 15 eager young reporters in uniform – plus a few pigeons – lined up for the invasion of France, several of them recruited from North America. General Dwight Eisenhower was to be Supremo in the assault on Europe, and Cole carried out a lightning recruitment raid to ensure adequate Reuter representation with the invading armies. He picked winners like Charlie Lynch and Marshall Yarrow from Canada; Bob Reuben, Bill Stringer and John Wilhelm from the United States.

Life in Reuters' Head Office now became a bit cloak-and-dagger. No one knew to what extent his colleagues – or bosses – were in the picture, what they knew or were meant to know. Towards the end of April, messages started to reach me at Reuters from 17 Egerton Gardens in Knightsbridge, a press relations office of SHAEF, the Supreme Headquarters Allied Expeditionary Force. They bore the illegible signature of a half-Colonel and were variously marked 'personal and private', 'restricted', 'secret', 'top secret' and 'most secret'.

On 24 April one arrived, marked most secret. ('How secret is that?' I thought). It read:

Will you please report to me at the above address at 19.15 hours on Monday 1 May, as I have an assignment for you. You should report in uniform, with full Field equipment properly labelled.

You will be away for approximately one week, but you should not make engagements for the period following your probable return.

The necessity for complete security cannot be overstressed. On no account should you discuss your movements with anybody outside this Headquarters.

'Blimey,' I thought, 'I don't like the sound of "probable return".' But I began a will o' the wisp existence. I came and went, seeing demonstrations of assault rafts for anti-tank guns; clearing roadblocks and mines; booby-trap plans; cliff casualty exercises. Sometimes Churchill and the South African leader, General Jan Smuts, also turned up.

I took notes compulsively, but occasionally wondered what relevance such demonstrations and exercises could have to a reporter joining the British after a beachhead had been established.

Another communication from the illegible half-Colonel who was organising us as half-soldiers arrived on 5 May:

Now that you are accredited, there are a number of matters which will need your early attention.

1 Immunisation and Inoculation. *Will you please render to me as early as possible, a certificate to the effect that you have been inoculated etc., as under: (a) TAB – Typhoid; (b) Tettox – Tetanus; (c) Typhus; (d) Vaccination – Smallpox.*

If you wish this to be carried out by the Army Medical Service please let me know and I will make the necessary arrangements.

2 Steel Helmet etc. *Please let me know that you are fully equipped with steel*

helmet and latest type of respirator and other anti-gas equipment.
3 Please supply me with a brief biography of yourself, giving such details as your
full name, nationality, education and general details of your civil career and war
reporting experience.

Not everything was shrouded in 'Most Secret' stickers. On 18 May a message went out:

TO: All Unit Commanders, Allied Expedition Force
At my first Press Conference as Supreme Commander I told the War Correspondents that once they were accredited to my headquarters I considered them quasi-staff officers . . .
As a matter of policy, accredited war correspondents should be accorded the greatest possible latitude in the gathering of legitimate news . . .
They should be allowed to talk freely with officers and enlisted personnel and to see the machinery of war in operation in order to visualize and transmit to the public the conditions under which the men from their countries are waging war against the enemy.
Dwight D. Eisenhower, General, U.S. Army

And even before D-Day, things did get published. On 12 May I reported:

Mr Churchill and three Empire Premiers saw a new weapon demonstrated today in a fast 60-mile tour during which they inspected invasion troops. It is a weapon that may play a big part in spoiling Rommel's Atlantic wall and Mr Churchill asked a lot of questions about it.

That was published on 13 May, less than a month before D-Day.

On 16 May I attended a confidential conference. The briefing we received was from General Montgomery – the same confident Monty as in Italy, though dressed a bit more formally than in the sweater and corduroys he wore on the steps of his caravan. The day before, he had briefed King George VI, Churchill and his cabinet, Eisenhower and the Chiefs of Staff. He was said 'to have permitted himself uncommon openness and breathtaking optimism about prospects of the grand assault'. Now, at St Paul's School, Hammersmith, standing at the front of a sloping stage carpeted with army blankets, he put about 100 assault correspondents clearly in the picture.

He warned that for the first few days censorship would be very strict and said, 'Confine yourselves to what you see going on, describing what the soldiers are doing, and do not attempt to tell how the battle as a whole is going or what is likely to happen . . . I think it will be a terrific party, a real first-class party. I am quite absolutely confident we will win it.'

Despite the instruction about secrecy, I wrote up almost every word he uttered, left it with a military censor and wondered when, if ever, it would be released. For historians, perhaps? No, it was published on D-Day, and prominently.

Our final London briefing was from a Brigadier at Army Group HQ, who told us we were to go to a 'press camp' from which we would be called up as wanted:

When we call you — you are all on 36 hours notice — slip away as quietly as possible . . . Everybody will be allowed 60 lbs [27 kg] of kit exclusive of what they can carry. That means a valise and small bag containing type-writer. Another 40 lbs [18 kg] of kit can be packed and lodged to follow later . . .

Correspondents must provide their own copy paper in the early stages.

Correspondents who write weekly articles and do regular broadcasts should write their stuff now to leave behind them. Once you are called up you will be treated in exactly the same way as the rest of the army . . .

To start with everything written outside the country will be pooled . . .

We have certain correspondents (rather a lot) who will be called 'assault correspondents' . . . They do not necessarily go in with the first wave but we have picked them to cover assault operations. We want every part of this show covered.

Communications (early stages):
. . . On paper, communication arrangements look very good but don't bank on them working 100 per cent satisfactorily. Wireless communications will be pretty shaky. We hope to have other means – carrier pigeons may be used.

Censorship:
Censors on the beaches have instructions to be very drastic. That is the period when you should write what it is like rather than try and give a general picture of what is happening.

The reference to carrier pigeons had a special resonance for a Reuter man. Paul Julius Reuter, the German genius who founded Reuters, had used them to beat the Brussels–Aachen mail train and be first with the news in 1850. The agency's contingency plan for D-Day also involved them, though I was never offered one and anyway would have refused.

Monty Taylor, a Reuter war correspondent with the RAF, released a Coastal Command pigeon named Gustave at 08.50 on D-Day and, despite a 30 mph headwind, it managed to reach the English coast at 13.46 with his account of the landings and the absence of enemy aircraft.

Bob Reuben, the young American correspondent, jumped before dawn with the 101 American Airborne Division carrying a homing pigeon. He had pre-typed a despatch with the magic dateline 'Normandy' and all he had to do was stay alive, land and send off the pigeon with his copy in a leg-band capsule. The pigeon was released before daybreak but according to one report the bird was so scared it didn't know whether to fly high or low. It did reach Dover, with the message, but after Taylor's.

These adventures lay in the future, though, when towards the end of May, very quietly, we slipped away from Fleet Street to Wentworth Golf Club near Virginia Water, west of London. We became non-persons, unable to contact our families or offices, sealed in a high security zone, where the only noise came from birds and leaves rustling in the wind. Correspondents who had covered fighting from Alamein to Anzio now heard the news they had waited for so long – which units of the invasion force they were to join.

Our final briefing on our roles in Operation Overlord, the Second Front, began in a large room where the elegant silver-haired Colonel Philip Astley, the husband of film star Madeleine Carroll, intoned, 'Woodward, airborne, D-Day.'

'I beg your pardon?' said David Woodward, heavily built correspondent of the *Manchester Guardian*. Had he heard correctly? The Colonel repeated it. David looked surprised. (He went in a glider.) Then came my name, 'Campbell, Marine Commandos, D-Day.'

I heard with incredulity, ecstatic delight. Magic! I was going with a crack British force on the very first day. There was nothing about waiting until a beachhead had been established. I had once seen a film called *Commandos Strike at Dawn*. Now I could play the part for real, I wanted to shout, 'Yippee!' What a break. Could any war correspondent ask for more?

When the long list was finished, we trooped into the garden with mugs of tea to discuss our postings. Not everyone could cross on D-Day. Some had to wait a week or more. One complained, 'But this is the biggest story since the Crucifixion!'

'Yes, but they managed that very well with four correspondents,' returned a staff brigadier.

Next day I met the commandos. Their Brigadier, Lord Lovat, was a real leader, tall, slim, with charismatic presence. A man of action, he led from the front, where his men could see him – and try to keep up. And without any suggestion of softness, he had exceptional sensitivity. What other commando chieftain would reminisce on the eve of D-Day about willow wrens nesting beside his tent?

Lovat smiled as an orderly deposited me before him with two or three grip-bags. His questions were crisp and to the point. 'No,' I confessed, I had never been on a commando exercise, much less an operation. Hoping that this legendary warrior, all the while sizing me up with less than heroic enthusiasm, would think I had seen at least some action, I told him my bags contained 'a few civilising comforts from the Cassino front'.

'You'll get everything you need in a commando pack,' he said tersely.

'Including a typewriter?'

'Yes, including a typewriter.'

I was with No. 1 Special Service Brigade, made up of Nos 3, 4 and 6 Army Commandos, No. 45 (Royal Marine) Commando, and the 1st and 8th Troops, composed of Frenchmen belonging to No. 10 (Inter-Allied) Commando.

Although proud to be given and allowed to wear a green beret, I was under no illusion that I was the real thing. Indeed, I seemed to be the only non-commando in this camp of several thousand men. After two or three days it was shattering to meet a fellow-intruder: a tall swashbuckling American with a black patch over one eye and leggings like stretched spats, a war correspondent and, what was worse, one from Reuters' most formidable competitor, Associated Press.

In the event Roger Greene, mature and wise, with old-world courtesy and impressive professionalism, was to prove a most congenial adversary and colleague. We were later to joke that we had shared a jeep 'from D-Day to bidet', though we did wonder what poor Lovat had done to deserve being lumbered with a one-armed Scot and a one-eyed Yank!

The troops among whom we lived came from formations which had fought in the fjords of Norway, the jungles of Madagascar, on the sands of Africa and in the docks of St Nazaire. For months now, on unfamiliar beaches, they had rehearsed various forms of attack, stretching stamina and weapons to the limit. They had had demonstrations of German arms and lectures on escape tactics. Every daylight hour they loosened up and practised assault tactics. A spirit of camaraderie prevailed, an almost tangible feeling of belonging to something rather special. Cooks, clerks, officers and batmen, as well as fighting men, those leaping over obstacles, swinging from trees or engaging in other feats of physical prowess, they all belonged to one unified assault force. They shared a sense of pride in their insignia and in their role and record in battle. They were also a friendly lot, with whom conversation was easy and uninhibited.

We had meals together, and slept in round bell-tents. On my right I had the padre, and we chatted at length about commandos, the state of the church and lots of less godly matters.

On Sunday 4 June – D-minus 2 – the padre took the pre-assault church parade. Several hundred big brawny commandos sprawled or squatted on grass banks and in shallow trenches under a canopy of ancient trees. The pulpit was a mound of earth and the canteen piano did for an organ. 'Eternal Father, Strong to Save' they sang with gusto, and bowed their heads.

The padre, preaching without notes but with an evangelical tone, told them:

I believe this fight we are in is God's fight. If I didn't I would not touch it with a barge-pole . . . Now lads, we are going into this party with a grin on our faces, hurling defiance at the enemy and feeling pretty good about it. But we are going to feel that way by facing up to what it is. We are going to see some pretty nasty sights on that beach and perhaps later on. God be with you.

An audible sigh echoed round the camp. The mood was awful, calamitous. Sensing it, Lovat strode to the makeshift pulpit. He spoke for about two minutes, reviving the men's morale like Henry V at the battle of Agincourt. Speaking first in English, then in colloquial French, he congratulated them on being chosen to fight together as the cutting edge of the Expeditionary Force, and concluded, 'We have been given a proud task, and I expect the Brigade to fight in such a manner that history will say, "They were men, they were giants in those days." '

There was a sequel. After lunch on our last day in camp, I was walking to my tent when I heard the sharp crack of a rifle shot, and the sound of the tent canvas stretching where the bullet had ripped a hole. The padre had shot himself dead.

I heard he had taken his life on being told by the Brigadier that he was not going in with the first wave. In Lovat's own memoirs, I read later that:

the new padre preached a rotten sermon about death and destruction . . . There were a number of complaints and the cleric was suspended and told to return whence he came. Poor fellow . . . the unfortunate clergyman killed himself . . . and . . . was put down as a battle casualty.

What a hassle it was getting everything (portable typewriter included) into my commando pack, then trying to stand straight and walk. A commando pack is not just heavy and cumbersome, it makes you feel like a beast of burden with it harnessed to your shoulders. Balancing with difficulty, I staggered to the bus taking us to Southampton docks and then on to the landing-craft.

The commandos were buoyant, whistling 'Lillibullero', though everyone was keyed up to the imminence of a momentous mission. With embarkation, tension eased and it was a pleasant summer evening as, at about 6 pm, we sailed down the Solent. Lovat's piper played in the bows of the first of the 22 craft in line.

A few hours later, our landing-craft skipper summoned to his cabin the officer in charge of the commando troop, my 'conducting officer' or minder, a Captain Hamar Bagnall, and me. As the clock struck nine, he opened an envelope heavy with official seals and marked 'Top Secret'.

'Gentlemen,' he said, 'it's on: this is where we are landing.'

By lamplight, we studied maps and saw the estuary of a river. Someone recognised it as the Orne, but I hadn't a clue where the Orne was.

If everything went according to plan, we should hit Sword Beach, a 2-mile swathe of sand on the extreme left flank of the invasion area, at about 9 am, only two hours after the first seaborne units had reached France.

The immediate objective was to destroy a battery and garrison in Ouistreham, a mile from the beach. Minesweepers had gone ahead, clearing channels to the coast. Units of the 6th Airborne Division would already be on the ground waiting for us. What I didn't know was that Sword Beach was covered by 140 German guns, some protected by 17 ft (5 m) of concrete, and was also within artillery range of Caen, 8 miles away.

The skipper passed round a bottle and each of us took a hefty swig. Then, back on deck, we lay down as flat as the cramped conditions allowed while the little boat pitched and groped across the Channel. We were warm, if we could avoid the knifing wind. We hardly talked. Excitement and uncertainty stifled any sense of fear. Sleep, like food, seemed irrelevant.

I was too hyped-up, there was too much happening to be afraid. But one awful thought kept recurring: a torpedo or even a bomb might kill any chance of getting the news back to London. The only thing that mattered for me at that moment was the story. The news – how to convey even a detail of this mighty mosaic – transcended everything. And when to write it – now, when there was no light to see? Or in the morning? But might not the matter of staying alive then rate priority over drafting despatches? Never. This was not the first time, nor would it be the last, when getting back to Reuters the first flashes of instant history became an obsessive commitment.

'God,' I thought, 'suppose I find myself in the drink.' Should I take George off? I couldn't float, much less swim, with George and the pack. Too late to worry about that. Bizarre thought – but for George, would I be here now?

Since before daybreak, bombers and fighters had cascaded their cargoes on German gun emplacements and pillboxes, scoured the skies for the *Luftwaffe* and probed ahead for tactical targets. This was war in its totality, theatrical and terrifying. The greatest combined operation in history was under way and this time I was not just in the stalls but on stage.

A smudge, brown on black in the far distance, marked our landing-area. The craft zigzagged the last mile or two, dodging the shells now coming out to meet us. There were ships everywhere, one or two smoking or even sinking, some fouling uncleared obstacles, but most of them swinging massively and majestically towards the hazy coast-line that was Normandy.

For the final lap, the skipper opened the throttle, and at 09.06 we rammed Sword Beach. The ramp thrown down from the landing-craft was steep and slippery, and I fell chest-deep into the sea lapping the mined beaches. The commandos, their faces smeared with cam-ouflage grease, charged ahead. I struggled. My pack, sodden and waterlogged, strapped tight round my shoulders, seemed made for easy drowning. But a lunge forward, helped by a heave from a large corporal already in the water, gave me a first toehold.

Ahead lay the beach. It was a sandy cemetery of the unburied dead. Bodies, some only half-dead, lay scattered about, with arms or legs severed, their blood clotting the sand. Behind me, through foun-tains of water raised by exploding shells from the coastal batteries, lit-tle ships were nudging into the shallows, and behind them a vast armada of battleships, cruisers, destroyers and close support vessels put down a paralysing bombardment.

It would be no good trying to bolt up the beach with the commandos, though many of them were also carrying collapsible bicycles. For me, every step was an effort under the backbreaking load of my pack. Dripping wet, like my trousers, it felt as if it weighed a ton. While the commandos surged ahead until swallowed up in the brooding woods, I edged along the protective shelter of a garden wall, crossed the pot-holed road into a field and stumbled into a ditch about 200 yards (180 m) from the beach. There I stayed, with the wounded.

We fought to stay alive in that shallow furrow, clawing at the soggy soil for depth that at least made us feel a little less exposed to the withering mortar and shellfire. Whether falling short or whistling overhead, it never let up. Earth spurted in with every near miss and more water seeped through our clothes. But we thanked God for that damp dirty ditch.

With every pause in fire, I was wrestling to ease myself out of the commando pack harness. When it was finally detached, I opened it almost furtively, and found my portable typewriter undamaged. I got a sheet of paper in and started pecking at the keyboard, but it was hopeless; every time I tried to type, a mortar exploded a few yards away or hit the lip of the ditch and a shower of dirt clogged the keys. So I tore a page from a school exercise book and scribbled a few lines from 'A ditch 200 yards inside Normandy'. It never reached Reuters.

Leaving the ditch, I wriggled and crawled back to the beach, flinging myself flat every few yards, then spurting forward again when I imagined the Germans might be reloading. Dr Robert Desmond in his book *In Tides of War*, said I had a pigeon on the beach. I did not even see a pigeon, or a censor, on the beach that morning, but a naval officer, operating a shuttle between Normandy and the English coast, agreed to take my grimy bits of paper and try to get them back to Reuters. I gave him £5, and never saw him again.

The German fire was by now murderous, hosing parts of the beach with mortar, as the beachmasters carried on unloading men, guns and trucks amid a shambles of twisted steel defences and battered boats sticking up out of the low tide. Some of the bodies had been covered by bits of tarpaulin, some were half-buried in sand. The din was deafening as I crept back to the ditch, past the now crumbling wall, the barbed wire and pulverised pillboxes, over the pot-holed road, wary of mines and booby-traps among the dunes and scrub.

The Germans had us hemmed in on the east and south, so my captain and I headed west, thumbing a ride D-Day style – a foothold on an armoured car. We ended up in an orchard where soldiers were urgently digging fox-holes. I borrowed a tool and tried to dig, but the ground was hard and unyielding, bullets were getting too close for comfort and rumour had it that German tanks were almost on top of us, so we beat it, fast.

Traffic was now building up. There was a non-stop crackle of shots from snipers up trees, in hedgerows and bracken, in cellars and attics, in ruins and church steeples, a favourite vantage-point.

But in Ouistreham, at the bottom of the garden of a fairly substantial-looking villa, I found a trench. It smelled like (but surely could not be?) an open drain; it was very damp and might well have contained rats or mines, but I was content with it. After a sleepless night, and 12 hours of being knocked dizzy by mortar and shellfire, I was mentally and physically so exhausted that I was ready to flop anywhere that seemed to offer any degree of shelter and safety, however small.

It was heartening to look up at the darkening sky and see the giant force of bombers, transports and troop-carrying gliders overhead, with fighters weaving protectively through the massed formations. The procession lasted nearly an hour and the din was fiendish as the German anti-aircraft batteries tried desperately but in vain to stop it. The sound of gliders diving in to land was a symphony to our ears.

When it got really dark, the *Luftwaffe* made a token appearance to bomb the beach and troop positions between the beach and the front. I saw one plane shot to bits as it caught the beam of a searchlight. Another fell as a flaming ball.

I had an agonising D-Day night, shivering and sneezing in my garden ditch. At first light I went to the house, a detached three-storey villa, with fluted wooden shutters on the windows of the first two floors. An elderly French woman greeted me and offered a chair, in which a German officer had been sitting an hour or two earlier. The old lady prepared an omelette and coffee.

'*C'était très joli,*' she said of the night's air display. She was one of only 400 inhabitants who remained in Ouistreham before the invasion, out of a normal population of 4,000, but one-third of those 400 were killed and one-third wounded.

In the town, we bumped into Leonard Mosley of the *Daily Sketch*, who had parachuted down behind the German lines at 1 am. I stayed within reach of the beach because no organised transmission service showed up and I was nervous about losing communications, however primitive. Some copy went by naval despatch boat at top speed across the Channel and the red-and-white courier bags were rushed to London from the coastal stations by motorcycle and jeep, or despatches were teleprinted to press headquarters at SHAEF. My copy, like that of one or two other assault correspondents, was pooled for the first few days.

To find the commandos from whom I'd parted company soon after landing, we drove next morning along a dusty road, snaking through fields where poppies grew in profusion amid the bloated carcasses of cows and horses, sometimes on their backs with hooves in the air. Then a Disney fantasy scene unfolded: hundreds of pancaked gliders, some intact, some nose up, some in ditches, some half-hidden by walls into which they had crashed, together forming a crazy pattern covering several acres.

We went across an orchard, a dormitory of slit trenches, and through a hole in a wall to the squat scarred farm-buildings where Lord Lovat had his headquarters. No one used the sand-bagged front gate. It was only 50 yards (45 m) from the farmhouse, but the Germans had been outside it last night and were still not more than 100 yards away. Lovat, however, looked relaxed. In a loose pullover and open-necked shirt, he might have been out for a stroll on his Highland estate, but for the green beret and the rifle slung over his shoulder.

He told me the operation had been 'one hundred per cent successful'. His men had carried out their mission and more. Within two or three hours of forming up off the beaches, where they had been met with a 'charge!' tempo on the bagpipes, the commandos had swept through several villages, neutralised nests of resistance, and advanced 5 miles inside Normandy.

Lovat did not say so, but this meant they had to take some routes seeded with Rommel's 'devils' gardens' of lethal impediments to join forces with the British airborne units dropped overnight by glider and parachute to secure the bridges spanning the Orne and Caen canal. He simply said they had attained their objectives and linked up with the airborne troops holding on to the captured bridges.

I learned that, in typically carefree and casual style, Lovat had come swinging up the road to meet the paratroops with a Scottish piper playing on either side of him. Wounded a few days later, Lovat sent a message to his men, 'I have become a casualty but I can rely on you not to take one step back. You are making history.' His gallantry as a commando leader brought him the Distinguished Service Order, the Military Cross, and several other decorations.

Three days after landing, I received the following hand-written note from Cole:

Thank God you are safe!

What a despatch you broke that good news. I am getting this down in the midst of an avalanche of routine because I want to tell you that you will never write a better piece than the villa.
  We are all proud of you: particularly
  Yours aye, Walton A. Cole
  Good luck. More power to you.

This intoxicating praise was echoed in my first letter from London two days later, from his personal assistant, Joyce Hulatt:

I have never in all my life read such a marvellous piece of descriptive as I've just seen in all the papers. I feel I've been sitting in that villa, and shivers are still running down my spine. Congratulations.

These were my medal ribbons.

The remainder of June was a confused welter of contrasts and a time of learning, about the news business and my fellow journalists as well as about war.

There was a slightly wild punch-drunk note in both my letters home and my feature pieces:

With the Advanced Allied Force – Fleas and 1923 champagne, the fragrance of wild roses and the persistent smell of cordite; mess tins and elegant French china; earsplitting barrages and the dead quiet of a cemetery; guns and cornfields, twittering birds, brown earth, lush green grass, animal and human corpses – it's a pretty grim picnic even as four-day-old bridgeheads go.
  I've had at least a dozen billets, from dank trenches to château boudoirs and cellars, from the base of an apple tree to a hole in the wall. When the bombs stop falling the shells start screaming, and snipers take over from the mortars.
  Last night the Luftwaffe *strafed us and bombed us for four hours solid. Broken glass and falling masonry heaped up on my German blankets. In the middle of an*

air raid today, when I was in my familiar posture of hugging the earth, the local mayor brought up the champagne. Two bottles of 1923 vintage – 'cent francs' *or 5s.* [25p] *a bottle . . .*

I spent last night with the rats, in the cellar of a French château about eight miles inland in which Germans had lived for several months . . . A little viscountess prepared a noble meal, really good after 72 hours on 'compo' rations . . .

Two parcels addressed to Germans were delivered. One contained two pounds [1 kg] *of Danish butter, the other a collection of hinges, screws, nails, darning wool, silk thread and needles. Hundreds of houses along the sea front and inland have blown up and are still disintegrating. I hope this house is not mined . . .*

But also the calmer:

Bayeux is the oasis of this bridgehead, a French town the war passed by. The shops are full and crowded with buyers. Life goes on as it did when Germans strolled along the cobbled streets and leaned against the bridge where British soldiers now stop for a smoke and a chat . . . and there is a posh hotel where you get a sumptuous double bedroom with all the amenities of the West End . . . A blue ink double line in the register indicates when the Germans cleared out to let the Allies move in . . .

French men wear gabardine or linen suits and the women mostly wear frocks of coloured prints and light costumes . . . elegant gowns in the shop windows and plenty of shoes . . . the French are living as well as many British families . . .

A recurrent feature of Normandy reporting was briefings by General Montgomery. A day or two after the landings, he had parked his caravan and set up Tactical Headquarters in the grounds of Cruelly Château, not far from Creully's Hôtel St Martin, taken over by the war correspondents as press headquarters.

A few paces along the High Street our censors and wireless operators worked in the remains of a feudal castle, where William the Conqueror was reputed to have planned the 1066 invasion of

England. In the hotel's stone-flagged restaurant we savoured the delights of *la cuisine normande.*

Summoned to a briefing on D-Day plus 6, about 50 of us met him in a green glade, a small clearing fringed by holly trees and firs and sweet-smelling white blossom, which he said was similar to the setting of a press conference he gave at El Alamein. He was wearing corduroys and no less than three grey-and-khaki pullovers. We squatted on the grass; he sat on a little collapsible canvas chair, and several times shivered despite his layers of clothing.

As a war briefing, he told us, 'We have won the battle of the beaches . . . I am very happy, very pleased indeed with the situation so far.'

He also told us the situation regarding his toilet arrangements. He said his caravan contained no chamber-pot, so the mistress of the château was asked for the loan of a vase 'suitable for the General's flowers'. Madame had produced a small *pot-de-chambre*, ornamented with pink flowers.

I enjoyed these occasions because I thought I had an unbeatable technique. First a series of two- or three-line 'snaps' on the highlights: 'won the battle of the beaches'; '7,000 prisoners taken to Sunday night'; 'German women snipers killed'. Then a near verbatim report of the whole briefing, and an overall lead containing touches of colour.

I reckoned a censor would clear quickly a brief message he could read in one glance without effort. On the full report, my shorthand gave me the edge; the serious papers at that time would take every word Montgomery was reported to have uttered. The final lead or 'intro' was ready-made for the tabloids. The result was a lovely spread of credits; and that was the name of the game then – get into print.

It was a technique never learned by my friend and rival Roger Greene of AP. The journalistic standards of AP were much the same as those of Reuters: no angling or slanting, quotes and sources a must, accuracy essential, speed a high priority. Roger was a good reporter and perhaps an even better writer, but when we started to receive copies of the British newspapers, I could see the erosion of his morale as he glanced through them.

We had been to the same part of the front, got the same quotes from the same people, gone in tandem to the censor's office, yet there was hardly ever an AP credit, always Reuters, usually with my byline. He even accused me of getting up to tricks, doing a deal with the censors – but it was simply the use of the right technique.

Whereas my first take would say, 'St Honorine captured', Roger might compose something like, 'Troops of a famous British regiment captured the village of St Honorine, four miles north-east of Caen, after a fierce battle fought among green fields full of rich crops.' My version got away quicker, and the sub-editors on the London desk knew from previous stories exactly where St Honorine was, and what the build-up to its capture had been.

Roger Greene and I were together in combat zones, bars and bedrooms for most of a year. He was 15 years older, at least 3 in. (7 cm) taller, and one of the best newsmen, and gentle and kind characters I have known. Together we jeeped to the front, buttonholed Monty if he turned up in our sector, cowered in cellars, listened and took notes from briefing officers. We would commandeer ('liberate', we said) a house or farm and send our driver or conducting officer to get food while we hammered out the story on our portables.

Once or twice when things got a bit hot and we'd missed a lot of sleep because we went on working as long as we had light, we could get a little tensed up. Roger would threaten to bash my brains in but for my missing arm and I would threaten to smash him to pulp but for his Cyclopean eye. Then we'd have a drink.

He wrote to me in 1957 on the day he was appointed AP's news features editor:

I guess there were never two guys who went through quite so much together over so long a time over a pretty rough period in our lives . . . It's still all too big in memory to remember, and yet . . . remember the little pinch-mouthed Captain who was our conducting officer for a while, and took us up to shell-bursting Caen and back again, down the long, long road to Bayeux, with Jerry planes slogging bombs around and about and spitting a few machine gun bullets and this chap at the wheel – Jimmy something – pushing that jeep to its wildest extremities, hurdling shell holes in the road at a speed which I, at that moment, personally believed was impossible, and a Jerry plane with some rather ugly guns came over us making a great vast noise and thup-thup-thupping cannon shells at us with vast violence, and I remember we all got out of that goddam jeep and crouched behind walls, and then, queasily, got into it again, and by God, Jimmy started roaring like mad down the road to Bayeux again at such a clip I wished the hell I was back in Caen and not going down that long, long road to the Lion d'Or.

Like all guys who went through it, Doon, our story will never be told. But what great gorgeous belly laughs went with it, too!

Alan Moorehead, a short neat compact man like a coiled spring, was part of a triumvirate with Alexander Clifford of the *Daily Mail* and Christopher Buckley of *The Daily Telegraph*, who were almost in a class of their own in the army of journos following the war in the 1940s. Clifford, a former Reuter man, was square-shouldered, cool, reserved, with uncompromising eyes behind his glasses. Buckley, tall and rangy, never looked too comfortable in his battledress. Their track records, consistent style and flair in covering and interpreting war gave them special status and easier access to generals and others in authority. To their colleagues they were never other than helpful and generous. In less congenial company they could distance themselves with ease.

They had their own conducting officer who seemed pleasant enough, but who used always to be watching me taking shorthand notes, transcribing them, sending urgent snaps and short takes. I assumed he was thinking ahead to a possible postwar job with Reuters, so when he told me one day that he had heard Tony Cole was coming over, and asked me to reserve an opportunity for him to dine with Cole, I thought, 'Like Hell. Cole won't want to be stuck with you.'

Cole, who was the press member of a delegation appointed by Eisenhower to deal with press communications, duly arrived and we met in the courtyard of the Lion d'Or in Bayeux. Suddenly Cole turned away from me and warmly embraced someone I had not even spotted: the importunate conducting officer.

'Did you fix dinner?' asked the officer.

'Sorry, not had time. I have only just this minute met Mr Cole.'

I then learned the officer's identity. He was Philip Dunn, who owned most of the *News of the World*.

I had superb colleagues in the struggle against the competition of AP and Dunn's team of Fleet Streeters. A better bunch could not have been assembled. They worked hard, loyally and with tremendous verve for Reuters. Those closest to me were Seaghan Maynes, a marvellous little bundle of Irish flair and fun who seemed drawn like a magnet to action wherever it happened to be, and Charlie Lynch, a bear of a Canadian whose exceptional touch proved unbeatable in his sector.

There was Desmond Tighe, with the navy, who had previously been a Reuter war correspondent in Finland, then Norway. After witnessing the occupation of the Norwegian capital, Desmond walked through streets filled with enemy troops to the main railway station, strode past a picket of German soldiers at the barrier and boarded the last train to Stockholm. He was later mentioned in despatches for work with the British Navy.

The RAF had Montague Taylor and Harold Mayes, who also did valuable work with the ground forces.

Of Reuters' North Americans, Bob Reuben and Bill Stringer were in the Cherbourg peninsula, and I had most contact with Marshall Yarrow, a carefree Canadian, and John Wilhelm.

Marshall, though no chicken, went in on D-Day with glider troops to 'a country of stinking swamp and hidden snipers' behind Utah Beach, and wrote one of the most memorable lines of the campaign, 'I left my face prints in the mud of Normandy's ditches.'

John Wilhelm, young, impatient and venturesome, was assigned to me after he came adrift with authority in an adjoining American sector over his attitude to regulations. Cole sent him into my care with the message:

Assigning Wilhelm to you as reinforcement. Wilhelm is essentially a decent sort of chap and I think you will make quite a lot of him. He will be a test to you because he is inclined to be impetuous and in his enthusiasm knows all the answers. He must adhere to instructions and not take the bit between his teeth . . .

He was told to report to you at once and sent a cable a few days later saying that he was coming over here [London] and if he was to be stopped we should reply at once. He was told not to come but arrived. Apart altogether from committing a cardinal fault . . . he foolishly provided ammunition to the American PROs with whom he has been having a private war . . .

I felt the safest thing was to slot Wilhelm into a jeep party with a few of the more establishment type of British war correspondents. After a few days, one of the other two tackled me brusquely, 'Where's Wilhelm? More important, where's our jeep?'

Eventually, Wilhelm turned up with the jeep and drafted this service message:

Pro Walton Cole exceedingly regret inform you apparently inevitable has happened eteye violated British regulations taking vehicle sans driver through German lines. Your friend Brigadier Neville has taken seriousest view this unintentional bad form my part etordered me Londonward profurther consideration. Waiting prolast minute conference with Doon sevening but apparently must return prohell from SHAEF, you, etal. It never rains but it pours. Regards etapologies.

75

I followed this up with a chaser about youthful impetuosity and his professional, if madcap, motivation in slipping through German lines into a French village to witness its liberation from inside, and so on. The final outcome was that the eager-beaver Wilhelm survived as a correspondent, though in another theatre, where he later helped liberate Reuters' Paris office. He eventually became Dean of the College of Communication at Ohio University.

A sympathetic account of our lives and performance at this time appeared as a three-page spread in *Picture Post* under the heading 'The Men who Send the Front Line News'. It said that out of a total 800 accredited war correspondents, perhaps 25 contributed the bulk of the first-hand battle news, and carried pictures of 13 of us, including me and the Moorehead–Clifford–Buckley trio.

The article was by Macdonald Hastings, father of Max Hastings, who was later to distinguish himself as a war correspondent in the Falklands and go on to edit *The Daily Telegraph* and the London *Evening Standard*. His article, dated 14 October 1944, said:

To begin with, it's high time that somebody said that the men of this war have done a far, far better job than the war correspondents in the last . . .

The despatches that the war correspondents are sending back this time are the story of the war as the front-line soldier sees it. Indeed, the correspondents in this mobile warfare are front-line soldiers themselves.

The evidence of it is that, relative to their numbers, more war correspondents have been casualties in this war than in any other unit in the forces. Since D-Day in France, six have been killed, and ten wounded.

The reporting of this war, if it's only occasionally been brilliant, has generally been accurate, and nearly always first-hand. When it hasn't been first-hand, the fault has been the failure of the army to provide proper facilities; it's never been the unwillingness of a reporter to take the battle risks . . .

Every day, in every sort of climate, they've tumbled into their jeeps, and started out on some hectic battle adventure. They've been wounded, blown up, lost, hungry, filthy dirty, frightened and exhausted. Yet, every day – somehow, some-where – they've got to their typewriters at the end of it, and, laboriously tapping with one finger, hammered out the story which has brought you the latest word picture of the war.

It's all very well saying soldiers have to go through just the same sort of thing. They don't . . . Soldiers aren't in the front line so long. And they don't get into trouble so often. And when they've finished a day's fighting, they don't have to sit down and write a despatch about it, and argue with a censor. The strain is fear-ful. The atmosphere is hysterical. And, week in, week out, the war correspondents never get away from it. It's a helluva life.

Apart from the stimulus of working with colleagues and competitors, I was spoiled and nannied by a flow of messages from London, mixing analysis, information, praise and support, often with a shrewd eye to motivation. No other news organisation gave their correspondents comparable attention from editor, news editor and desk.

Herograms came in like, 'Congratulations good allround coverage new offensive which linked nicely with copy from colleagues. Your work tonight first class regards Mason'; 'You alone with late message yesternight on new dispositionings calvary hill etc. splashed everywhere good luck Cole'; 'Your copy has reached a level where it cannot go much higher regards Mason'.

Sometimes there were also personal letters; an early one was from Sid Mason:

To come to first things first, you seem to have had a very rough passage but at no time was I aware that you were going in with the Commandos . . . I wrote to your father and mother today and told them you were getting lousy for want of soap . . .

I believe I asked you for a story which would support one sent by Bill Stringer that Normandy was a prosperous country. The reason for this: the French were going for us over the story, just because it had been sent out by Reuters. Everybody else had it too, but it did not matter much.

It was not quite in its proper perspective in as much as Normandy always was one of the granary areas . . .

I don't know whether I really explained to you previously what happened on our initial coverage, but it was so good that for the first time in Reuter history the Board placed on record its appreciation of various people including the war correspondents by name . . . That does not sound very handsome but as a departure from tradition I think it meant a lot . . .

And another instructional letter from Sid at the end of the month:

From enclosed evening papers you will deduce that your copy was treated properly. What happened was that this came through me at SHAEF. Time of arrival was about 2.20, and from your first and second pages, three snapfulls [the third level of priority rating after flash and snap] *were done. At the end of your second page, the item about the breakthrough of the German infantry lines I saved . . . until the strategic time of 3 pm when it broke into all late evening papers and stayed there. . . . Transmission from the beachhead is averaging roughly anything from three to four, sometimes five, hours . . . 50 words reaching here at 6.30 will get somewhere, and your follow-up of anything from 250/400 words if it lands anytime between 7 pm and midnight will get used . . . Your copy at the moment is just right.*

P.S. We are doing every week an article of about 500 words for a Swedish client. What's needed is a despatch sent off during Saturday to reach us during the evening or first thing Sunday morning, but no later, giving a punchy, intimate personal description of the fighting and a short concluding paragraph summing up what we might be about to do. In any case, no one will let you write the latter, but we can probably fix it. This wants vivid treatment . . .

Too many such requests for specials and 'thinkpieces' could become burdensome, and though on the whole Mason showed understanding, there was little let-up in the demands for copy.

With a fluid front and three or four running action stories, these 'specials' could sometimes be difficult to fit into a 12- to 14-hour day. I had to restrain myself from allowing testiness to creep into acknowledgements. From long experience Mason and Cole expertly spotted such symptoms and reacted:

Doon [instead of the usual proCampbell] *listen to me. Unnecessary and nobody expects you downwear self. Suggest inpull Marsh Yarrow to cover your present assignment infilling him cumwhats needed and then you go Bayeux sleep proweek take things easy generally. No dithering over this. Do as eye say and rest regards Sid.*

But this was followed by a message from Cole:

Yarrow outpulled and informatively confidentially have independent medical report which explains this. Arranging Maynes replace Yarrow British zone and have informed him to work in to your plans. You going great guns good luck Cole.

I had received, and rejected, an offer to work for AP at twice my Reuter salary, and I told my father about it in a letter which also indicated my state of mind:

Have not had a proper bath since D-Day. We have torrential rain. I do two things: work and scrounge. I scrounge eggs and butter and beef and strawberries. Came away from the American sector yesterday with half a hundredweight of tinned bacon, several hundred cigarettes, several gallons of tinned Carnation milk. But, gosh, I do get tired. Utterly exhausted, too tired to sleep. Sometimes I think of packing it in with Reuters and taking a whole month's real rest . . .

On one occasion, after working myself to a frazzle, I did whip off a note to Cole – in the middle of a battle – questioning whether churning out pages of bylined copy was really worthwhile, and wondering if it might not be better to spend two years on sabbatical, reading history through an extra-mural university course. Cole, the psychiatrist, was always quick to apply the appropriate treatment: extravagant praise. He wrote on 20 July:

A personal note to say how proud I am of your work. You have certainly applied every lesson that has been passed on to you and your enthusiasm and enterprise are reflected in the grand show all your despatches have been receiving.

They are just what are wanted and you yourself are aware that all the time there is a consistent improvement in quality content, an improvement learned by experience.

You are doing a fine job for Reuters and what is more it is thoroughly appreciated . . . Continue as you are doing and all that you wanted to attain in this fine profession of ours will be realised . . . In you I see, and have always seen, the correspondent who will make Reuters the great force it must be in world affairs, and particularly in ensuring that what we both believe in journalistically is attained.

One tip: avoid sweeping generalisations like 'Rommel has had more than enough for the time being'. You can get the same effect without boomerang phrases and understatement is always more effective than over-playing . . .

A couple of weeks later I received a six-page letter from him, again reassuring me about my future, but telling me I needed a lot more experience first and advising against accepting other offers. Here are some extracts:

Do not imagine that you are prematurely important . . . I was exactly the same age as you when I started being taken notice of in the Street. I should imagine I have had exactly the same sort of experiences as you have had.

First of all there were offers that I well knew to be fantastic and others that appealed as having possibilities on a long term aspect, and I believe that the offerings of agency work more than balance the bait preferred by other units in this profession.

Straight news, honest to goodness assessment of it and not proprietorial, factional or policy interests mean more to me than spondulicks or personal byline.

I am not such an awful lot older than you but I have seen scores of people who felt otherwise disappear from the byline sphere in popular papers and elsewhere and others who are more or less Fleet Street's forgotten men through being all burnt up . . .

You have a brilliant career in front of you here with the world as your beat and the pick of the world news stories as your assignment. There was no one more aware of your shortcomings than myself, and the only way these will be remedied will be in the same way that I am remedying mine – by experience.

You know me sufficiently well to realise that I have no selfish interest and that I am capable of taking the widest viewpoint.

There is more tommyrot and fatuous talk about careers in journalism than in any other profession and there are all too many well intentioned beings who are ready to act as counsellors.

Forbid that I ever enter the sphere, and I am certain that if you follow the line that I have given you, you will have no regrets, and that furthermore your desire to possess the complete qualifications will be met.

There is a tremendous field that is awaiting you here in this organisation in the not so distant future. If, after sampling that, you still have reservations about the background you are wanting and our ability to give it to you, then there is abundant time to feel that some breather is required.

After reflecting on these concerned messages, I mulled over all the options and, putting my trust in Cole, decided not to jilt my 'magic mistress'. I was immediately glad I had made that decision.

5
From the beaches to the Rhine

General Montgomery was a major focus for much reporting of the British sector of the invasion which, Cole had made clear in another of his letters, was the part on which we must not be beaten by the American correspondents, no matter whether they beat us on the American sector. When King George VI came to Normandy to hand out medals ten days after D-Day, it was Montgomery who walked beside him, and who called for 'hats off and three cheers for His Majesty', and it was Montgomery who sat beside Winston Churchill when the Prime Minister visited the devastated city of Caen five weeks later.

Churchill's visit had been kept a very close secret, but once he was there it was hard to miss the fact that there was a Very Important Person about, as he swished along the Caen–Bayeux road, sitting with Montgomery in the back of a big Humber car with a Union Jack on the front and a 'Priority' sign on top, preceded by a military police jeep sounding its siren, and followed by a third car carrying an officer and a civilian.

By accident I dovetailed into the VIP convoy as it passed through mile-long columns of jeeps, scout cars, ambulances, Bren-gun carriers, lorries loaded with ammunition and clumsy clanking tanks. I had never driven faster down that road – not even when German shells were pot-holing it on the day Caen was captured – than when trying to keep up with Churchill's convoy. It wove in and out of traffic jams, through the ruins of villages and on past the twisted steel skeletons of hangars at Carpiquet airport. I could see Montgomery leaning over to point out details of the aerodrome which cost the Canadians so much fighting.

At the crossroads below Franqueville, where General Miles Dempsey was waiting, Churchill got out to have a closer look at Carpiquet, then changed cars, clambering into a tourer to drive up a narrow muddy lane past the gaping battered Abbaye Ardenne through the shambles of Authie to a point just over a mile from Caen. Hundreds of soldiers mending the road, digging trenches or eating from their mess tins in cornfields by the roadside looked up, startled, as the cars swirled by in a muddy spray. One or two waved, but I heard only one 'Hurrah for Winnie', as the cars were on them before they had a proper chance to see who was inside.

Churchill stood up, climbed on to the seat and looked across the ruins of Caen to the country below where Allied armour and infantry were still slogging it out with the Germans. In what appeared to be a deliberate gesture, he faced towards the German lines, and relieved himself against a ruined wall, before driving on to see the horrors of Caen itself.

I saw quite a lot of Montgomery around this time. Whenever I spotted his car I would turn round the jeep and follow him. He was always approachable, always good for a quote, and what he said was always printed prominently. When circumstances did not allow a chat he would sometimes acknowledge my presence with an old-fashioned wink.

Whenever I saw him he seemed in good spirits. I recall him leaning against an apple tree in an orchard west of Bois du Homme, where the Germans had had a camp only 72 hours earlier, and telling me, 'Progress is excellent. We are hitting the Hun a good crack. It is all going very well. I am satisfied and delighted with the whole thing. The Americans are doing splendidly too. The whole thing is excellent. The question now is – when is the war going to end?'

In response to service messages that the opposition (mainly AP, BUP and Extel) were getting into print with telling criticism that instead of making a lightning movement inland, as indicated before the invasion, Montgomery's forces were overcautious and making slow progress, I got hold of a senior staff officer at Montgomery's headquarters who rejected that view, and gave me an inspired forecast.

He said the Allied campaign was exactly on schedule, even including some stages which were slower because of Montgomery's policy of building up large reserves before assaulting German defences, and that the coming stages might be quicker than originally expected, with 'tremendous' German disasters in many places in the next few weeks. Only one week later the German army was fleeing eastwards towards the Falaise Gap in headlong retreat, under savage air attack, and Montgomery told his men that the German armies in north-west France had suffered 'decisive defeat'.

By 24 August the Allies were racing for the Seine, trying to catch up with the Germans, and I noted, 'The enemy nowhere in sight. I have been looking for the front since eight o'clock yesterday morning and my gauge records nearly 190 miles.'

One of the Corps commanders, Lieutenant-General Sir Brian Horrocks, issued an Order of the Day on 28 August, urging his men on by telling them the countryside they were entering was the area from which Hitler's flying bombs and rockets rained on southern England, so every yard they advanced reduced the launching area and helped 'to free our homes, our wives and our children from German attacks'.

It was impossible to keep up with the speed of the advance. From Amiens on 31 August I reported, 'The front is somewhere between

here and Berlin, but I can't find it.' I asked some of the officers from
the British administrative HQ where they were going, and they said
they were heading towards the Somme. 'We will keep moving until
we bump into the Russians. There is nothing ahead,' one said.

Amiens and Arras both appeared little damaged, and the girls
there smothered the British troops with kisses, fruit and flowers. I
took the road for Brussels, passing thousands of prisoners. The local
fire-engine roared past with its complement of Nazi prisoners and
with cheering Maquis hanging on to its mudguards and rails. There
was a never-ending stream of cars, cabs and carts full of prisoners –
SS men affecting yawns of indifference, Austrians in Tyrolean hats,
Mongols, Japanese, Swiss, Russians.

The British spearhead was speeding towards the centre of Brussels
at the same time as the German columns were trying to get out.
Many snipers were still lurking, and from time to time there was the
sharp crack of a rifle shot to be heard above the yelling of the enthusiastic crowds, who were in a state of hysteria, milling around, kissing
and hugging the soldiers.

There was nothing to suggest a battle. The city was clean, the
Belgians well dressed and well fed. Allied flags draped almost every
house, and huge 'welcome' signs sprawled along the rooftops. In the
Metropolitan Hotel, chic women were sipping their drinks and, I
reported, 'dolly birds in silk stockings, Chanel and little else have
moved into the double bedrooms'.

The army set up a press billet and mess in the then rather lush
Canterbury Hotel. In this mink-lined fox-hole we relaxed with choice
wines, oysters, *foie gras* – and news stories galore. It was not long until
the pressure for extra effort began again, this time partly arising
from an escapade by Seaghan Maynes and five other correspondents
who entered Paris the day before the Allied forces. Seaghan told it
like this:

I was with the American General Patton's tanks, which had been ordered to halt at Rambouillet on the outskirts of Paris to allow the Free French forces, which were well behind us, the honour of entering the city first. We frustrated correspondents were forbidden to go in ahead of the troops.

With the help of correspondent Ernest Hemingway I linked up with a French Maquis guerrilla group he was unofficially running. We penetrated the retreating German rearguard and charged into Paris a day ahead of the allied armies.

The Maquis took me to their underground radio, which the BBC monitored, and I broadcast as a Reuter correspondent an eyewitness account of the street fighting between the Maquis and the departing Germans.

My broadcast was accompanied by requests to the BBC to pass it on to Reuters. It was punctuated by rifle fire. There were no censors around and the radio was the only way to get Reuters a world beat on the historic liberation story. I knew the risk. I figured it was worth taking. Supreme Headquarters frowned and I was suspended.

He and the other two British and three American correspondents who sent their reports over the radio were banned from the Continent for a period. Cole gave me the bad news:

Just had news Maynes with Howard Marshall others suspended 60 days which upfollowing. Fresh demands other areas put us hopeless position temporarily . . . can you reshuffle dispositionings? Tighe Lynch both doing well meet situation or incall Maynes. Sorriest but know you understand.

If at all possible require soonest 2000 words La Libre Belgique, *clandestine paper published Brussels during occupation. How edited and distributed, how staff Gestapo-hunted, how presses seized and forced move, how people lost lives in effort distribute truth. Anxiousest get this one.*

Mason followed up:

Unknow where you situated but whenever chance upplay Dunkirk contrast 1940 ettry parhook crook get beach scenes of German surrenders if possible. Dont know if possible cumyour [with your] *tieup but leave you decide whether possible route messages through teleprinter Canadian HQ Bayeuxwards whence transmission instantaneous SHAEFwards . . . remember if you land Holland sometime want cover stories Dutch resistance during German occupation life generally under Germans. Whats Rotterdam look like remembering savage bombing.*

By 11 September I was indeed near the Dutch frontier, after heavy fighting in which, I was told, more Germans had been killed than in the whole 200-mile run to Brussels. Little more than a week later, the British troops had swarmed across the Escaut canal in assault boats and rafts, then bounded on 50 miles to Nijmegen.

Several of my despatches from here were lost when, soberingly, a motor-cycle despatch rider was killed while ferrying them from Nijmegen to Eindhoven. This was one individual tragedy in an over-all picture of destruction as the *Luftwaffe* used everything from bullets to a glider and a piggy-back bomb to try to smash the great bridge across the Waal. The Allies managed to cross the river, the Dutch section of what is elsewhere called the Rhine, but failed to reach Arnhem in time to save the paratroops trapped at the 'bridge too far'.

At Dunkirk, from where Sid Mason was so keen to see my cover of the British revenge for their 1940 evacuation, the civilian population was being allowed its own evacuation, in the opposite direction.

A 5-mile long, four-deep queue of people with babies, livestock, parrots and aspidistras stretched from Mille Brugghe to the other side of Dunkirk. Before noon on 5 October almost 13,000 civilians, including a few Germans in mufti, had passed through the 'international zone' on their trek inland.

According to an intelligence report I saw, the German garrison ration was one hot meal a day, half a pound (225 g) of bread per day per man, sometimes a small piece of horse flesh, but no cigarettes, no spirits or wine, no soap, and no chocolate except for officers.

87

The report said the Germans seized a large quantity of food by looting civilian houses, and added that it 'often happens that one finds on a prisoner-of-war three sets of civilian underwear under his uniform, a couple of fountain pens and half-a-dozen watches in his pocket . . . gold rings are also preferred souvenirs'.

One young German lieutenant accepted my cigarette, and told me, 'I know basic English. I can say basic "I love you" and "Goodbye".'

'*Au revoir*,' I said.

'*Heil Hitler!*' he replied, giving the Nazi salute.

Although I was reluctant to abandon the excitement and stimulation of such visits to the scene of action, Brussels was press HQ, where twice-daily briefings updated the overall battlefield picture – a 'must' for news agency reporters.

Briefings usually couldn't compete with graphic eyewitness reports of a skirmish, or first impressions of a captured town, or what it was like in a German bunker, but between every such report, a dozen or more editions of morning and evening papers were crying out for the latest news, obtainable in approved form only from briefings.

My room at the Canterbury Hotel meant a bed was available the occasional night I got back from the Maas front or Hertogenbosch or wherever forward units of the 2nd Army were. The hotel was the scene of the occasional spontaneous party, like the time Alan Moorehead's wife Lucy brought over the records of the Broadway smash hit *Oklahoma*.

Brussels was a glitzy sin-city, with countless bars, night clubs and cabarets catering for most known conventional and unconventional forms of entertainment. At the Canterbury, George X, a captain with a catering background, was the soul of discretion, indicating by a tick against correspondents' room numbers on the mess list that they had company.

The routine in Brussels was to jeep from the Canterbury to the rue de la Loi press office for the daily briefings by army and RAF officers, one of the best of whom was Alan Melville, the author and writer of such revues as *Sweet and Low*. The technique at the briefings, which were held on the ground floor, was to get your typewriter on a table close to the door. The censors were on the floor above, up a short flight of stairs.

The moment the briefing ended, news agency correspondents belted out a couple of highlights or snaps, and raced them upstairs. The name of the game was to get these bulletins through the censor and on their way to London ahead of the competition. Seconds counted.

Early on I noticed a civilian, bareheaded and wearing a long dark coat, who was hanging about outside the briefing room. He had a style and bearing which caught my attention. He seemed to be watching me belting upstairs. He offered to help, and went up the stairs like a rocket.

This was my first encounter with Serge Nabokoff, one of the contact men *par excellence* on the European political and diplomatic circuit, which was to develop into a relationship I valued for more than 45 years. To formidable intellectual and linguistic gifts, Serge added immense charm and a gift for friendship. Through him, I obtained the use of a room in an elegant house behind the rue de la Loi, so that if I worked late I no longer needed to find a taxi to take me back to the Canterbury.

At first, while awaiting London's authority to engage a 'stringer' (part-time correspondent), I could reward him only with an occasional carton of cigarettes. Eventually, he became a Reuter staff correspondent and bureau chief in Brussels.

On 27 November, Major Geoffrey Keating, a discriminating press relations officer who did not bestow favours with abandon, asked if I would like a special and exclusive out-of-town assignment. Geoffrey was a rare spirit, whose robust brisk nature, flamboyance and independence of action had caught Montgomery's eye, and I went along with his mystery offer.

It turned out to be a meeting between Eisenhower and Montgomery – recently promoted Field-Marshal. After a long boring drive, I was allowed to stand in pouring rain to witness Ike's arrival. He greeted me with a remark about the weather – I must have looked water-logged standing outside the door – and hustled inside. I had no fill-in on their talk, nothing, and I was annoyed at giving up two briefings just to get a momentary sight of Ike, and a soaking.

The only hard news was that Eisenhower and Montgomery had conferred in a house on the Belgian–Dutch border, and that Eisenhower's presence had been kept secret till he arrived. But the atmosphere at Allied HQ at this time was confident and I wrote:

A rendezvous in Belgium
General Eisenhower is conferring tonight with Field-Marshal Montgomery in the third-storey sitting-room of a bleak house near the Dutch border. They are design-ing the final defeat of Germany . . . there is a sense of urgency about the whole business.

The two men have been in conference upstairs for more than two hours at the time of writing – 8.30 pm. Rain is beating on the windows, and a howling wind is flapping loose shutters and unfastened doors . . .

I am able to state on high authority that relations of the Higher Command in this theatre have never been closer or more cordial . . .

There had been not much news at that day's briefings, so several papers went to town on my story and several correspondents had requests for a 'matcher'. I was summoned to the office of the Chief of Staff, Major-General Sir Francis de Guingand, who wanted to know how I had got on to the story, what briefing I had been given, and every other detail.

I was under no pledge of confidentiality, much less of secrecy, so I told him everything. Finally satisfied, he could not fault one fact in the story. He voiced concern about the prominence and size of headlines it had attracted, but I convinced him that newspaper treatment of an agency story was outside my responsibility. That was the nearest I ever came to being carpeted by the military.

The year ended with American forces under pressure in the Ardennes and at Bastogne, but less going on in my sector, bringing the inevitable suggestion to cut down on cable costs. Sid Mason wrote to me on 13 December:

Between you and me, the office is very much overspent on cable tolls which, for reasons of policy, must be reduced to a certain figure before the end of the year. Hence my service message yesterday asking you and Charlie [Lynch], *while the front is quiet, to cut down a bit and to send any features through Ministry of Information channels. I did not mean by this that you and Charlie are overfiling – far from it – but the cumulative effect from several centres is pretty terrifying sometimes, when one sees the aggregate total . . .*

Seaghan [Maynes] *whom I regard as a regular good little guy, is doing extremely well on his new sector. I imagine he is so small that the opposition is sometimes inclined to overlook his presence, with the result that he gets in first . . .*

I dare say we shall be getting the usual 'Christmas in the front line' sort of story. If you or Charlie are doing this try and get the real story, the story of the men up in the front line, as distinct from those in the rear where there may be plenty of beer and skittles . . .

From then on I spent the next three months watching the Allied forces crunch their way towards the Rhine, through the defensive Siegfried Line, and squeezing the Germans into narrow boxes around the western bank of the river. I felt I was doing a worthwhile job in Brussels, and did not solicit an operational assignment until I thought I had been denied one.

I had been named in charge of Reuter war coverage from the 21st Army Group and, in that role, pulled Charlie Lynch back from the Canadian sector in late March for a few hours of R and R (rest and relaxation) among the flesh-pots of Brussels. We were in a night club when, just after midnight, an army despatch rider came looking for us. He passed a cable to my Canadian colleague. Charlie's face registered a mixed reaction as he read it.

'Let's see,' I said, and he passed it across the table. It was from Reuters in London and read, 'Are you prepared undertake important but hazardous assignment which may involve parachute drop?'

What the hell was London playing at, sending such a message to Charlie?

'Look, Charlie,' I said. 'The war's just about over, you've a wife and family back home in Canada and it's too long since you've seen them. You owe it to them to get back in one piece. Let me handle this with London.'

So I drafted a message to 85 Fleet Street, 'After weighing everything and discussing with me, Charlie reluctantly declines. Why I not offered "important but hazardous assignment"?'

London's reply came with the sobering light of dawn, 'It's all yours.' But the army would not let me jump. They said you needed two hands to use a parachute. I could not challenge that, since I'd never heard of a one-armed parachutist either. Seaghan Maynes was sent to parachute down with the British troops, while I was assigned to a glider attached to a combat team of the 17th American Airborne Division, under Major-General Matthew Ridgway.

He had commanded glider and parachute forces in North Africa, Italy and Normandy, and had seen the error of Arnhem: the failure of armour and men driving through to link up with and rescue the airborne units. Now he was determined that his command would not be trapped on the far bank of the Rhine through failure of ground forces to cross the wide fast-flowing river in time. So it was agreed that the Allied assault on the river would come first – with Ridgway himself among those crossing by boat – followed by the airborne attack on the further bank.

The American combat teams assembled near Paris. The evening before the assault, someone turned on a radio and Radio Berlin blared forth, 'Allied landings on a large scale to establish bridgeheads east of the Rhine must be expected. We are prepared.'

Switching programmes, we heard that Eisenhower had come into possession of a secret German High Command order about the execution of airborne Allied soldiers and had warned the Germans against trying to carry out that order.

Nobody slept much that night. We were roused shortly after 5 am and served with bacon and eggs, pancakes and syrup, peaches and cream – a hearty breakfast as specified in the cliché about condemned men – before making for what the troops called the 'cardboard coffins', though they were in fact made of canvas and plywood. Ours was No. 39, a Waco CG-4a named 'Chattanooga'.

I sat in the back of an open jeep harnessed to the floor of the glider, my good arm resting on a box of grenades. A tiny shift in the jeep's position, I was told, would send us into a terminal dive. There were four men in that jeep and I hardly had room to move a muscle, yawn, or toss anti-sickness pills into my mouth – not that they gave much reassurance anyway.

'The heaviest load I've ever carried,' remarked the pilot, and I fretted that the moment we were airborne the whole caboodle of jeep and grenades would come adrift from the fragile and overloaded glider. Still, it was a lovely day, the war was hurtling to an end, and here I was operational with the American airborne elite, *en route* to the Rhine and the heart of Germany. Magic!

Then the glory and excitement gave way to sick-making terror as the flimsy glider cavorted madly in the slipstream of the tow-plane. I was one microscopic detail in the largest single-day airborne operation of the war. Why, oh why had I been daft enough to go chasing after this?

We glided, or rather yo-yoed, over one rubble heap after another, for about three hours until, approaching the Rhine, we were unhooked. Ahead lay a dirty grey-black screen of smoke as thick as a London pea-souper fog, and bullets began to rip through the wings, convulsing the glider.

Fear now gave way to fatalistic feelings. What relief it would be, I thought, if flak or a German 88-mm. shell hit the grenades – I would be blown up without even knowing it had happened, and spared the indignity of tumbling in the back seat of a jeep through 2,000 ft of nothing, helpless, without a parachute. Then an opening appeared in the smog and the pilot got Chattanooga into its last dive. We were now about 300 ft (90 m) up, free-falling at 90 or 100 mph, with no manoeuvring possible. Ahead lay a fence and, beyond it, a white-walled farmhouse. The pilot just managed to catch the fence, as a sort of trip wire, and the glider lurched to a halt, its nose smashed. The glider immediately behind us missed the fence and exploded against the wall of the farm.

But we were alive and on the ground. We got out through the emergency hatch, to see gliders everywhere and still coming, gliders plunging down like torches, gliders disgorging men and machines in mid-air, gliders hurdling ditches, wrestling with telegraph wires.

We tried to get our bearings, but mortar and machine-gun fire seemed to be coming from all sides. We made it to a ditch full of American troops. A man, shot alongside me, was operated on with a trench knife.

'Say, son, where d'you reckon we are?' asked a young officer, trying to read his silk-handkerchief map.

'Up creek, *sans* paddle,' I replied. There we were, lost, in a ditch with our noses in the dirt, when a barrack-square voice from the nearby wood hit us, 'Get up and out, you slobs, this way.' It was the Corps Commander, General Ridgway. I got out of the ditch and tagged along behind him, hoping to come to a press relations unit, but by this time a screen of Germans blocked our access to the river.

Desperate to get my copy out, I rode round our tiny perimeter looking for glider No. 48, which had the trailer with our transmitter. I saw two generals leading 25 men on a patrol through the wood. A white cloth fluttered from a German pillbox, but when the Americans moved in, a shot rang out from a strong-point on the flank and went through a GI's forehead.

Six hours after landing I located the transmitter trailer – just in time for the nine o'clock BBC news. I watched a colonel listening to the broadcast account of the assault he'd led, 'We have established a sizeable bridgehead . . .'

So much was happening – first it was a case of staying alive, then ditch-hopping, then observing the Americans and their adversaries: the Chief of Staff leading a patrol, a general sorting traffic, a German dog in the front seat of a jeep, a German cart-horse pulling our mortars, a German motor-cyclist giving a lift to two GIs.

Seaghan, as I was to learn later, was also having quite a day: landing near a German machine-gun nest, he sheltered behind a tree and yelled, 'Hands up!', then watched as five Germans emerged to surrender to a British paratroop captain, the only other person present.

We were both on top of the world, and my salary was raised from £650 to £750 a year. Sid Mason wrote:

I was thankful indeed to get Charlie's message that both you and Seaghan were all right. It must have been a hell of an experience judging from your story and it was hard luck about the transmitter. I wired and also wrote to Pat [Cameron, my fiancée] *telling her that you were all right and also mentioning the glider Wings and Combat Star* [medals presented to me by General Ridgway]. *You deserve both.*

In a letter home, I told my father:

The airborne operation was fun – but I sweated it out quite a bit. I knew last time I was home that I was on this show and only a last minute balls-up landed me with the American 17th Division instead of the British 6th Division to which I should have been attached. However the Americans were such a thoroughly civilised and combat-conscious crowd that I did not kick.

It was worth foregoing the splash in the British Press – which naturally went to Seaghan with the British outfit – to get this experience with our ally. It gave me a good insight into their approach to battle and conduct in the field – well worth obtaining.

Since then I have reverted to 2nd British Army coverage, taking over by degrees from Charlie Lynch. This was also at my own request.

I am happy again calling at Brigades and Regiments and really getting the atmosphere. I know that much of what I write is true because I have seen it for myself. Life in Germany is not at all bad for correspondents. We help ourselves to everything. We eat well, work hard.

Back in the field, I travelled hundreds of miles following the British and American divisions as they swarmed over the wasteland of the East Rhineland. By 2 April, the troops were more than 100 miles across Germany and I was racing along an autobahn, past a flood of tanks, to get to the action, find my story and race back to the transmitting centre. Such breakneck trips could be dangerous. My letter home ran:

I have been in a jeep accident. The driver had a blackout on a bridge when we were travelling at 40 mph. We bounced off the left parapet, smashed through the right parapet, toppled nine feet into a river, and all got out alive.

Thought I was a goner for a moment because my left arm was trapped under the water between the spar, holding the roof of the jeep, and the river bed, but I was able to wrench it out.

I wired Reuters – 'Regret report involvement in jeep accident with arm smashed – fortunately left one. Jeep write-off. Lettering.' I've been over the bridge twice since and cannot see how we were not all finito.

It was common to see German women and children tramping the roads looking for refuge. Looking into one house, I saw a junk heap of glassware, bottled food, cases of beer, pictures of Hitler and propaganda leaflets all thrown together. Sometimes the walls showed the German eagle over a china crucifix, or a portrait of Goering or some other Nazi leader. But I was surprised to find that German families east of the Rhine had more eggs than they could eat, more milk than they could drink, and more meat than the British civilian's ration. I did not see a hungry German, and I saw no social contact between the British troops and the German civilians.

I spent two nights in one farmhouse, keeping myself warm under back numbers of Goebbels' newspaper, *Das Reich*. The farmer's family appeared every morning, but we never said, 'good morning' or 'excuse me' when we passed on the stairs. It was the same in most German houses where British soldiers were billeted.

One German I was able to interview was the Cardinal Archbishop of Münster, Monsignor Graf Clemens von Galen. He had taken the oath of allegiance to the Nazi regime in 1933, but Nazi propaganda against the Church earned his contempt and he became known for his sermons attacking the police state, saying his faith was stronger than the Nazi party.

He had been bombed out of Münster five months earlier, his palace flattened and his cathedral destroyed. When I saw him at the Hospital of St Francis in nearby Sendenhorst, with Allied armour clattering down the road outside and white flags hanging from every undamaged window in town, I asked this outspoken clergyman if he had anything to say about the new order which must prevail in post-war Germany.

'I am a German,' he said, and he would make no statement that might have repercussions, not only on himself but on others still under Hitler's authority, 'when there is peace, then I will speak . . . I want peace on earth for all men, British, Americans and Germans.'

97

For what it was worth, this was his first interview since 1939. The hospital room where he received me had no carpet on the wooden floor, but there were fresh daffodils on the table. Most of the 300 patients were tuberculosis victims, not war wounded.

One of the dangers at that time was that of a typhus epidemic. Several cases of typhus had broken out in a camp of about 100,000 liberated slave-workers near Frankfurt. The US 3rd Army medical corps carried out a mass inoculation – the first in Germany – and arranged to burn down the entire compound of the former concentration camp. Concrete buildings were blasted to bits and all the rest were set on fire.

In other villages I saw Poles, Czechs, Russians, Belgians and Dutch, freed after five years of slave labour, making merry on German gin as they danced in the streets, wearing fancy hats and straw boaters. One of them even sported a pink crinoline.

Hundreds of children, to whom occupation or liberation were still very much of a novelty, lined the streets waving and shouting, 'Chocolate, chocolate!' The name of one street had been changed to Churchillstrasse. British troops were everywhere – sleeping on top of rumbling Bren-gun carriers, writing home on paper held up against the tank turrets, or trying to make bully-beef sandwiches while speeding forward at 30 mph.

On 13 April, I watched Montgomery formally open a Bailey bridge over the Ems–Weser canal, the thousandth built by his engineers since D-Day. He told the 500 troops who were in the field:

It has been a long, long journey, but the end is nearly in sight. The Germans have been well and truly defeated . . . completely and utterly finished. But the German military machine, which is in the hands of the Nazi party, will never surrender – they will just go on fighting to the last.

A few days later, the Allied troops liberated 20,000 prisoners of war from camps near Fallingbostel, including men who had fought at Dunkirk and Alamein, commandos who had assaulted the beaches in Italy and Normandy, troops overrun in the German offensive in the Ardennes or captured at Arnhem.

A sergeant of the army Medical Corps, who had been in the camp since October, told me, 'Thirty paper bandages was the week's issue for 156 surgical cases. We got some penicillin from the British Red Cross. The Germans were stingy with surgical instruments, drugs and hospital equipment generally.'

But any distaste this caused was pale by comparison with the almost simultaneous news of what had happened at the Belsen camp near Bremen. This is what I wrote on 20 April:

Belsen Concentration Camp, Saturday
War seems nearly wholesome compared with the black spot which lies beyond big red-and-white 'Danger – Typhus' notices strung along the road more than three miles from the entrance to Belsen.

Men I saw there a few hours ago will certainly have died by the time you read this. Over 17,000 prisoners, men, women and children, are said to have died last month. I cannot tell the whole searing story. Much of it may be given only in medical reports because it would offend public morality if published in any other form.

In one hut 50 men huddled sore to sore. One seemed to have a rail over his head – then you recognised arms. One seemed just bone – till you went close and saw stretched skin. One with so many scabs could only see through narrow slits of eyes. One was biting – trying to eat – rotting wood. One was trying to stand on string-like legs that dangled from a body the thickness of a naval hawser. But they all said 'Hello' and tried to smile . . .

About 400 Hungarians are on guard duty and 150 are digging graves. About 40 SS men and 20 SS women are loading and unloading into deep pits bodies of the dead . . . Everybody says the SS women were the most vicious Nazis in the camp.

Josef Kramer, SS camp commandant, lived sumptuously in a big barrack-like building near the bottom of Adolf Hitlerstrasse as the carnage went on. He had an orchestra which played Strauss waltzes while men, women and children died and the wounded wailed.

'Kramer came from the infamous Auschwitz camp in Poland,' said an English-speaking Polish woman in one of the camp cookhouses . . .

They are still dying like flies in the camp. In the hours I was in the camp I saw a man eating coal-dust and another dipping a hard crust of bread into a filthy puddle because he could only digest slops . . .

Kramer was sitting, brooding, on a short-legged stool, when I met him. The inmates would have torn him limb from limb but for his British guards, and they too would have liked to see him hurled into the death pit with all the indignity of the corpses for which he was responsible.

'I worried about conditions at the camp,' he said, 'but thousands of prisoners kept flooding in, and things got out of hand.'

A few days later, I watched six bearded black-coated burgomasters, from nearby towns, stand mute and motionless as they gazed at the spectacle of graves, dead and dying people, filth and disease. The camp's loudspeakers blared, 'What you see provides the final condemnation of the Nazi Party. It contains complete justification for any measures the Allied nations may take to extirpate the Party.'

I could not express what I felt about Belsen when I went there, but it was encapsulated by whoever wrote:

The most unspeakable achievement of those camps was the extent to which they seemed to drain human existence of all meaning, and to reduce each individual existence snuffed out in them to apparent insignificance by the sheer unimaginable scale of the evil that was at work.

There was, however, only about a fortnight now until the end of the war in Europe, a period which for me included another accident while jeeping from the front to the press camp, but also the thrill of entering Germany's second city, Hamburg, on 3 May, more than three hours ahead of the first British soldier.

Private John Holbert was at the wheel of the British army staff car as we drove in at one o'clock to witness the hand-over.

The western approach was a huge wasteland of burned-out tenements, charred houses, whole blocks of buildings razed to the ground. Civilians came out on the ruined suburban streets to gaze at the lonely British car.

Inside the city itself the streets were empty of civilians, but more than 20 German military personnel, officers with automatics and soldiers with rifles, stopped us, until they realised Holbert belonged to the other army.

The Town Hall, though chipped and windowless, looked the most intact building in the city. A German army photographer joined us in the office of the Burgomaster, Carl Vincent Krogmann. A picture of Goering hung on the wall, and one of Hitler stood among the daffodils on the desk. The photographer told me, 'Krogmann is a naughty boy. He has gone over to the Nazis. People are not satisfied with him. Until they kill all the Nazis there will be no peace.'

Krogmann said, 'You are not supposed to be here for another hour. There must be no shooting when your army commander arrives. All the people have been ordered to their houses. I don't anticipate trouble but there are always the stupid radicals. I am charged with maintaining order, and I mean to see that it is kept.'

'You are the first soldiers I have seen,' he added, fidgeting nervously while questioned. 'My people are quiet and behave splendidly. There was no demonstration or ceremony over Hitler's death. The worst raids were in July 1943 when more than 50,000 men were killed. There are now about one million people left. Many of course have gone to the front. Half the buildings in Hamburg have been destroyed. Less than one-third of the city is still habitable.' There was no gas but there was water and rationed electricity. Citizens observed two 'economy days' every week, when there was no light.

The garrison had been confined to barracks, although the SS had wanted to stay at their machine-gun posts in the town. More than 100,000 leaflets had been distributed warning of the arrival of the occupation troops and telling people, 'If you behave there will be no trouble; if you don't, the occupying force will deal with you. The police are responsible for maintaining order.'

Dozens of German policemen were indeed scuttling about, giving the Hitler salute. One had a blanket slung over his shoulder, and a loaf of black bread under his arm. After reading the proclamation the *Wehrmacht* photographer declared, 'I'm not going to be captured. I'm off to Lübeck.' We let him go. He would be captured anyway.

At 2.30 pm a German general arrived in a small blue Opel saloon, and swaggered by with a flourish of Nazi party greetings. All kinds of people came up and said, 'I am Dutch,' or 'We have waited for you,' or 'Have you a cigarette, please?'

After four hours with the Burgomaster and the German military and police, but no sign of the British troops, we felt it was time to go home. We travelled 3 miles into the suburbs before running into the spearhead British battalion, and stopped them, waving a white hand-kerchief in case of mistakes. Then we turned round and led a small convoy of two Honey tanks, three scout jeeps and an office truck in a triumphal procession to the Town Hall.

We finally got back to the 2nd Army press camp just as the briefing officer was looking at his watch and telling correspondents, 'In five minutes leading units will be entering Hamburg.'

'Excuse me,' I interrupted, 'I've just come back from the centre of Hamburg . . .'

When I bumped into Alex Clifford of the *Daily Mail* afterwards he grinned and said, 'Told the paper I'm not filing tonight – they should use Reuter.'

It was the sort of remark that is music to a wire-service man's ears. Back in Hamburg two days later I went to Reichssender Hamburg, the main radio station, from which William Joyce, 'Lord Haw-Haw', the British Nazi with the mock-aristocratic accent, broadcast his nightly propaganda, always beginning with what sounded like 'Jairmany calling, Jairmany calling . . .'

Joyce had made several references to Reuters, including this comment on 11 April:

One of Reuters' correspondents reports that a British officer serving with the 2nd Army, in commenting upon the optimism that has been stimulated at home, exclaimed: 'It is very far from being all over.' He admitted the severity of British casualties and remarked that the troops themselves certainly did not share the hopes which seem to have gained currency among the civilian British public. The officer was merely expressing impartially and without any propaganda motive, the feelings of British soldiers who have had to encounter the fighting men of Germany fanatically defending their own land, and beyond that the whole future of Western civilisation. The positions which are occupied to-day by the British and American troops, and those which may be occupied in the future will not in any way serve to decide the results of this war. The issue lies now, as before, between National Socialist Germany and Soviet Russia. If the German Wehrmacht *were to collapse, Stalin would be Lord of Europe, and eventually of the greater part of Asia. He would command military forces incomparably stronger than those of Britain, and Mr Roosevelt, as I have said before, would never take up the cudgels against the Bolsheviks on behalf of British interests. He would utter platitudes, he would remonstrate, he would express indignation, and he would finally withdraw from Europe, leaving this continent to the mercy of the Soviet conquerors.*

At the radio station, dozens of his 'Views of the News' scripts were lying around, many dated and signed 'William Joyce'. I picked up some of them as souvenirs, including the script quoted above.

There were up-to-date copies of every British national newspaper, of the *Glasgow Herald*, *The Scotsman*, the *Manchester Guardian* and *Yorkshire Post*, and a book titled *Jewish Influence in British Life*.

But the chief censor at the station told me Joyce himself had left by car, in a convoy heading for Denmark, 36 hours earlier. I never got to interview him. He was eventually captured and was executed for high treason.

The day before the final unconditional German surrender, I was at Wismar, the little Baltic town where the British and Soviet armies first made contact, to watch a meeting between Montgomery and Rokossovsky, one of the heroes of the battle of Stalingrad, which raged about the same time as Alamein.

Montgomery, who flew to the meeting from his Tactical HQ, was as usual in battledress. Rokossovsky, in the uniform of a Marshal of the Red Army, drove from Lübeck in a black Packard, preceded by a jeep full of Red Army photographers. Two or three inches taller than Montgomery, he looked more like a benevolent philosopher than a legendary warrior.

They met in a cobbled lane, in front of a paratroop guard of honour, and their handshake lasted a full minute and a half. Rokossovsky, beaming so that the gold fillings in his teeth glinted in the sun, nearly drowned Montgomery's first words with a torrent of welcoming sentiments, calling him 'a great soldier of this war'.

The last 2nd Army troops in fighting contact with the Germans were men of the 51st Highland Division probing in a village outside Bremerhaven. Germans there said they were being attacked 'while the surrender negotiations are going on'.

When the cease-fire order went out to the 51st Division front at 05.23, it was not because the commander knew anything about the high-level negotiations at Montgomery's Tactical HQ,, leading to the signature of the surrender documents half an hour later. It was because he was negotiating his own terms for the surrender of 11,000 troops of the 15th Panzer Grenadier Division, which the Highlanders had first encountered at Alamein. The lightning speed with which Montgomery finished the negotiation of the capitulation staggered even senior officers. Many found the news hard to believe.

Then more than 100,000 British troops in Germany celebrated VE day with a wild night of bonfires and Very lights, singing and drinking victory toasts until early morning in every mess and billet from the Baltic to Brussels. Lights blazed from unshuttered windows and headlights were dazzling. The talk was of reunion with families, about village locals with dartboards, about jobs, social security.

For me, too, peace meant going home, to Scotland. There Pat Cameron presented me with several volumes of cuttings of my stories. Unknown to me, she had been subscribing to a press cuttings agency, and had a record of all the main operations ever since I had first donned my uniform as a war correspondent.

6

'Come East, Old Boy'

After two weeks' leave in Scotland, I returned to Fleet Street, and received a message from Tony Cole, who was then in India, 'Come East, old boy, here's where the action is.'

I went to Bombay, and had two or three long days of briefing from Cole, John Turner, Reuters' chief in India, and Sam Jackett, news editor in Bombay.

Reuters, which had been in India about 80 years, owned the profitable Indian domestic news agency, Associated Press of India (API). My programme was: go to New Delhi, cast a critical eye over the whole Reuter/API set-up, appraise about a dozen staff, mainly reporters, maybe write one or two pieces; then go to Calcutta and on to Burma, where the war was still going on.

I got to New Delhi and, sweating profusely in the 110-degree (44° C) temperature, and with a ghastly rash of prickly heat, went to the Reuter office, where I learned that next day the Congress party leader Jawaharlal Nehru was leaving by train for Simla.

It was time I met Nehru.

Taking a rickshaw to the station, I elbowed through the squash – vast numbers of noisy Nehru fans in the station, and the usual scrum round Nehru himself, who had already taken his seat in the stationary train. I got into the carriage the only way possible: by climbing through an open window and struggling through the heaving mass.

I eventually found myself next to the great man. He was a bit taken aback by the sudden appearance of a Reuter reporter in such circumstances, but I was able to ask him about forthcoming talks, how he viewed prospects, how he found relations with the British, how he saw the outlook for long-term peace – straight, simple, obvious questions. He answered in the non-committal and wordy way that was Nehru's style, a style with which I was to become familiar in later years.

Then, as I was leaving, near-disaster. I leaned out of the carriage window to open the door and my upper denture came adrift, dropped out and bounced on the platform. But it settled, intact, clear of the surrounding mass of filthy feet, some sandalled but mostly bare. With as much insouciance and dignity as I could muster, I picked it up, dusted it off and, with a prayer that Nehru had not seen the pantomime, I popped it back where it belonged and went off to file my story. There was a happy ending: the interview scored well.

I was less happy on my first brief visit to Calcutta. Cole had fixed for me to write two columns for a leading Indian newspaper about the last stages of the war in Europe, and my reward was to be a splendid dinner in a Calcutta restaurant or hotel of my choice. But I had no stomach for food in Calcutta.

The Calcutta scene was too raw to allow enjoyment of food. The whole place seemed a festering sore – the combination of sticky heat, obnoxious smells, flies, beggars hideously deformed, an obscene sprawl of bodies using pavement space as public dormitory, a naked teenaged girl dementedly trying to cross a street of snarling traffic.

I flew on to Rangoon with a new Licence, No. 152, of accreditation to the South-East Asia Command (SEAC). It differed from my SHAEF licence, not only in being green instead of blue, but in that whereas the SHAEF licence under 'Distinguishing Marks' recorded 'Nil', this one – incorrectly – had 'withered left arm'.

I got to Burma in time for only the fag-end of one of the bloodiest and muddiest campaigns of history. Few war correspondents were left in the dingy wooden structure which served as press HQ in the operational area, and only one other from an agency, Lawrence Atkinson of the Exchange Telegraph, a keen newsman and an amusing one. Here I first got to know Ian Morrison of *The Times* and Michael Reynolds of the BBC. Morrison was later immortalised by Han Suyin who fell in love with him and, after he was killed in Korea, told their story in the autobiographical *Love is a Many-Splendoured Thing*.

Son of 'China Morrison', a famed Victorian missionary said to have been the first person to translate the Bible into Chinese, Ian was a gifted newsman with a strikingly attractive personality. He spoke to me often and tenderly of his family.

A colleague said he had 'the easy gait of a dancer, the languid clear voice that turned the accents of Winchester and Oxford into music . . . chuckling verbal wit and kindly teasing conversation . . .' Ian gave me an excellent quote on the China situation from the British businessman Tony Keswick, 'The writing is on the wall all right. But it's in Chinese, and no foreigner knows what it means.'

Generally, the spirit at press HQ was good and we all got on well. My colleagues certainly showed charitable tolerance of what must have seemed the maddening enthusiasm of a brash 25-year-old fresh out from London.

They had lived through all the savage and splendid moments between the fall of Rangoon in 1942 and its recapture in 1945. Now I had arrived when the story was right down-column. As Larry Atkinson said, 'There seemed to be a mistaken impression in Britain that with the Rangoon Victory parade [of 23 June], the war in Burma was over.' Together, he and I decided to get the last battle of Burma into the papers.

Soon after I arrived, I had a unique break. The acting Army Commander met me and asked if I would come to his 'prayers' next

day and give his officers a first-hand account of the final defeat of
Germany, relations between Eisenhower and Montgomery, the link-
up between British and Russian forces, and so on. Thus, in less than
a couple of hours, I became known to most of the officers commanding or attached to units doing the fighting, and they could pre-
sume I had the blessing of the General.

As in Europe, most days we correspondents jeeped to forward positions, picked up whatever information was available, and returned
for briefings before filing our despatches. We slept on makeshift beds
under mosquito nets and swallowed lots of pills to ward off malaria
and kindred ailments.

We saw few Japanese, alive or dead, though their 'tiger boys' or suicide infantry were digging in and consolidating perimeter positions of
a 3-mile-deep bridgehead established west of the Sittang. From jungle bunkers and bamboo huts, they fired on the Allied troops wading
chest-high through flooded fields in a push towards Myaungkashe.

All day and night monsoon rain cascaded down from low clouds.
It was not clean, refreshing rain, but sticky and steaming, coming in
under the roofs and rusting the rifles. Food, blankets, papers – everything got soaked. The soldiers were nearly as wet when asleep as
when on one of those nightmare patrols.

At one point in mid-July, violent rain lashed the waterlogged battlefields for 18 solid hours, the worst deluge of two monsoons. In
those conditions, rivers can rise more than 7 ft (2 m) in a night, and
squelching mud swallows the legs up to the knees. It was like six wars
wrapped in one, with the Allied soldiers fighting insects, disease,
space, nature and geography as well as the Japanese.

War in Italy, Normandy or Germany was never as rough, tough or
terrifying as the routine business of soldiering in Burma. There was
no defined front line. The Japanese organised ambushes along roads
during the night, when Allied traffic was 'frozen' in garrison pens
dotted along the route.

It was a different world back in Rangoon, where a new city was rising out of the rubble which Allied forces had found when they entered it early in May. There were plenty of goods on sale, and Burmese maidens strolled about with a parasol in one hand and a long cheroot in the other.

Bombs, shells and demolitions were estimated to have destroyed half the houses, but already people were repairing them, electricity was coming back and the water was running. People queued at the pumps to splash buckets of water over each other. Children sailed paper boats in the puddles.

I put the war back in the headlines with a despatch on 22 July which began:

The first big face-to-face battle of the whole Burma War is opening out today with large-scale skirmishing round Zaha railway station, 140 miles north of Rangoon . . . More than 3,000 Japanese were last night observed concentrating in the jungles . . . This morning 200 of them launched a frontal attack on Indian infantry positions . . . More than 7,000 Japanese may within the next few days make a desperate life and death dash for the farther bank of the Sittang river. This will be the signal for a major battle.

From Calcutta came a herogram saying, 'Your despatches absolutely first rate getting grand display India. Colour and atmosphere just right.' But there was also a letter from Alan Humphreys, senior war correspondent in the area, based at South-East Asia Command HQ in Ceylon (now Sri Lanka), enclosing a cutting of my story published in the *Ceylon Daily News*. He commented:

I do not know whether this is as you wrote it or whether London have been doing some free rewriting. If this is as you wrote it then, for your background information, I must tell you that the present battle can in no way be compared with the vastly bigger campaign carried out by the Japanese in Manipur last year, when the battles for Kohima and Imphal went on for some months. Three complete Japanese divisions – more than 50,000 men – and a larger number of 14th Army men were involved in what was easily the biggest battle, and a stand-up face-to-face one at that, yet fought in this theatre.

I accepted this squelching in the spirit in which it was offered, though my story had been an accurate reflection of what senior officers had told me. I balance it against a flattering paragraph which Larry Atkinson gave me from his manuscript of *The Forgotten Front*:

The first war correspondent to come to SEAC after the fall of Germany was Doon Campbell of Reuters who was among the most quoted war correspondents on the Western Front. For handling hot news he is the fastest factual reporter I have ever met . . . A terrific worker, he misses nothing.

Early in August I was summoned to Ceylon, with several other correspondents, for a briefing by Admiral Lord Louis Mountbatten, Supreme Allied Commander, SEAC, who was just back from the Potsdam Conference, where Truman and Stalin had conferred first with Churchill and then with his newly elected successor, Attlee.

I'd never met or even seen Mountbatten, whose gift for showmanship, high-handed action, name-dropping and getting things done won him enemies as well as friends. He was in cracking form, pleased at the way his war was going, and full of anecdotes and racy descriptions about his 'new political masters', including Attlee and his Foreign Secretary, Ernest Bevin.

From what Mountbatten said or hinted about the military future, added to what I had already picked up in Burma, it seemed to be on the cards that a major operation would be mounted before long to reoccupy Singapore, which had been in Japanese hands since 1942. Through army and air force contacts, that I had carefully cultivated over the previous few weeks, I felt reasonably sure that

I would find a place among the first troops back in Singapore.

This became an obsession. Speed, plus being there and being first, were very much my dream. Banner headlines about Singapore filled my mind. Besides, intelligence indicated that vigorous Japanese resistance was unlikely. But I could not communicate any of this to Head Office. So when London cabled to tell me to go to China, I replied, 'For good reasons and in Reuters' interests feel important I remain Burma protem.'

'Go to China,' London repeated. Rashly, out of the conviction I was right about being able to give Reuters a classic beat on the recapture of Singapore, I tried again, 'Your message noted understood but plead reconsideration in company's interests allow me stay here just little longer. Events will justify wisdom such decision.'

London's reply, peremptory, final and with no customary 'regards' sign-off, said, 'Campbell, your instructions are to go to China. Get moving and advise when on way.'

It was another lesson learned: you may know better than Head Office, but you'll never win. When I was eventually able to tell Sid Mason why I had resisted so hard, he asked why I hadn't told him. But I couldn't have told him. Instead, cursing, I went to RAF headquarters and arranged a flight next day to Calcutta.

At the API office there was a long message from Cole. He said he was sorry about the way he had 'jerked me out' of Burma, but the 'transcendent' story in the United States was China.

America had a huge financial, military and political investment in China, as well as something of a China fixation. Reuters, in dire financial straits, was bidding hard to strengthen its outlets in the American market, and no running story there was more important than China.

A master at making you feel everything depended on you, Cole certainly left me believing the company faced a hammering unless I pulled out every stop and hit the China news jackpot. His telex

directed, 'Go to RAF liaison office in Calcutta, along the street from
API. Get hold of Wing-Commander Harold Dickson, show him my
telex to you and he'll fix everything.'

In the foyer of Calcutta's Great Eastern Hotel I saw Clive Graham
of the *Daily Express* (horse-racing's 'The Scout' when not a war correspondent) looking disconsolate.

'What's the form?' I asked.

'Trying to get to China . . .'

'Big queue, long wait?'

'About three weeks so far.'

At the liaison office I met the redoubtable Wing-Commander
Dickson, a former *Daily Sketch* executive. He didn't waste words. He
read Cole's telex, fished in his desk, and pulled out a batch of priority air travel forms, all already signed 'W. A. Coryton' (Air Marshal,
Air Commander, RAF Bengal–Burma), and instructed me to be at
Dum Dum airport RAF office at 7 am next morning. A Dakota flying tyres to Kunming could probably squeeze me in.

'Where's Kunming?' I asked, feeling stupid.

'It's in China,' Dixon exploded, with a rich lacing of expletives about
beggars not being choosers. 'You've to go to China, haven't you?'

He pressed a bell. It was answered instantly by a young officer in
the uniform of an RAF pilot. As it turned out, I was to know this
bright and knowledgeable young man for more than 40 years. His
name was Mohsin Ali, and he was to be with Reuters in Delhi,
Karachi, London and finally as diplomatic correspondent working in
most of the world's capitals, still bright, knowledgeable and youthful
in mind and body when he finally left to write for *The Times* in
Washington.

In those days it was quite a thing to fly 'over the hump' from
Calcutta to Kunming. The mountain region was plagued by clouds
which tossed aircraft about like toys. The pilot called me to the cockpit to see the cumulo-nimbus just ahead. For the rest of the journey I

lay stretched flat on the bare metal deck, surrounded by piles of tyres.

When we arrived at the RAF staging post at Kunming, I could almost hear the questions bubbling in the minds of officers and men: who was this odd bod? What was he after? Why was a journalist in their camp?

I quickly made it clear I had no professional interest in their affairs, and the bottles of Scotch in my kit lubricated relations enough to get an answer to my only question: how could I get to China's wartime capital, Chungking?

They told me of an eccentric American major who flew his own aircraft to Kunming every two or three weeks to load up with supplies of goods which were short in Chungking. He was in Kunming now, and they indicated the compound where he was sleeping.

Next day I went there and found him getting quietly pickled as he washed his smalls. I introduced myself and, after a few more jars, it was all set up. I was to be at the airstrip at 6 or 7 next morning, with minimal luggage, and he would fly me to Chungking.

The whole exercise was arranged in such an alcoholic haze that I had doubts if, with dawn, it would still be on. But come daybreak, though suffering a monumental hangover, he managed to get the little plane airborne, and it was monsoon aerobatics most of the 400 miles or so to Chungking. We tickled treetops, climbed, banked and swooped in alarming fashion.

The major – I never got his name and I'm sure mine never registered with him – was becoming more sober all the time, and now realised his predicament. Without any check on credentials, accreditation or papers of any sort he was carrying me into a highly sensitive security area. For all he knew I could have been a political extremist or even a terrorist.

I saw the problem and made it clear I had no wish to embarrass him. So we agreed he would drop me at the perimeter of the landing zone and from that moment I would be on my own. He didn't know me, had never set eyes on me. And that is exactly what happened. He set me down, and I walked off and thumbed a lift in a jeep to the famous Chungking Press Hostel.

The Hostel was known as 'Holly's Hotel' after Hollington Tong, a Chinese Government vice-Minister of Information who opened the first establishment in 1939. Reuter correspondents Graham Barrow and Henry Bough, both old China hands, were there awaiting my arrival, about which for understandable reasons they had had no precise details. After installing me in one of the Hostel's cluster of shacks, they went their separate ways: Graham to a club across the Yangtze, Henry to friends in town.

So I was alone, and hoping to keep a low profile at least until I could concoct a plausible account of how I got there, or at least fudge the details. But the American correspondents were soon rushing about, filing their heads off on what appeared to be a major political assassination.

Their excitement was infectious. Instead of keeping my head down, I followed their example and cabled about 600 or 700 words. It turned out to be worth about a paragraph – a politician had been shot dead, but only accidentally, by a trigger-happy sentry.

Reuters understandingly sent me only the usual reminder about watching my cable costs, but I learned a more important lesson from this Chinese news baptism: stay cool and unfussed; never be influenced by your rivals' activity, however frenetic; remain detached and follow your own judgement.

However, the illegal nature of my arrival in Chungking never did attract official notice, and I became part of the life of the Press Hostel, where the foreign correspondents worked, lived, played and entertained cabinet ministers, generals, officials, visitors and girl-friends – the latter mainly from embassies and American offices, though there was also a young Chinese lady who dressed like a model and shared her favours between the Hostel and the diplomatic community.

The Press Hostel was an institution, to which came ambassadors, philosophers, academics, business tycoons – including the *taipan* of Jardine Matheson, Henry Keswick – to seek updates on Chinese and world news. There was a daily flow of news contacts and translators.

It had started life as Pa Hsien Middle School, a large rambling building of mud-and-plaster atop a hill on the outskirts of the city. In its converted form it began with 13 rooms – 11 rented long-term, two reserved for transients – was bombed twice, rebuilt, and grew to a 48-room cluster of shacks.

Although flimsy and tacky by Western standards, these one- and two-storey wooden-frame buildings were better than many of Chungking's squalid tenements. The windows had real glass, when not broken during rumbustious parties. Each room had a small drum stove burning wood or coal, and a real fireplace warmed the 'Blue Room', a modest social area next to the dining-room. Showers and toilets were shared.

There was only one resident woman correspondent: Charlotte Ebener of the International News Service (INS). The men included Theodore H. White (*Time/Life/Fortune*), Tillman Durdin and Henry Lieberman (*New York Times*), John Roderick and Clyde Farnsworth (AP), George Wang (UP), George Weller (*Chicago Daily News*), Phil Potter (*Baltimore Sun*) and A. T. Steele (*New York Herald Tribune*).

I started off with a cell of a room with bed, table and one or two hard chairs; basic but almost adequate. It opened on to a veranda running the length of the unit. After a few weeks, my status as a Reuter correspondent having been regularised and recognised, I graduated to the luxury of two rooms.

I had a lounge cum office with a desk and cupboard, plus a bedroom. The walls were wafer-thin, and it was a goldfish-bowl existence, everyone knowing just about everything about everyone else. No correspondent could hope to tap typewriter keys during off-peak hours, say between 9 pm and 9 am, without attracting the intrusive

attention of his colleagues. Creaking floorboards and heavy breathing often betrayed the efforts of a young American naval doctor, a frequent visitor, to dispense something other than medicine to the
young Chinese lady.

My rooms were over those of the doyen of the hostel, Spencer
Moosa of AP, and his wife Nina. They had little privacy. Tall and
quiet, Spencer was a good and loyal colleague, and probably knew
more about Generalissimo Chiang Kai-shek and his government
than most of the other correspondents. A British subject, he was born
in Shanghai in 1905, became chief editor of Reuters there, joined AP
in 1939, was in Chungking from 1941 to 1946 and followed Chiang
to Taiwan in 1949.

My bedroom had a washing-bowl and I was soon mystified to find
marks on my soap as if someone had scraped it with a comb. The
mystery was solved one night when, turning over in my sleep, I heard
a noise. Putting on the light, I saw a rat as big and as fat as a cat clawing and gnawing at the soap. I was glad of the slight protection of the
mosquito net. Rats infested much of Chungking.

Taking account of the state of the drains, and the dingy hovels
some of us penetrated in the search for shark's-fin and birds'-nest
soup and other culinary delicacies, it's surprising that our ailments
were seldom worse than dysentery, diarrhoea and the occasional
attack of piles.

Shortly after I reached the hostel, the cook died of food poisoning.
By candlelight, we showed respect, forming a slow-moving procession round his body, with a live cockerel tied to the chest, presumably
to frighten off evil spirits.

For six months of the year Chungking, which is in the Szechuan
hinterland at the confluence of the Yangtze and Kialing rivers, was
enveloped in a thick damp mist. When the sun broke through, we
served drinks in the garden ringed by our shacks, patches of lawn
with stone-flagged paths, banana trees and sunflowers. The drinks

were local gin, vodka, cherry brandy and Chungking D (D standing for Death or Double Strength). That patch of grass became 'Hangover Square', meeting-place of the 'Good Clean Kids Club', which featured elbow-bending prowess high among its qualifications for membership.

Only an alley separated the Press Hostel from the Information Department of the Information Ministry, where conferences were arranged, press releases (often propaganda) were issued, and where one found censors and filing facilities, by cable and voicecast. It was a compact set-up.

Having had no briefing on China and no time or opportunity to read up on the situation, I was appalled by my near-total lack of background knowledge. Of more than half-a-billion Chinese, I knew the names of four: Chiang Kai-shek and his wife, and the Chinese Communist leader and his deputy, Mao Tse-tung and Chou En-lai, who headed the Chinese Communist Liaison Office in Chungking. Even these names I knew only in print; when a Chinese official spoke of 'Massadoong' and 'Joe 'n lie', it took me several days to realise who was meant.

On 14 August 1945, the day the Japanese surrendered after being at war with China since 1937, Chiang invited Mao to come to Chungking from his base in Yenan for talks. The invitation was repeated on 20 and 23 August, and finally, on 28 August, Mao flew in, accompanied by Brigadier Patrick Hurley, the American Ambassador.

The story we had was that Mao had refused to come unless Hurley accompanied him from Yenan. Hurley, an extrovert Oklahoman who sometimes startled the Chinese by breaking into an Indian war dance punctuated by high-pitched 'Yahoos', had been to Yenan the previous year, and gave Mao his personal guarantee of safety.

So for the first time in 18 years, the two Chinese leaders shook hands. Mao stayed for 41 days. He had talks with Chiang, and Chou had talks with Foreign Minister Wang Shih-chieh, while millions of Nationalist soldiers were locked in the wasting civil war against Communist regular and partisan troops.

Although very much a new boy, the youngest and most ignorant in a foreign Press corps of exceptional calibre, I was bursting with enthusiasm and a couple of weeks after Mao arrived, without seeking guidance from anyone, I brashly drafted 12 questions and addressed them to him. A week passed, and then Mao replied, bypassing a string of similar – if more academic and convoluted – requests from better-informed and established newsmen who had been analysing and interpreting the Chinese scene for years.

I was summoned to his modest house for this, his first exclusive interview with a foreign correspondent since the talks began. Physically, and in his bearing of unaffected authority, Mao was impressive. He was inscrutable, but seemed to radiate something, a sort of chemistry. We shook hands, and I was given his answers to my questions, typewritten in English. He never dodged or fudged a reply. I read them in his presence, and asked a few supplementaries.

He spoke no English, and everything had to be translated, but his answers were spontaneous and offered without a moment's pause for reflection. Of course, I had no idea whether he was really saying what the translator said, much less what he was thinking. Then I drank two cups of tea, shook hands again, and left.

As always, I filed the interview dead straight: an introduction quoting his words, 'I am confident in the outcome of the present negotiations – they cannot break down', then giving questions and answers almost verbatim. The Chinese Nationalist authorities handling transmission did not alter a word.

This is how part of my cable to London read in its raw state:

Within few hours of announcement of 'no civil war in China pact' between Kuomintang and Communists, Mao Tse-tung Chinese Communist leader told me

119

tonight, 'Eyam confident in outcome of present negotiations – they cannot break down'. This first exclusive interview given Allied correspondent since his vital talks with President Chiang Kai-shek began three weeks ago. At outbreak of parley which would decide war or peace Chinawise both leaders pledged themselves to silence. Mao Tse-tung tonight broke the silence to answer twelve questions eye post-ed to him moren [more than a] *week ago. Here are questions etanswers: Can civil war Chinawise be averted by agreement without resort to arms? 'It can because this will be accordwise with the interests of ruling party Chinawise. What China needs presently is policy of peaceful reconstruction – no other policy. Therefore civil war in China must be determinedly averted.'*

Word filtered back to me through the Chinese Communist Liaison Office that Mao had appreciated the way the interview was handled. At the Press Hostel, several correspondents were sour. Men with vastly greater knowledge and experience of China than I would ever have naturally felt that if Mao had anything to say, he should have said it to them.

I understood those feelings, but I also knew that experts sometimes get so involved that they can become incomprehensible to the average reader. Mao spoke to me because he saw straightforward questions, not loaded or angled, and because he knew Reuters would not twist or distort his words or take them out of context. He also knew, of course, that through Reuters his words would be guaranteed to reach most of the world.

I was able to capitalise on that interview for the rest of my China assignment. The Nationalists, equally with the Communists, ensured that Reuters always had competitive access to whatever information they were releasing, and I was never aware of either side ever feeling let down.

I wrote about Mao in a letter home in mid-October:

I met Mao several times when he was in Chungking powowing with the Gimo

120

[Generalissimo Chiang]. *He is stuffed with all the good old clichés – unity, democracy, prosperity.*

How little was accomplished during the five weeks of talks. They haggled, bargained, bickered over ambiguities and the Communists refused to put things down in writing. No minutes of the most important meeting of a decade for China's 500,000,000!

The Gimo showed Mao off at social get-togethers and cocktail parties as much as to say, 'Look – isn't he a prize exhibit?'

To judge from that letter, I was fairly pleased with myself. It began:

c/o Press Attaché, British Embassy, Chungking, is still the best address, though letters take three weeks to a month to reach me . . .

More nice cables from London. Geoffrey Imeson, an old China hand who is presiding over the editorial in Cole's absence from London, has just cabled, 'You have put Chungking on the map so far as Reuters is concerned keep it up.'

You may not know that I was the second correspondent in the world to send an uncensored despatch out of China for seven years. A correspondent of the American news agency, Associated Press, was first.

Gosh, I'll never be an accountant: my September budget was half-a-million dollars (Chinese). I've sweated two days accounting for it all.

Had picture taken with Chiang Kai-shek yesterday. He invited foreign correspondents to a tea party and afterwards posed with us all. The photograph may appear in Life, *Henry Luce's magazine.*

The Generalissimo – we call him the Gimo, General 'Vinegar Joe' Stilwell used to call him 'peanut' – is an imposing man.

He has very soft, delicate hands and enormous charm. He speaks no English but tries -'seet down'. He smiles, nods, keeps repeating good-humouredly 'ho-ha-ho-ha', which in Chinese means 'good' (and he and his wife have been heard addressing each other as 'darling').

Madame is quite dishy - it isn't fright that sends shivers down your back when you shake her hand. She is one of the most attractive 40-year-olds I have come

121

across. Her poise and make-up are impeccable. She speaks English fluently, loads her conversation with literary quotations and classical allusions . . .

The Chinese are a happy people. They smile when Indians would scowl. They are disturbingly cheerful under the most trying conditions. Tolerance and patience above all else are required in the foreigner. He will never make the East West. It is no good thinking in Western terms in the East.

There is none of the practical efficiency or of the commonplace civilising amenities as we know them in China. China seems to have stood still for a century. And the reawakening is evolutionary . . . Their homes, religion, politics, public services, their lives – everything in China and of China is feeling the impact of a new age.

A Chinese cabinet minister said to me the other day: 'I understand your politics, I understand American politics, but our politics – they beat me.' That's how it is.

But there is not much hope of early settlement between the two major parties, the Kuomintang and the Communist Party, because neither side trusts the other and will not make the first worthwhile concessions.

Each side is out to prevent provincial bloc building by the other. Each wants territorial, military, civil, political control. Yet each side claps hands for democracy, unity, freedom, nationalisation of the armies. The Kuomintang has Soviet and American backing.

Chinese chow is good and rich, but it lies heavy. It is good manners to belch after a Chinese meal and to leave the table-cloth a pile of bones and noodles and sauce and sweet and sour pork. It is vulgar to use a fork. Fingers are socially correct with awkward bones. Life can be fun in China – but for the roads and rats and heat of Chungking. Certainly I would like to stay quite a bit longer . . .

Life was fun in some ways. Correspondents with common interests formed pairs or groups and shared jeeps to call on news sources. The jeeps could only crawl in streets chock-a-block with traffic, rickshaws and people, including men and women harnessed to heavily-laden carts, and an estimated 250,000 street squatters.

I usually accompanied Spencer Moosa, to benefit from his card-index mind on China. At least once a week we called at the British

LEFT: On the front steps of Craigmailen manse; with Urquhart (right), perched on Dad's knees

BELOW: With Jan and Urquhart (right)

ABOVE LEFT: NUJ card, 1942

ABOVE RIGHT: Walton A. (Tony) Cole

ABOVE: Reuters'
London newsroom,
which housed many
specialist writers in
the 1940s

RIGHT: The area of
the general desk
where I twitched as
a newcomer

CASSINO ABBEY-FORTRESS
ALLIED BOMBS AND GUNS

Speedy Reduction to Crumbling Ruin

DOUBLE ONSLAUGHT FROM THE AIR

Germans Scramble Out as Walls Collapse

From DOON CAMPBELL, Reuter Special Correspondent
NEAR CASSINO ABBEY, Tuesday Night

I SAW Cassino Abbey shattered to-day when Allied bombers struck in the morning and again in the afternoon at German troops sheltering within its walls. It was a sight terrifying, spectacular and dramatic.

Heavy bombers made the first attack, and mediums followed up in the afternoon. Both struck in three waves. After the last bombs had fallen a Cockney soldier, Private William Clark, of Lambeth, who had been close-up, said: "The place is hollow. Its inside is smashed to pieces. With the aid of glasses I could see the walls beginning to crumble and fall away in large chunks. It has been a terrible beating up."

From an observation post less than two miles away I watched the attack on the abbey begin at 9.20 this morning after a period of ominous silence. The first 30 heavy bombers droned high overhead, l trails. Soon I saw the bombs fall. The seemed to creep through the sky towards th first bomb found the target. It hit the left-hand corner of the abbey with an explosion at rocked our look-out post.

Great 20-minute Attack

That was the prelude to one of the most intensified 20 minutes of aerial attack against a pin-point target in this war. Stick after stick of bombs rained down from these black-half-inch smudges some 20,000 feet in the sky above.

Flame spurted and clouds of yellow dust shot up more than 1,000 feet. The whole monastery began to shake and quiver and then disintegrate.

I counted at least nine direct hits. When the dust subsided the steeple had gone.

More bombs fell as the dust cleared, and now a big gap was torn in the eastern wall and clouds of smoke began to billow from the abbey.

The country for miles around seemed in the throes of an earthquake. It quivered as the building on the hill took the weight of the heavy bombs.

There was not one burst of anti-aircraft fire throughout the attack.

No Sign of Monks

After the first wave of "heavies" had dropped their bombs there was a pause during which Allied heavy artillery took over the attack. They pumped shells into the abbey as Germans scrambled from the shattered walls. German batteries returned the fire, but were eventually silenced.

After the second wave of bombers had struck, about 200 more Germans deserted the home of the Benedictines which Hitler had turned into a fortress. There was no sign of Italian civilians or black-robed monks.

The significance of the attack seemed to communicate itself to the hundreds of troops who watched it. They realised that it was a holy place on which the bombs were raining and that something which had withstood the ravages and vicissitudes of 1,400 years was now being destroyed in a few hours.

Silent Spectators

The soldiers had heard reports that the attack was due soon, and they had been hanging on to see it. Whenever one appeared with field glasses he was

ABOVE: My report of the devastating Monte Cassino raids (*Yorkshire Post*, 16 February 1944)

RIGHT: With Richard McMillan (centre) and Christopher Buckley (right), hearing General Montgomery thank war correspondents for their 'help and kindness and patience', Vasto, January 1944

ABOVE: In a Piper Cub lent by the American 5th Army commander, General Mark Clark, taking off for an aerial view of the battle for Cassino and to get a close-up of erupting Vesuvius

3rd March, 1944.

British War Reporter Flies Over Blazing Volcano

VESUVIUS MORE IMPRESSIVE THAN BATTLE

By DOON CAMPBELL, Reuter's Correspondent

I HAVE just flown over Vesuvius less than 100ft. above the tidal wave of brown-purple lava relentlessly flowing to the sea. Thick gaseous fumes poisoned the air and choked the cockpit of the tiny Flying Cub.

As I looked down the lava crushed another pretty little pink-roofed house in its irresistible course to the sea.

Thousands of Italian civilians and refugees cluttered and jammed the roadways as they fled from the path of the molten mass tossed it about. I had just flown from another erupting volcano in the Italian mainland—Cassino.

The force of angry nature is a thousand times more impressive than the battle between men.

Cassino is the fuller incident—sharp flashes of orange flame, puffs of smoke, and tiny khaki-clad figures bustling about guns

ABOVE: This unusual angle on the news about Monte Cassino helped me to win a place in Reuters' D-Day team (23 March 1944)

MONTGOMERY'S I

GENERAL'S "INTO-BATTLE" TALK

"Absolute and Complete Confidence in Outcome"

RIGHT: Despite instructions to the contrary, I wrote up almost every word spoken by Montgomery on 16 May 1944, leaving copy with a military censor. The story was widely published in full on D-Day (Edinburgh *Evening Dispatch*, 6 June 1944)

ABOVE: In army uniform, 1943

Doon Campbell, Reuter correspondent at General Montgomery's Army Group H.Q., says:—

General Montgomery was in confident mood when he talked to Press correspondents on the eve of the landings.

"I have absolute and complete confidence in the outcome," he said. "The party is in first-class shape to win the match."

was the same "Monty" of the
t and Italy—competent, and
ient, reassuring without mask-
his assessment of the old
y.

Tribute to Eisenhower

e scene at his spacious Army
p H.Q. was a bit more formal
when the slight figure in a
ter used to appear on the
van steps, blink in the sun,
out correspondents in the pic-

wore battle-dress, stood at
front of a sloping stage car-
i with Army blankets. More
100 British, Dominion, and
rican correspondents faced

touched on the study and
ication of human nature in
battlefield, the common enemy
German, his personal adversary
l - Marshal Rommel, the
ration of the Allied fighting
hine going out to war. He had
ess at Rommel's tactics.

paid tribute to General Eisen-
r, "who is tremendously
d himself," and said it was a
great honour to serve under American command.

Correspondents Warned

General Montgomery warned
correspondents that they must
expect very strict censorship during the early stage of operations.
He pledged himself to keep correspondents as up-to-date as was
possible on what was going on.

"Initially, when we start fighting, I have no doubt you will want
to send off all sorts of information

about the battle," he said. "W
will have to be terribly carefu
about what is put out, and see tha
there is no loss of confidence here
or over there, and that wron
stories don't get out.

"You may find that for the firs
few days the censorship will b
very strict, and my advice is this
In the first few days it would b
far better to confine yourself t
what you see going on, describin
what the soldiers are doing, an
not attempt to tell how the battl
as a whole is going or what
likely to happen.

"When the moment comes th
I feel it is possible to put you i
the picture then that informatic
can be given to you collectively.

"It is important that the peop
in the home countries of the Alli
know how their soldiers are gettir
on, and what they are doing. B
they must know it right."

Rommel Too Impulsive

"I think that whereas the Ge
man soldier is fighting to-day ju
as well as he ever fought, I do
believe that the standard of high
German leadership is as good
it was. I don't believe the Germ
general has the same grip on t
battle as he used to have.

"I regard it as a great comp
ment that Rommel has taken co
mand on the other side.

"I think Rommel is too imp
sive for the set-piece battle. He
not a general who likes to fi
a set-piece fight. I think
strong point, his forte, is disr
tion. I think he will go for
spoiling tactics and try to p
us back into the sea straight aw
I think he is too impulsive a
wants to get cracking in the bat

"We are a great Allied tean
a terrific Allied team.

"I don't know when the w
is going to end. I don't beli
myself that the Germans can
on much longer with this b
ness. They are fighting on f
fronts—Russian, Balkans, Itali
and Western Europe. I don't
lieve they can go on doing it.

"I think it will be a terr
party, of course, a real first-cl
party, but I am quite absolut
confident we will win it."

PES

On D-Day, June 6, 1944, the first British correspondent to hit the beach at Normandy was Reuters' man Doon Campbell. He wrote the story of the invasion while lying in a bullet-swept ditch, near the shore. After the invasion, Reuters' men once again made use of a pigeon post service, this time to relay vital messages across the channel to England.

TOP: Forty-eight hours after landing on Sword Beach with the Marine Commandos on D-Day (PA News)

ABOVE: A cartoon from the *Eagle* comic depicts me scribbling my first report from France (28 August 1965)

SAT AT VILLA WINDOW AND SAW OUR MEN WIPE OUT TWO GERMAN SNIPERS

24 Hours of Shelling: 'Thank God for the Good Earth'

From Doon Campbell, Reuter's Correspondent
(Advanced H.Q., Allied Assault Force, France, Thursday)

SNIPERS bullets, whining shells, diving planes, and the thunder of a great naval bombardment which shoots the typewriter off my knee every few seconds, are the rather disturbing conditions under which I am writing

I am several miles inland and a mile behind the frontline trenches. Between 9 and 10 last night the sky filled with hundreds of Allied planes cheered by the men on the ground.

I counted 400 Spitfires and Marauders nipping in and out of cloud as they escorted a giant force of Marauders and scores of troopladen gliders.

"C'est tres joli," said French civilians who say of the Allied invasion "C'est tres chic."

It is a miracle that I am alive to write this story, that I have survived 24 hours on this bridgehead bag of wicked tricks. Bombs, shells, bullets and mines, to say nothing of booby traps, make each hour an age of grim experience.

The dead lie about, covered by a piece of tarpaulin or half-buried in the sand.

I was pinned down for an hour by a withering barrage of enemy shell fire yesterday. The beached craft got the full weight, but men were also hit. The wounded dropped unobtrusively away the whole afternoon.

The Good Earth

Most of my 24 hours here have been spent lying flat out on my face burrowing into sand or earth, the good earth.

Every forward soldier thanks God for soft earth. It makes him feel safe at least.

The beach group maintain a well ordered bustle in landing and unloading the men, war materials, tanks, guns, lorries and supplies amid a shambles of twisted steel defences protruding above the low water, battered boats, shell holes, and bomb craters.

One of many German prisoners who have been ferried across the Channel to England in the past two days.

troops between the beach and the front.

A Flaming Ball

I saw one fall, a flaming ball, a victim of extraordinary intense A.A.

ol a privet border, and two German snipers.

I can see the whole drama through the front window of the villa in which I am sitting. It is happening in the garden. The soldiers have been through the house twice already.

They suspected a sniper might be upstairs; then they thought he might be in the dug-out at the bottom of the garden. I stayed the night in that dug-out. Two bullets have already come through the window, and a third is not far away from the direction of the fire.

I watched a hundred German prisoners being marched along the beach. They were mostly very young, and they seemed staggered at the amount of Allied shipping lying in the bay.

"Quiet and Gentle"

There has been a steady flow of prisoners into Allied cages ever since "H plus Two." They include Italians and satellite troops.

"Germany finished?" I said to one blond boy in green uniform. "Maybe now," he said. "Before invasion—no."

Private W. Nicholls, of 89, Chertsey-road, Addlestone, Surrey, told me: "They put up a bit of a fight at first, but were not long in coming out, waving handkerchiefs and pieces of white cloth.

"They had strong steel and concrete reinforced shelters electrically fitted and large stocks of wine and spirit. But they seemed quite happy to give themselves up."

ABOVE: This despatch, a composite of several messages filed on and after D-Day, was front-paged in the London *Evening News*, 9 June 1944

LEFT: Commandos going ashore, some carrying bicycles, on the Normandy beaches (photograph courtesy of the Imperial War Museum, London)

TOP: Troops dug in on a Normandy beach (photograph courtesy of the Imperial War Museum, London)

ABOVE: Fifty years on, visiting the site of the ditch in Ouistreham where, 'shivering and sneezing', I spent D-Day night

ABOVE: At General Montgomery's first press conference after the Normandy landings, in the grounds of Cruelly Château, on the far left

"BLIND DATE WITH DEATH"

Mon. 26·3·45

Dispatch
26·3·45

Doon Campbell, Reuter correspondent with a combat team of the 17th American Division over the Rhine, says in a Sunday night message:—

I have crossed the Rhine twice in 24 hours. I glided over the swirling waters after noon yesterday. I reached the west bank again 24 hours later.

Some of the boys who glided and parachuted on to the scarred soil beside me kept a "blind date with death."

East of the Rhine there is now a sprawling, raw waste land. German people are there, bowing and scraping until one sickens of them.

Allied forces met no organised opposition, but machine-gun bullets and mortars were trained like a hosepipe on the gliders as they groped crazily for some solid brake, sometimes a fence, sometimes a house.

As the Germans slammed 88 mm. shells into the defenceless craft they disappeared in flames.

The men say the landing was rougher than D-Day or Arnhem.

Bu~~t yesterday's~~ bridgehead is ~~colu~~mns of traffic ~~and G~~erman carts ~~of am~~munition, are ~~... more than six~~ ~~m~~ine.

German prisoners—the Division to which I was attached took more than 3000—goggled at the spectacle.

There was a mix-up on landing due to a smoky haze. A hundred feet from the ground I saw a fence and behind it a solid house. We became groundborne in time to hit the fence.

A glider which followed hit the house. Bodies are still in the wreckage.

I rode eight miles round our tiny perimeter trying to locate glider 48 which had the trailer containing the Press and radio personnel.

Soldiers stopped each other to ask if the~~y had seen their friends.~~

Over th~~...~~ or brushw~~...~~

A tren~~...~~ as a sur~~...~~ two Gen~~...~~ patrol t~~...~~

I saw~~...~~ fluttered~~...~~ when th~~...~~ in, a bul~~...~~ point w~~...~~ head.

Search~~...~~ bore fr~~...~~ landing~~...~~ personn~~...~~ compon~~...~~

We h~~...~~ the Col~~...~~ the ass~~...~~

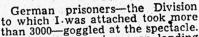

Award To Scots War Reporter

THE Commander of the 17th U.S. Airborne Division has awarded Glider Wings and Combat Star to Reuter's correspondent, Doon Campbell, who landed in a glider with the Airborne Army's H.Q. across the Rhine.

A 25-year-old Scot, Campbell, writes a "Daily Record" reporter and former colleague, is Britain's youngest war correspondent. In the last two years he has covered the fighting around Cassino, landed with Lord Lovat's Commandos on D-Day, and reported the whole course of the Western Front campaign. Twice he was cut off during the fighting around the Nijmegen salient.

Educated at George Watson's College, Edinburgh, he is the younger son of the Rev. A. A. Campbell, Craigmailen Manse, Linlithgow.

TOP: The story of my glider voyage across the Rhine (Edinburgh *Evening Dispatch*, 26 March 1945)

ABOVE: In army uniform, 1943

RIGHT: The *Daily Record* reports the award of Glider Wings and Combat Star after the airborne crossing (27 March 1945)

William Joyce

"Views on the News"   11.4.45

On the battlefields of Germany to-day, British soldiers are laying down their lives, are enduring the hell of modern warfare, are submitting their bodies to be maimed and battered, and the illusion that their efforts and sacrifices will lead to an early or a satisfactory peace is being rapidly dispelled.   One of Reuter's correspondents reports that a British officer serving with the 2nd. Army, in commenting upon the optimism which has been stimulated at home, exclaimed "It is very far from being all over".   He admitted the severity of the British casualties and remarked that the troops themselves certainly did not share the hopes which seemed to have gained currency amongst the civilian British public.   That officer was merely expressing impartially and without any propaganda motive, the feelings of the British soldiers who have had to encounter the fighting men of Germany fanatically defending their own land, and beyond that, the whole future of Western civilisation.   The positions which are occupied to-day by the British and American troops, and those which may be occupied in the future will not in any way serve to decide the results of this war.   The issue lies now, as before, between National Socialist Germany and Soviet Russia. If the German Wehrmacht were to collapse, Stalin would be Lord of Europe, and eventually of the greater part of Asia.   He would command military forces incomparably stronger than those of Britain, and Mr. Roosevelt, as I have said before, would never take up the cudgels against the Bolsheviks on behalf of British interests.   He would utte........................would remonstrate, he would express indignation, and h..... from Europe, leaving this continent to the mercy..... The power of Bolshevism would not doubt be subst..... absorbtion of Germany into the Soviet Union, and..... politicians who retained any feeling or regard..... most heartily wish that they were confronted on..... of August 1939, in order that they might be e.....

ABOVE: An original 'Lord Haw-Haw' radio script, found in the Hamburg radio station where he made his wartime broadcasts

RIGHT: Lord Haw-Haw, William Joyce

TOP: At Chungking Press Hostel, popularly known as 'Holly's Hotel', 1945

ABOVE: Chinese accreditation card, 1945

BELOW: Within hours of the announcement of a temporary agreement to end civil war in China, Mao Tse-tung, the Communist leader, received me at his headquarters in Chungking. The despatch sent on 3 September 1945 was unaltered by the Chinese censor

via press wireless
press reuters newyork
official one 52200 excampbell chungking colon within few hours
of announcement of quote no civil war in china pact unquote
between kuomintang and communists mao tse tung chinese
communist leader told me tonight quote eyem confident in

outcome of present negotiations dash they cannot break down unquote
stop twas first exclusive interview given allied correspondent
since his vital talks with president chiang kai shek began
three weeks ago stop at outbreak of parley which would decide war or

peace chinawise both leaders pledged themselves to silence stop mao tsetung
tonight broke the silence to answer twelve questions eye posted to him
moren week ago stop here are questions etanswers colon can civil
war chinawise be averted by agreement without resort to arms query stop

quote it can because this will be accordwise with the interests
of ruling party chinawise stop what china needs presently is policy
peaceful reconstruction dash no other policy stop therefore civil war
in china must be determinedly averted unquote stop what concessions

are communists prepared to make to reach agreement query stop quote under
the condition that peace democracy etunity will be realised in whole
country chinese communist party is prepared make important concessions

including reduction number troops in liberated areas unquote stop
what compromise or concession on part of central government is required
satisfy communist claims query stop quote the chinese communists demand

kuomintang government to recognise the popularly elected governments etpeoples
armies of liberated areas comma permit them participate in work of receiving
the japanese surrender comma severely punish traitors etpuppet

troops comma equitably etrationally reorganise armies comma protect freedoms
etrights of people etestablish democratic coalition government unquote stop
are you hopeful of settlement or even temporary agreement emerging

from present talks query stop quote eyem confident in outcome present
negotiations stop eye believe that permutual effort etmutual concession
an agreement comma not temporary in character comma but one which will

ITH GENERALISSIMO
CHIANG KAI-SHEK

ABOVE: Generalissimo Chiang Kai-shek (in uniform and cap) stands between Spencer Moosa (AP) and the Chinese Minister of Information, with foreign correspondents including (second row, left to right) Charlotte Ebener (INS), me and Henry Lieberman (*New York Times*), with Phil Potter (*Baltimore Sun*) just behind and between us, the moustachioed Ed Ward (BBC) in the fourth row, and correspondents from Tass, Nanking 1947

Embassy to see Geoffrey Wallinger (later British Ambassador to Brazil), who belonged to an effective and totally unstuffy brand of British diplomat: intelligent, informed, always ready to swap news on an adult basis. His potent pink gins were almost as stimulating as his pungent commentaries on the Chinese scene.

I dined as often as invited with the Dutch, French and Belgian Ambassadors. Food and wine at these tables made an agreeable change, and each mission had its quota of attractive girls. The Americans, Australians and Canadians were also invariably friendly, generous and made good news contacts. Embassy dress was nondescript – mine was usually an olive-green gaberdine monkey-jacket, as favoured by American officers, with fawn trousers.

I recall one visit, to a modest but attractive brick house which could almost have been in Surrey. It was only a short distance from the city centre, though it took an hour to reach in the traffic. This was the home of one of the most colourful and exciting soldiers of his age, Winston Churchill's personal envoy to Chiang, Lieutenant-General Sir Adrian Carton de Wiart, VC. Still a splendid, swashbuckling figure at 65, he had a black eye-patch where he had lost an eye in fighting the 'Mad Mullah's' dervishes in Somaliland before the First World War, and was also missing one hand, lost in combat at Ypres. He had led his men over the top with a light walking stick and a bag of hand grenades, pulling the pins out with his teeth.

A very English tea was served, and I became aware of the old warrior watching my one-handed technique for spreading scones: holding the scone in position at the side of the plate with my thumb and bringing the knife loaded with butter across it.

'Campbell,' he said. 'Why don't you put the thing on the table-cloth where it won't slip?'

He was right, and I have never since buttered scones, toast, rolls or biscuits any other way.

But if life was pleasant in some ways, covering the civil war itself was the most frustrating assignment I had encountered. Chungking was a sort of neutral area, 500 to 1,000 miles from the fighting. The Communists were operating an army group headquarters inside the Nationalists' capital. Their officials were under no restraints; they could go where they liked and do or say what they liked. It was as strange as if Field-Marshal von Rundstedt had had his officers snooping around in General Eisenhower's compound before D-Day.

There were no fronts near Chungking, no communiqués, no official briefing officers, the communications were shaky, and all news was late. It was not unusual to spend an entire day interviewing military experts, war zone commanders, Nationalist and Communist spokesmen to get six lines of copy attempting to establish a single fact. Neither side claimed a military initiative; both claimed to be on the defensive. Each side had its own operational maps, and each side told a different story.

The Communist headquarters sent the Press Hostel a daily stack of handouts headed, 'Stop the Civil War', which might, for example, charge Nationalist Kuomintang troops with using poison gas. The correspondent would check with General Kuo, the Government spokesman, at his office in the alley off the south end of Tseng Chiangai. When the tea tumblers and rice bowls had been removed, and the Communist allegation roundly denied, the General would unfold reams of rice paper, carrying the intelligence reports received daily from the fronts. The Kuomintang might declare that Communist troops had been looting, raping and killing civilians.

It could take hours to drive the 3 miles to the other end of Tseng Chiangai to the Communist clearing house at No. 50. Kuomintang troops in black helmets made a note of every visitor. Chickens, dogs, beggars and flies competed for breathing space between charcoal-burning pots and hawkers' stalls that led up to the doorway. Inside was a peek-hole, at which the correspondent would ask, 'Is Kung Peng in?'

Kung Peng was the unnamed 'Communist official' quoted in our despatches. The soft-spoken daughter of a wealthy Shanghai official, she was known from the Yellow River to Tibet. In a little room furnished with wicker chairs and cuspidors, high on a cliff-face overlooking the Kialing River, Kung Peng gave an informal daily press conference. She had an engaging manner, knew her job inside out, was always in the picture and was very competent.

I saw her chief, Chou En-lai many times – he had a good relationship with all the serious correspondents – and the only reason I did not see him more often was that Kung Peng was so good. But anyway, the check on the Kuomintang account of looting and pillage would result in it being denounced as 'utterly false', and there was no way to check either story.

After the day's battle of words, there was an old-school-tie gentility about the encounters between the two sides. Generals from both camps would lend cars to each other and exchange pleasantries over embassy cocktails, while up in the Northern Provinces more than a million of their men were violently squabbling – or worse – over the legacy of the Japanese surrender.

Being single-handed in Chungking, trying to provide competitive cover of both the military and political battles and General George Marshall's efforts to mediate, and at the same time handling more and more requests for 'think-pieces' and 'in-depth articles' of up to 2,500 words each, sent by air mail to save cable tolls, I was not unhappy to be free from contractual responsibilities.

I did ask about such points, including a new contract with the Chinese Central News Agency and a possible English-language bulletin service in Chungking, but was told to concentrate on the news, and seize the chance to widen my experience of political reporting.

The service messages were full of praise: 'you doing splendidly', 'we making utmost use your material', 'our China coverage now completely competitive and independent report from America said similar there'. The succession of complimentary messages was flattering, but words alone could not bridge the thousands of miles or all the other, often more meaningful, strains of separation.

Although I never mentioned her, Patricia Cameron, my fiancée in Edinburgh, figured prominently and importantly in my thinking. Pat was an attractive 17-year-old when she left school in 1942 to join *The Scotsman* as secretary to the chief reporter, J. W. Herries, well known in Scottish literary circles as an erudite poltergeist. I lost no time in dating this tall dark-haired free spirit, seeking her company for evening and weekend assignments – theatres, concerts, even political meetings at the Usher Hall.

Sometimes we visited friends or went hiking on the Pentlands. I took her home to Craigmailen manse – and to the church – and even to Skiddaw. She knew of my clandestine exercise to have a total dental extraction and had me home that weekend to meet her parents, baking a cream sponge soufflé, the sort of food you could swallow without chewing.

I often wondered afterwards what her parents in genteel Barnton thought of her choice of a first beau – five years older, with an artificial arm and no teeth at 22!

Our courtship flourished and, after I left Edinburgh for Reuters in London, we maintained a near daily contact by phone and letter. From *The Scotsman*, Pat moved to the British Council as PA to the director, Harvey Wood, who found a pretext to send her to London, where we had a long weekend at Gowing's Hotel.

Thereafter she painstakingly kept cuttings of every published despatch, filling several volumes (now with the Reuter archive). If I had been less hyped up by the challenge and less totally absorbed by my work, I would have contrived to get Pat with me. As it was, she showed great patience, never grumbled about the long separation or caused me to precipitate any crisis with Reuters.

There were other aspects of alienation. The diet, even though I loved rice and spice, could become distasteful – too much stomach-churning, fried rubbish. Bouts of sickness and internal disorders kept recurring, and the stuff you would normally pick up from the village store to settle the stomach and related ailments just didn't exist in this city of open drains and sewers, vile climate and ghastly overcrowding.

Being a Reuter correspondent meant more to me than anything, but in this black mood even work began to pall. There was no let-up in the grinding daily routine. I was always worrying about words – had I got in first with the news, or had I wasted company money? What was I doing in Chungking anyway? Savouring life? Cooped up much of the time in a shack hardly more civilised than a garden shed, watching rats guzzling my soap, nightly dodging the dive-bombing mosquitoes?

In one such uncharacteristic fit of depression, in February, I intemperately shot off a cable reminding Reuters that I had a personal life to think of, as well as being another cog in the news-agency machine.

The conciliatory reply was that my cable was understandable and reasonable, and Christopher Chancellor was prepared to offer me a three-year contract, at £750, then £850 and £950 a year, based on a 'continuing and developing career', in China for the immediate and foreseeable future.

'Thanks. Considering. Will advise,' I replied. The next from London was an Exocet:

ProCampbell. Terms your latest cable quite unacceptable. You showing unfortunate prima donnaish tendencies recently. Must insist immediate unqualified apology to Mister Chancellor. Cole.

Phew! Such language in an open cable flummoxed me. I was anxious to convey to London, without grovelling, the genuine distress I felt over the way my reply had been misinterpreted, and cabled:

ProCole. Regret text and spirit my latest cable tragically misconstrued as unthinkable eyed show such cavalier attitude and disrespect to Chancellor to whom herewith unqualified apology. At same time episode shows manifest lack of trust under which it impossible continue, so herewith also resignation for implementation soon as convenient to you. Campbell.

The exchange ended with Cole conciliatory again:

Unlikeliest we be in position relieve you proapproximately three months but doing best. Eye Americawarding cummister Chancellor until end February and confident we can rely on you for next three months whereafter we want to bring you home and talk everything over together and arrange your future in way which will be best for you and all of us. All good wishes from us both. Cole.

7
The bamboo curtain

I returned to London in March 1946 to be met at the airport by two favourite Reuter mates, Geoffrey Imeson and Hilary Green, editorial secretary (later to become Mrs Imeson), and offered the chance to stay at the Reuter country house, Gatton Point, between Redhill and Reigate.

Reuters had acquired it as a bolt-hole from London's bombs and rockets for transient correspondents and managers. Harold B. Carter, company secretary, his wife Betty and their three children lived there with staff including a cook, nanny, maids and a gardener. For a dog-house, it was a very cosy kennel!

Two days later, Cole and his family arrived, and after lunch he and I paced the lawn.

'Girl friend trouble?' asked Cole.

'Girl friend, no trouble.'

'Want to marry her?'

'Haven't had a chance yet to decide anything.'

'OK, son. Take a couple of weeks off and let me know.'

Next morning, I was off to Scotland. My feelings towards Patricia were unchanged, but she was still only 21, the only child of caring Edinburgh parents who understandably preferred her to be within reach of Scotland.

I was not prepared to leave Reuters, for love or money. So, with reluctance on both sides and to the regret of my parents, after three days we called off the engagement and I wired Cole, 'No wedding. Ready reassignment.'

'Congratulations,' he wired back. 'Want you return China via Palestine.'

After my leave, I had a few days at Head Office, did the ritual squat on Sid Mason's wastepaper basket, and saw on top of a pile of papers on his desk a carefully-placed internal memo to Sid from Cole, 'Alright by me if you feel it necessary to cut young Campbell down to size . . .'

Sid didn't mention the memo, and Cole never referred to our exchange of cables in Chungking. I never mentioned it either, but at the beginning of May I was given a three-year contract on the terms laid out in that exchange, naming me correspondent in Nanking, the new Chinese capital, where I would be under the direction of the Shanghai manager, Bill O'Neill.

Within a week, I was in the Reuter office in Jerusalem, where we collected and distributed news from the first floor of a modern office block. That made a change for me, though there was a curfew, and it could be an ordeal sending cables after dark, with a soldier on the roof pointing his gun in your direction.

Reuters had a high profile and good standing in Jerusalem. A prominent businessman named Cedric Mulford had overall steward-ship and the senior correspondent was an extremely competent and widely-trusted Scottish newsman named John Calder.

One of the most interesting of the others was Julian Meltzer, who worked part-time for Reuters as well as handling a portfolio of other journalistic interests. Julian was a big man, with a big personality, who could produce near-perfect copy at great speed. I could listen to him for hours, talking about his theory that the good journalist work-ing in Israel must know and be able to quote the Bible.

He said the Psalmist had reporters in mind with his pronounce-
ment that, 'His word runneth very swiftly,' and claimed that the Book
of Proverbs, chapter 25, verse 25, contained the first mention of the
foreign correspondent's work, 'As cold waters to a thirsty soul, so is
good news from a far country.'

The most exciting story on my brief Palestine assignment was a
midnight taxi drive across country with AP correspondent Carter
Davidson to meet the biggest single transport of immigrants to reach
Palestine since 1939. The ship, a 761-ton Greek vessel called the
Smyrni, crammed with 1,750 stateless East European Jews, including
370 children, had been sighted from the air off Haifa.

As we raced towards Haifa we were several times halted by patrols,
which poked rifles through the window to challenge our identity and
purpose. We reached the port before dawn, but the effort, strain and
expense seemed wasted when a dock official refused correspondents
permission to approach the 'hell ship' by motor launch.

Davidson and I dodged behind a shed, and slipped aboard a small
craft carrying Jewish Agency officials. As we neared the *Smyrni*,
escorting British destroyers fired warning shots to signal us to keep
away. But by that time we had close-up eyewitness material of the
floating slum, where people were squeezed into holds and corridors
like sardines, but singing the 'Hatikva' with a gusto that drowned the
loudspeaker of the escort destroyer.

There were gnarled and bearded grandfathers, dirty and bedrag-
gled parents, ragged children and babies. Some were half-crouched
below deck, clutching their bundles of possessions, with scarcely
room to lie down. Some hugged the mast from which the blue-and-
white Jewish flag flew. All were smiling and waving as they came
within sight of Palestine.

At 11.40 in the morning, a few days after leaving harbour in
Rumania, a 16-year-old girl named Gittel Ginsburg, in a crumpled
brown skirt and torn red sweater, walked down the gangway to her

131

promised land. Behind her were refugees from Hungary, Poland, Rumania, Czechoslovakia and Yugoslavia, nine of them hospital cases. The Rumanian master and his 19 crew were arrested.

Working in Jerusalem, I retained an obsessive dread of breaking the curfew, behaving badly resulting in embarrassment, or of even being suspected of any hanky-panky with a female member of staff. However, intent solely on strengthening colleagueal links with staff, I accepted an invitation from a knowledgeable and outgoing girl in the office to have a drink at her apartment. The conversation flowed so smoothly that curfew time passed before I noticed, and there was no alternative but to stay the night. The muslin curtain separating her bed from my couch, however, remained undisturbed all night.

A less dangerous temptation was a delicate gazelle of a girl, who definitely did not work for Reuters, but turned up for breakfast one day at my Jerusalem hotel, the Eden. I feasted my eyes on this beauty, but before I could find out who she was I was moved on to Amman, to cover the end of the British Mandate in Transjordan and the creation of the Hashemite Kingdom of Jordan.

In Amman, I stayed at the Philadelphia Hotel opposite the Roman amphitheatre, but was invited one night to dine at the hillside villa of the Reuter business representative. Who should adorn his table but that exquisite creature who had so captivated me at the Jerusalem Eden. She was his daughter.

After the tension of Palestine, Jordan was a joy, the sort of laid-back place where you could telephone the palace and find your call answered by the Crown Prince or Prime Minister. Ten of the rooms at my hotel, with private bath, were available for £1 a day.

The only problem with Amman was that the Post Office was not used to press cables, and unmoved by 'urgent press', 'double urgent', or even 'extra super urgent'. It was quicker to drive back through the frontier posts to Jerusalem to file.

I got an exclusive interview with the diminutive, bearded Emir

Abdullah, ruler of Transjordan since the expulsion of the Turks, a few hours before he was to become King Abdullah. A rotund and pompous Court Chamberlain accompanied me to the palace after glancing at the questions I had prepared.

The Emir shook hands with a smile, said he was sorry he couldn't ask me to breakfast because he had 'so many things to do' that morning, and motioned me to a seat opposite him. I sat down and, adopting my usual posture, crossed my legs, balanced my notebook on my left knee, using George to hold it in position, and grasped my pencil in my right hand.

To my horror, the Emir froze, and frowned thunderously. I wondered desperately what I had done to occasion this dramatic change in mood. He fixed me with a steady eye, then just as suddenly relaxed and began to chat. How had I found Amman? Was it my first visit? And so on. He took my questions, answered every one, shook hands warmly, and said he hoped I would come back and see him 'when things have quietened down'.

'God! What the hell happened there?' I asked the Court Chamberlain as soon as we were out of the room.

'You crossed your legs. The sole of your shoe was pointed at His Majesty. I can hardly imagine a greater insult to an Arab.'

What had happened was that the King-to-be had been instinctively offended by my posture – it is an insult to point your sole because it has touched the dirt – but then had seen the glove on my left 'hand', and understood the difficulty I would have had in holding the notebook any other way. I told the Chamberlain I would have appreciated a briefing before the audience.

However, the interview won splash play, and it was not long before my next move.

The cable said:

Want you proceed Teheran next two or three days. When arrive like know soonest

133

whats transport position etpossibility proceeding Kabul [capital of Afghanistan]. *Unwant you file spot news ex Teheran unless sensationalest but continue flow airmailed situationers which appreciatedest.*

There were rumours of war in Persia, but if I had thought Chungking was frustrating, Teheran in June 1946 was to prove even more so.

As a place, it had just about everything: a bit of Ruritania and a chunk of Boom Town, a flavour of Oriental tradition and a slice of Western sophistication. There were limousines and archaic horse-drawn *doroshgehs*, diamond-ringed millionaires and ragged beggars. Fountains and noble monuments to Reza Shah and the poet Ferdowsi skirted opium dens, cabarets and dirty hovels below the gutters. A blistering sun heated the open drains, creating an aroma which mingled with the scent of exotic perfume.

An American car cost £2,000 and the shops were well stocked with silk and satin, skis, skates, shotguns and everything you would expect in a first-class international department store. In the bustling bazaar quarter you could get a telephone (with a number) and fittings for £135, a typewriter for £35, radio for £30, a three-piece suit for £12 and a pair of silk stockings for £1. The biggest shop-window, the pavement, offered all the content of American Post-Exchanges: a packet of Lucky Strike cigarettes for 3 shillings (15p), tobacco, gum, soap and razor-blades.

Scores of hotels and restaurants offered delicacies for all tastes. A table d'hôte dinner at the Ritz was 10 shillings (50p) and a portion of caviar 7s 6d (37½p).

For breakfast at my hotel, the Ferdowsi, I might have a tumbler of fresh orange juice, fresh peaches, and eggs; for lunch sweet-and-sour soup and American or Viennese steak; for dinner mushrooms and chicken, followed by strawberries and cream. Tea and sugar were rationed, more nominally than in fact; belt-tightening was an unknown expression in clubs and cafés. There were few privations or restrictions for members of a cosmopolitan society – oil agents, diplomats, adventurers, even young women wanting to be wives for long enough to get British or American passports.

To my £2 a day bedroom at the downtown and run-down Ferdowsi trooped a procession of contacts, tip-offs and translators – men who monitored Teheran, Azerbaijan and other radios, local papers and government ministries. There were reports that the Iranian army was preparing for war, that conflict threatened in Azerbaijan, of fighting between Kurdish and Iranian troops in northern Kurdistan. All were unconfirmable. My retinue called at all hours to tell me things I had to discard because I could not check.

I had no Persian or Farsi, no Kurdish, no Baluchi or Azerbaijanese. When the local radio or Tabriz broke into a music programme with a major announcement, I hadn't a clue. As for a coherent prior briefing, that was something to which I was not accustomed, though one or two executives did their personal best to give some sort of picture. Sid Mason, now with the title of chief news editor, had followed up his cable about going to Teheran with an instructional letter and a recommendation of the local part-time correspondent Mr Norman. The letter is worth quoting as a sample of his work:

There is no need to file spot news from Teheran. The downhold still continues, and firmly. You can safely leave this to the stringer, Mr Norman . . . Conditions, although unsettled, do not appear to be likely to develop to the point where any big-scale operations are likely between Azerbaijan and Teheran.

But what you could do is to continue the flow of airmailed situationers . . . Try your hand at stories on the following lines: What is the political line-up as against the Arab league? (The Persians are not really acceptable to the Arabs but, against Russian and British pressure, they might eventually be forced into the Arab Union if they are to retain their independence.)

Easy on this one, remembering Arab opinion, and check with Norman. Who is the real power behind the Teheran government? (We have all heard of Qavam es Sultani, but is he really the power that matters?) Do this profile style, with colour. The Shah, a shy young man, does not possess half the power his father did; how does he come into the picture in all this squabbling over Azerbaijan and power politics? The domestic side of it, because of his relationship with King Farouk, can be got locally for background and, although we do not want a story about this, it may have a bearing on any future relationship with the Arab rulers. Mr Norman knows what I mean about the Shah and Farouk. The Shah has not been interviewed for a long time and this may be difficult but . . . try it anyway . . .

I never did establish Mr Norman's status, other than as a part-time Reuter correspondent. He had a house with a swimming-pool and fruit trees, out towards the hills, where it was cooler than the city, and had something to do with the British Embassy or British Information Service, though was not on their staff.

He took me to meet the Iranian Foreign Minister, who immediately launched into a vitriolic diatribe against Reuters and Norman, going puce in the face. I thought he would have a fit. Norman left Teheran soon afterwards, leaving me to handle the Persian situation alone from my furnace of a hotel bedroom. Sid sent a supplementary briefing, but reiterated that the hold-down on spot news cables still held good.

I explored ways of getting to Kabul. At the British Embassy, an attaché suggested the only way to get there by road was to take a car the first 500 miles, to Meshed, then perhaps a camel to Kabul – altogether about 1,200 miles through bandit-infested and mountainous desert. I found a man prepared to do the first 300 miles, but at a cost which caused Reuters to abandon the idea.

On 12 June Cole told me to find a temporary stringer and get on my way to Nanking. So I arranged for a trusted tip-off man to cover us for £15 a month until a new Reuter staff correspondent could get there, and on 20 June was shoe-horned into a grossly overloaded

Dakota on my way to Cairo, Calcutta and then Nanking, where I arrived in early July.

The China story itself had hardly changed while I was away. The Nationalist or Kuomintang army was estimated at 2.5 to 5 million men, the Communists at 1.3 to 2 million, but nobody knew for certain how many were fighting. It was the same sad serial: the greatest civil war in history supposedly going on (or was it?) with the future peace of the Far East and perhaps the world depending on it, and the world paying minimal attention.

General Marshall, who had gone back to Washington in March believing his objectives had been met, returned after a month, with his policies in disarray, to resume his mediation efforts alongside the US Ambassador Leighton Stuart, and the endless talks with Chou and Chiang, illusory accords and hopes of breaking deadlocks.

For me there were three big differences. The Chinese Nationalist Government had moved to Nanking two months before, and accommodation in the city was at a premium.

We had no 'Holly's Hotel', but sweated it out in the fan-less, breathless and noisy Nanking Hotel. In suffocating heat, I flaked out and had to go to hospital to stop the spread of a skin infection. If the Nanking Hotel was awful, the hospital was worse. I could not get out soon enough.

Then there was galloping inflation – the Chinese dollar cost of a translator had already doubled and was doubling again, but I was now being financed by Shanghai in American dollars. Thirdly, while everything filed from Chungking had gone first to London, everything from Nanking went first to Shanghai, and got near-instant publication because the English-language *Shanghai Evening Post*, *China Press*, and *North China Daily News*, among others, picked up everything issued by the news agencies.

I asked Tommy Aldeguer, our senior editorial man in Shanghai, why we pampered them like this, and he agreed that it had not been

so in pre-war days, but said both AP and UP were doing it now.
Nearly all the Shanghai papers had splashed on their front pages a
'special' I had done on the Nanking Hotel. His letter went on:

*Your service is A1 and everything would be perfect if the telegraph people could get
it down quicker. Latest transmission times average 8–10 hours. Mr O'Neill*
[Shanghai manager Bill O'Neill] *is up to the neck trying to get the office on
a more businesslike basis, and he is making progress, except with the messengers,
who refuse to accept any compromise. Although working, on direct orders from
Mayor Wu, they are liable to walk out any time.*

The Shanghai newspapers often published three Nanking stories a
day. One which was prominently displayed in July covered the foreign
correspondents' campaign to be allowed to see the 'civil war' we were
told was happening on the far bank of the Yangtze River. My story
called the barrier against us an 'iron curtain'.

Pointing out that we were used to taking risks, we put a barrage of
requests to the Information Minister Peng Hsueh-pei, emphasising
the embarrassment of sitting in Nanking writing about the contra-
dictory statements of the two sides. Peng said he would refer the matter to the Defence Minister. We said we had already asked him, and
he had referred it to Peng.

'I don't think it is safe yet,' said Peng. 'There is too much fighting
going on. It would be most difficult for you to see what is happening,
because hostilities cover such a wide area and there are no communications. You would perhaps go for days without seeing anything.'

We pointed out that it would be difficult *not* to see the tens of thousands of troops each side was reported to have committed to the battle. But all we got was a promise that if we specified the towns we
wanted to visit, Peng would make inquiries. It was to be several
months before we got our way.

Interspersed with the efforts to cover inconclusive talks and so far unconfirmable military activities were letters from Bill O'Neill about the detail of financing our operation and, of course, holding down costs. Some samples:

[3 August] *As requested earlier in the month, please hold down your cabled wordage to spot news, and send us all secondary material by mail. This month we are faced with a cable bill from Nanking for nearly £150, reckoned on a basis of 2,000 words a day, and this together with the £150 you will require for running expenses makes a total of £300 or $1,200.*

I hate like hell to bother you for I know what you are up against but you know how desperate I am for finances and the efforts I am making to 'recover' this office without having to call on London.

Also, in the telegrams you do send, it is not necessary to be too detailed. For instance we continually get 'President Chiang Kai-shek', 'General Marshall', 'Ambassador Leighton Stuart', 'Kuling mountainside resort', and so on, whereas one word in each case would suffice, and economy in this way would make an impressive total by the end of the month. I suppose the opposition have the use of USIS [US Information Services] *facilities and hence can file as they please . . .*

[10 August] *You will be glad to hear that we are now riding high financially and I am in a position to finance you without any need to call on London or anywhere else. I even have the money for your jeep, when and if we can get one. If you have a friend coming down, will you please ask him to call and collect your* US$550 *for August.*

Thanks for cutting down on wordage and saving us expenses. Please send what you can by mail to supplement the situation. Please also let me have your July accounts immediately as our accounts are held up waiting for you. Don't forget that these days you are a businessman as well as a correspondent . . .

Things improved not only in Shanghai but in my domestic arrangements, particularly in the means I found to escape from the

Nanking Hotel. I told about it in a letter home on 2 September 1946, proudly headed:

Foreign Correspondents' Club, 1 Pinghsieng Shan, Hankow Road, Nanking
I have spent the last few weeks keeping abreast of the news and getting organised
. . . The first thing we had to do here was to find ourselves proper accommoda-
tion. We formed an association – Nanking Foreign Correspondents' Association.
I was elected vice-president, until a round robin from Head Office said no Reuters
representative abroad could accept office in such Associations without first getting
Head Office approval. So I resigned, but they put me on the house committee along
with the president, Walter Logan, a home-spun American of United Press. We
started looking for a house.

In mid-August we started moving from the slum that had been our head-
quarters in the Nanking Hotel to an attractive yellow stucco English-style villa in
the residential quarter here. The house belonged to the wife of the governor of the
Province and was acquired for us by the Chinese Ministry of Information for
55,000,000 Chinese dollars or 25,000 American dollars a year. That was
cheap here. Inflationitis set in months ago.

There was the catch one usually finds in Chinese contracts. The Ministry found
the house, rang us up and invited us to go look at it. Walter Logan and I went
along. We liked what we saw, not least the solid, comfortable furniture. The house
had nine bedrooms, three bathrooms, a good kitchen, central heating, four ceiling
fans – a first-class house by Nanking standards. We told the Ministry it was fine
but we would only agree to take it (on a subsidised basis) if furnished as we had
seen it. The Minister said that was understood. He paid Mrs Wang her 55 mil-
lion CNC early August, ten days before we were scheduled to move in.

By 9 August the place had been practically stripped – all the good armchairs,
the best carpets, the beds and the desks had gone. We kicked, told the Minister we
would not now take the house. We then saw the contract for the first time. Do you
know what had happened?

The Ministry had paid over 55 million dollars for a house 'with the furniture
as contained in attached list.' The 'attached list' came ten days later. It was very

incomplete. So Logan and one or two of us then went through every room in the house listing missing pieces of furniture and items – as far as we could remember. We then put our list to the Ministry with our terms: You find these articles of furniture or keep your house. It cost the Ministry another 8,000,000 Chinese dollars to give every bedroom a bed, carpet, desk, two chairs and so on.

Then we had to engage servants, buy a million dollars worth of spoons, forks, knives, plates and other kitchen items and equipment. We were such amateurs! We engaged the very best cook in Nanking and probably the best staff of English-speaking servants, without mentioning wages. Three or four days ago, the number one boy, who has sort of manager status over the others, reminded us that the servants had had no money for three weeks. It took us a day and a half to adjust wages to the satisfaction of personnel. And we have since learned that our rates are 50% higher than those paid in the British and American Embassies.

Many things are still in a very disordered state: the cook wanted US$200 to go shopping. Logan knew there was a US$100 note in my top desk drawer and another in Charlotte's purse [INS correspondent Charlotte Ebener] *so he took these for the cook's shopping. So I find it has cost me something like £120 to live three weeks in our experimental club.*

We so badly need a manager – what about coming out here and taking on the job, Mum?

There are five permanent correspondents, two semi-permanent, two transients. The second week, however, there were only four of us resident in the place and we realised to our horror that we were maintaining two cooks, two wash amahs, two house boys, a number one boy, a messenger, an odd boy who opens the gate and looks after the garden.

This business of setting up house on a trial and error basis has nevertheless been fun and needless to say our house is now perhaps the best known in all Nanking. Diplomats have taken an interest in it; the American Army Commander donated a king-size fridge, the girls at the American Embassy made our curtains – a real co-operative effort in the best spirit. We are proud of the place which is open to all guests from breakfast to midnight.

Our manners could stand improvement sometimes. Two of the American

141

Ambassador's private secretaries were in for dinner the other night when one correspondent wondered aloud how much it cost to entertain one guest! For the next half-hour our guests might not have existed – we haggled and argued over the price, which some said was excessive and others maintained was reasonable.

Actually the guests, nice girls, loved the whole unrehearsed performance – rightly or wrongly some people seem to think of correspondents as a shower of eccentrics and feel something is amiss if they do not behave rather oddly.

We have had General Marshall to dinner and most of the Ambassadors. A house warming party will be held shortly. It has been difficult fitting in all this extra incidental time and attention with the real work schedule but there have been no complaints. Bill O'Neill is the boss, based on Shanghai for the administrative side of things, while I look after the news front in Nanking. We work with a minimum of interference.

The climate is bad. I have suffered a lot recently from prickly heat, a seasonal affliction. We work and live in a world of our own out here. My stories are published every day in a dozen English language and in local Chinese newspapers. I write little for New York or London, but send a lot of copy by airmail. Five days a week I work from 9 am–2 am. Saturday/Sunday I work two or three hours each morning before trying to escape from work. Usually I join a young crowd from the Netherlands Embassy. We have discovered a gem of a pool – just like a Scottish hill loch – about 10 miles outside Nanking. We go picnics there, when weather allows, most week-ends, which are very crowded.

Take yesterday: 11 am – waffle breakfast with American naval attaché and wife; 1 pm – lunch with manager of Standard Oil; 3 pm – swim with the Dutch crowd; 7 pm – dinner with chief Communist negotiator General Chou En-lai; 10.30 pm – classical records chez Tass [the Soviet news agency].

[12 September] *Many thanks, Mum, for the gloves* [knitted to fit George]. *Life is very much more settled now although servant trouble, the mess bills, menu preparation and the like – these things occupy too much time. Our Club is really an enormous success, or rather it will be as soon as we can control 'squeeze' – an old Chinese habit – and the soaring commodity prices.*

Nanking is much more social, certainly more fussy about dress and convention than Chungking. I cannot think of one day this month when I have not had at least one breakfast, lunch or dinner engagement every day. I am also very friendly with the Australians. The Australian Minister, Dr Copeland, is an important economist, a sort of Keynes of Australia, during the war years. He has a well situated legation which has a diminutive pool attached. I've been in three times. Distance is still one of the big problems in Nanking. Sending every message involves a two-mile drive. Now I telephone almost every message. It takes an hour to get through to Shanghai but I can anticipate when I'll be ready to dictate.

We have had General Marshall to dinner again. He is an exceptional American, the most impressive American I've ever met, a great man by any standards. How Americans love their 'movies'. Marshall's aide, a young Colonel, telephones to say General Marshall invites us (really meaning summons) to see a movie after dinner, which should therefore be served at 7.30 pm. During dinner Marshall was wonderfully relaxed, reminiscing about his school days, his relationship with Roosevelt, Eisenhower and others. During the movie, delicious chocolate ice cream was passed round.

Dr Leighton Stuart, the American Ambassador, is another fine man – one of the most gentle and charming I've ever met. He is a missionary, one of the most respected and beloved foreign educationists ever to set foot in China, and diplomat. We feel sorry for him because of the slickster politicians who take advantage. In a similar way we feel it a great shame that a man of Marshall's years, calibre and record of service should now be the errand boy of Chiang and Chou and a lot of lesser beings . . .

With organisation, life at the Nanking Foreign Correspondents' Club became more interesting and agreeable. As President, folksy Walt Logan, who liked to regale us with yarns about his friendship with Katherine Hepburn, and the fashion house wardrobe he built up as UP's fashion editor, had the biggest and best room in the house. As a prime mover in finding and arranging the funding of the place, I had the next largest.

143

We had dinner guests every week, indeed most nights, Chinese and non-Chinese. Henry Luce, founder of *Time*, *Life* and *Fortune* magazines, and possibly the best known and most active American Sinophile, came to our table and afterwards took part in a question-and-answer session. It was quite informal, not for the record, but I was struck by how inarticulate he seemed to be, considering the publications he had edited so successfully.

My trunk full of clothes and blankets, shipped from London in May, reached Shanghai early in October. I took a weekend off to recover it from wharf and customs and to enjoy Bill O'Neill's hospitality at Broadway Mansions, the 16-storey red-brick building overlooking the famed Bund, which housed the Foreign Correspondents' Club of China.

Bill and his wife Peggy, whom he had married in Hankow before the war, insisted on making their apartment my home every time I visited Shanghai. Bill was a big-hearted, straight-shooting Irishman, the sort of man who enriches life. He was much more than my boss: he was a friend and father-figure.

With all his Irish blarney, Bill had an insecure streak. It showed up in an incident arising from his love of riding horses, not fashion-parade stuff, but for exercise. One day, he rode his horse over a level crossing, instead of dismounting and walking it across. He was charged with a technical infringement of ancient regulations.

The court treated the episode as a joke, but paid regard to the sanctity of the law by imposing a fine – one Chinese dollar, or about one-fiftieth of an American cent.

One of the Shanghai papers carried a tongue-in-cheek editorial on 'Buffalo Bill O'Neill'. Everybody found it amusing, including Bill, yet he was genuinely concerned lest the story got back to Head Office and might there be frowned upon, as unbecoming publicity for Reuters' manager in Shanghai.

He and Peggy were a considerate and caring couple, loved by all who knew them. When Bill died in 1984, aged 81, the obituarists wrote with an uncanny consensus and conviction about his compassion, kindness and companionship. They recalled how he was always shelling out pocket-money for anyone patently in need, beggars, messengers and anyone suffering.

Denis Warner, a Singapore correspondent in the 40s, said that as an Irish citizen in Shanghai, Bill could have escaped imprisonment by the Japanese if he had chosen to collaborate. Instead he first organised a clandestine operation to send food supplies into the prison-camp holding the British, then told the Japanese he was just as much their enemy as the British were, and in he went to join them.

Michael Davidson of *The Observer*, recalling his time with Reuters in Singapore, called Bill, 'one of the great figures of the Far East . . . Behind his roistering Irish jollity and that wonderfully handsome Irish face were an acute and sensitive mind and one of the sweetest, most humanly generous natures I've ever been lucky enough to meet.' Jim Henry, a former Reuter manager and Far East colleague, recalled that in Hong Kong, Bill had been affectionately dubbed 'the honorary Irish consul', while Monty Parrott, an editorial pillar of both Australian Associated Press and Reuters called him, 'Mr Reuter . . . his name and personality ranked far above anything else in the region associated with the news agency'.

My first break in Shanghai also gave me a chance to meet the other staff and see the Reuter office. I spent most time with Tommy Aldeguer, in charge of the editorial, and his number two, Julian Bates, who took me to lunch at home with his wife and her family. This was the start of a 30-year Reuter-based relationship with Julian. He had joined Reuters in Shanghai in 1941 and in 1945 helped to reopen the office, after release from internment by the Japanese. Later he became successively editor of Reuters North American services; North American manager for news and sales; then in London associate editor and executive editor.

Back in Nanking, we had a surprise break in November when the Ministry of Information, finally capitulating to our plea to see what we were writing about, arranged a 10-day facility visit to the northern war zone.

We flew in an ancient Dakota which had doors removed as we approached the battle area and, roped round the middle to avoid falling out, we edged close to the plane's exit to get a better look at the terrain. Not a soldier was in sight, much less a war; not the sound of a single gun, much less heavy artillery fired in anger.

In ten days, we saw no actual fighting, but we had many briefings and at least saw something, however staged, of the army in the field. On the ground we travelled in an armour-plated train, carrying a squad of soldiers with fixed bayonets, until it ran off the rails.

We were guests of the Nationalist army and they made a big effort to look after us. Every night was a banquet – an impressive array of Chinese dishes, including duck, spicy pork and sea slug, a Chinese speciality, and lots of fire water and cups of yellow rice wine.

Following custom at these parties, a toastmaster, a convivial character known for his alcoholic capacity, addressed each guest individually round the table, offered a toast and drained his glass. Once he had completed a round, the bottoms-up ritual would be repeated. And again, and again and again. On this occasion the wretched man, an army major, more than met his match and lost face. The newsmen downed their drinks with such gusto they literally saw the major under the table.

We slept in dingy cells, government guest houses and one night – memorably – in a cave. Before we retired to the privacy of our small separate caves within the large cave, a dozen village maidens were paraded for our choice as partners for the night. They were young, shy, giggly, spoke only Chinese and were protected from the freezing cold, as well as from amorous moves, by several layers of heavy padded tunics and trousers.

I found it difficult to make the most generalised judgement about China and the Chinese. I never saw China as a military threat, or as a glittering market. It had been both, but the long lethargy of its millions, their technological backwardness and lack of entrepreneurial know-how, meant decades of catching up. I liked them: they could show nobility in face of appalling adversity, a capacity to live through the most horrendous man-made and natural calamities without bitterness, a readiness to smile and be trusting, an industriousness, an innate friendliness, and at the same time glaring character contradictions.

'Nothing could be more fallacious than to judge China by any European standard.' That nugget of wisdom is attributed to the first British Ambassador to China, Lord Macartney in 1792. In fourteen months, I was never invited inside a Chinese home: they kept their distance. I saw a strong strain of xenophobia. They seemed a proud people, very aware of their cultural and racial superiority to foreign 'barbarians'.

Another character trait became apparent almost by chance. One day my translator had word that a suspected wartime collaborator was going to be publicly executed. We drove to an open prison, and through bamboo bars saw an old man, seemingly unconcerned, eating rice out of a bowl. Within minutes the whole scenario changed.

The old man's face registered terror as guards burst into his cell, tied his hands and roughly manhandled him into an open truck. We drove close behind to a vast allotment area, ringed by high ground, on which thousands of people, clearly alerted to be there, were assembled. It was like an open air circus.

The old man, in a long gown and felt slippers, was pushed and stumbled forward to a clearing in the centre of the audience. A officer with a baby face, looking too young even to be in the army, followed close behind. He pulled out a revolver and shot the old man in the back of the head. The crowd roared applause. This was a circus all right. The old man fell, blood oozing from his mouth, but still alive

– you could see that from his eyes. The baby-faced officer stood over him and fired again, this time through his heart, and the old man was dead. A rough unshaven-looking character, a Quasimodo type, then prodded the old man's chest with his foot, opened his tunic and, with a hideous leer, removed some papers. It was a ghastly spectacle, cheered by that crowd. It left me troubled because I had never seen this chilling, obscene streak in the Chinese character before.

Meanwhile in Nanking, the war of words, of charges and counter-charges, propaganda and lies went on. It was often impossible to know who was telling the truth. Out of naivety, Marshall once or twice believed success was at hand. He thought so in October when the Generalissimo, having learned late that the US Government, per-suaded by Marshall, was imposing a total embargo on military deliv-eries to the Nationalist Government, declared himself ready to continue to seek a settlement by mediation and consultation.

Marshall had reckoned without the Communists, who quickly made it clear they were no longer interested in a negotiated settle-ment. Instead of a truce, which would have left the Nationalists in a strong position after recent gains, they demanded that the govern-ment armies withdraw to positions they had held months earlier. Finding difficulty understanding such demands, Marshall told Chou he felt his mediatory efforts were 'futile'.

'I told you some time ago that if the Communist Party felt that they could not trust my impartiality, they merely had to say so and I would withdraw,' he said.

A last-minute attempt to bring the two sides together caused the Generalissimo to postpone a meeting of the National Assembly, but it finally met in Nanking on 15 November. Neither the Communist Party nor the Democratic League was represented and next day Chou En-lai denounced the convening of the National Assembly and asked General Marshall to provide transport for himself and other Communist representatives to Yenan the following week.

At a meeting on 1 December, Marshall was critical of the Generalissimo for neutralising his mediation attempts by military action. Chiang Kai-shek replied that the Communists had never intended to co-operate with the National Government; indeed, under Russian influence, their aim was to disrupt it.

On Christmas Day the National Assembly, without the Communist Party and Democratic League, completed drafting the new constitution. With no hope of a negotiated settlement left, Marshall asked to be recalled, and returned to the United States in January 1947 to become Secretary of State.

General Marshall never slipped from the pedestal on which I had put him from our first meeting. He set a standard of integrity which stood out in bold contrast to the pettiness and corruption often surrounding him and his mission. Throughout 'Mission Impossible' – which was how we saw it – he must have felt anger, frustration and exasperation at the duplicity surrounding him, but one saw little evidence of these moods.

I met him many times and while very occasionally, just once or twice, he wore a wrath-of-God expression over some diabolical letdown by one side or the other, he was patience personified. The only tiny lapse I ever heard from his normal measured utterances was in an aside about a certain well known Democratic League politician, a bit player on the political stage, who kept trying to put his oar in. 'The trouble with him,' whispered the mediator, 'is that he can't keep his pecker in his pants.'

Some non-American correspondents felt resentment over off-the-record talks given by General Marshall at regular intervals to the American press corps. Although nothing from these sessions could be published attributably, the General's analysis had considerable guidance value in the muddled situation. I was never fussed by this practice because one or other of the Americans invariably supplied a fill-in on essentials. Besides, I could usually see him privately if necessary.

Marshall and Chou were the stars on stage in Nanking whose lustre never dimmed. Like most of the foreign press corps, I had a high regard for Chou En-lai. He had enormous charm, energy, ability and humanity.

I do not think anyone at that time could imagine or claim that he was close to the chief Communist negotiator, but in various ways, including accessibility, manner and mood, acceptance of questions and general demeanour, I felt a certain rapport. In a personal gesture, before leaving Nanking Chou gave me a portable radio and several rolls of cream silk (which I had made into shirts), as part of the process of getting rid of possessions he didn't want to carry to the Communist headquarters in Yenan.

Amid all this I received in December one more official request for less expenditure on news calls and more airmailed features. It was a letter from Bill O'Neill:

Since you do not appear to take any notice of my repeated warnings relayed to you over the 'phone about the present cost of long-distance calls I am committing this warning to paper. When the shock comes, don't say that you were not told. You have been averaging about 40 minutes a day, which will cost us about £100 a month. This could easily be cut by half, without the service suffering appreciably.

You could cut down on some of the less important war and political items culled from the Chinese press and reduce the length of some of your own stories, especially where obscure places are involved. All this second-class material can be sent here by express mail and will reach us in good time.

Things are not so bad when we have two experts like Tommy and Yourself [sic] at either end of the 'phone, but when we have your Chinese assistant at that end and a beginner here then it's so much money poured down the drain.

Sid Mason has written as follows, in a letter of November 27:

'It is important for London to receive about four good situationer stories . . . each month from China. You may be able to divert some of the effort at present directed to "shorts" to producing one good world situationer a week.

These should deal as broadly as possible with such questions as the political sit-uation in China, the reconstruction of China generally – as opposed to Shanghai in particular – a broad picture of the food, industrial, manpower and such like problems . . .

In conclusion, please thank Doon for his contributions and tell him that the news service could do with more material of this nature if it can be managed, with-out imposing overmuch on a good and willing correspondent. Gallagher of Press Association has written asking for a medical feature along the following lines . . .'

Sorry, Old Son, to visit you with these headaches all at once and so near Christmas. Tommy tells me that you may come down for a couple of days and, if so, we'll bed you in the 'parlour' if there is no room available. We can also feed you, as we now have our own servants and kitchen. Am holding US$500 for you which I will send up at the earliest opportunity by hand.

But immediately after Christmas I had a more pressing cable from London, 'Proceed Saigon soonest.' Why had it always to be 'soonest', 'fastest' or 'instantest'? But I complied, soonest.

Everyone advised, 'Take plenty of greenbacks (US dollars) because inflation is rampant.' So I arrived in Saigon with US$1,000 in my pocket, which I was not asked to declare, and took a taxi straight to the Continental Palace, the biggest and best hotel, a monument to French colonialism. All 70 rooms were occupied.

Would I mind sharing?

'No, not at all, provided the other person doesn't mind,' I said. A visiting correspondent had to take whatever accommodation he could find in French Indo-China at that time. I was shown to a large room, high-ceilinged, with a connecting bathroom and a balustraded veranda large enough to take a breakfast table.

The floor manager was about to put a second bed alongside the king-sized double already there, but I asked him instead to put it on the veranda, because, under a mosquito net, that would be more comfortable in the sultry climate. It was a fortunate choice.

Deciding to shave and freshen up before taking a stroll along the boulevards, so inviting under the old tamarind trees, I still had soap on my face when all hell broke loose. A Frenchman was standing in the doorway, screaming obscenities, his face contorted. He must have been the resident occupant, and clearly the manager hadn't informed him about the sharing.

I couldn't get a word in, but the storm eventually subsided and the Frenchman stomped off. I hoped he had found another room. Eventually I got into bed, on the veranda. Through the mosquito net I could see into the still empty bedroom. About one or two in the morning, turning over in bed, I became aware of an unfamiliar sweetish aroma.

Now half-awake, I witnessed for the first time an opium-smoking ritual: a man, presumably a colleague, servant or call boy in the bathroom cooking the stuff, and ferrying it to the double bed, occupied by the Frenchman who had earlier gone berserk. Propped up with pillows, he was now slipping serenely into ecstasy while I watched. Headlines like 'Rooming with a junkie' and 'Sleeping with an addict' ran through my head until I fell into a dreamless sleep.

The Frenchman had gone by the time I got up, and I did not see him again until the small hours of the next morning, when a repeat performance took place. That second day, in the Saigon Press Club, a Reuter stringer introduced me to, yes, Monsieur X, my junkie bedroom companion. He gave not a flicker of recognition, let alone apology, but was charming and solicitous about my comfort, accreditation, contacts.

After three days, the hotel found me a smaller but quite adequate room to myself. I got to know and even like Monsieur X but I never did raise with him, nor did he mention to me, what went on in his bedroom.

Saigon was an enchanting city. Exquisite Vietnamese girls in flower-patterned *ao dai*, the ankle-length national dress, split to the waist over black trousers, strolled along the tree-skirted boulevards, chatting and giggling, posing and flirting, demure and elegant. Excellent clubs and restaurants, sophisticated and showing few scars of war, catered for high standards of eating and entertainment. Chanel perfume could be bought, by the litre, lobster and Chablis could be ordered, as could even strawberries with cream in midwinter.

On the terrace of the Continental, nicknamed the 'Continental shelf', French officers and their ladies exchanged gossip over *citron pressé*, or coffee and cognac. The city was still very French, *très chic*, and one sometimes needed reminding that since 1945 France had been trying to reconquer her former colony.

The reminder came in the uniforms, the wire-mesh screen shields against Communist Viet Minh grenades, or an occasional explosion in Cholon, the Chinese suburb south of the sluggish brown River Mekong. A little scary, but life at the swimming-pools and crowded bars and cafés was never seriously disrupted, and the war effort seemed less than whole-hearted.

Under cover of darkness one night, I was whisked from the Continental by car to an elegant villa not far from the centre of Saigon, where a courteous Vietnamese offered a choice of drinks while giving an update of the military situation from the Viet Minh side. He was but one of several senior Viet Minh sympathisers who had infiltrated French positions.

The advice I'd had about American dollars was very sound. Hotel employees and touts did not waste time before sidling up to ask, 'Any greenbacks? I pay best price.' The rate was seldom less than 26 piastres to the dollar, sometimes up to 40, but one had to show discretion and be seen changing sizeable sums at the counter at the official rate of seven to the dollar. I could not tell Reuters; the company would never condone irregular currency dealings. At least there was an effective restraint on over-filing: every word had to be counted and paid for at the Post Office before it was transmitted.

The biggest news name in Indo-China was Ho Chi Minh. In news terms he was to Indo-China what Mao and Chou were to China, what Gandhi and Nehru were to India. He operated from Hanoi. That was where the action was. With Ian Morrison of *The Times* and Dickson Brown of the *News Chronicle*, I flew to Hanoi on 10 January.

The capital of North Vietnam was at war all right – there were battered buildings and streets blocked by barricades. We would drive down a street as far as a wall of sandbags, several deep, 7–8 ft (2–2.5 m) high. Through a peep-hole one could see, perhaps 50 yards away, another bank of sandbags, and behind that the Viet Minh. That's how close the war was.

One day, a lovely day, we were driving down a quiet street with trees on either side and hardly any traffic, when we saw, straight ahead of us in the middle of the road, two objects, obviously placed there with some deliberation. They looked like a couple of pot plants.

When we got nearer we saw they were indeed pots, but instead of plants they had neatly severed, but still bloody, human heads in them. The victims were boys. What gruesome message their heads were meant to convey we never knew. It was terrorist language, atrocity articulation.

Nevertheless this first Vietnam war was not on the scale of the second, waged by the Americans. Vicious and dirty enough, it was still fought with artillery, grenades, spears and even bows and arrows, not the mind-boggling armadas of bombers and flame-throwers, the search and slaughter squads that were to come a generation later.

Hanoi's Hotel Splendid hardly lived up to its name but, considering everything, it was no great hardship. The French Governor, M. Jean Sainteny, was first class. The British and American Consuls were generous beyond the call of duty, feeding and refreshing us. With the Indian Consul they went out under truce flags about once a week to negotiate with the Viet Minh the return of hostages, mainly women and children.

The British Consul, a splendid man, agreed to take with him a series of questions which I addressed to Ho Chi Minh. Then we waited. After some days, in the absence of any response from Ho Chi Minh, I flew back to Saigon. About a week later, I got a phone call from the British Consul.

'Ho Chi Minh has answered your questions.'

'Great! How, in what form?'

'They are typed and signed.'

'How do you know it's his signature?'

'The French police and military are in no doubt.'

'What have they to do with it? Where's the copy?'

'They're photographing it – their security people are most interested. You'll have copy in a day or two.'

I felt bucked. Quite a scoop. 'Uncle Ho' seldom gave interviews at this time. The cleanly typed questions and answers, in English and signed with a pen, duly arrived, and I handled the interview in the usual way, a lead followed by straight treatment, 'Here are Ho Chi Minh's answers to my questions . . . '

The Post Office clerk took an age to count the words and calculate the charge, about £100 at the official rate. As always, I kept the receipts, and returned to the hotel. I felt sure the despatch would provoke positive London reaction – either a bouquet or a king-size brickbat for squandering so much money on the cable.

Two days passed with no word from Reuters. On the third day, I went back to the Post Office, produced my receipt and asked the clerk to check at what hour the message was transmitted from Saigon. He shrugged. I demanded to see the Director. After another wait, I was escorted upstairs to meet *M. le Directeur*. No change. He was not going to disclose such information.

'Right,' I said. 'I will be back at noon tomorrow with two witnesses to ask that same question. You'll have had time to think about it by then.'

Next day I went back with Ian Morrison and Dickson Brown. The Director still would not budge.

'In that case, I give you notice that regardless of the consequences I'll get a copy of that interview – together with an exposé of what has happened – out of Saigon for publication in Reuters world services.'

'We know press messages are being smuggled out of the country almost every day,' said the Director.

I added that Reuters abided by the rules; scrutiny, censorship or whatever, and insisted on their observance by correspondents. In this case however, the French did not admit to any censorship and the Post Office had taken money to transmit a despatch to Reuters in London. I had serious doubts whether it had ever been sent.

I typed a copy of the interview and took it, with a separate story on the suppression of the original despatch, to the RAF office in Saigon addressed to Reuters' office in Singapore for relay to London.

Two days later, Cole cabled congratulations on the Ho Chi Minh questions and answers, and thanks for the exposé on blind censorship which was 'causing a fuss and questions in French media and Government quarters'.

Next move was a curt summons to see the French High Commissioner, Admiral Georges Thierry d'Argenlieu, who had retired from the navy to become a Carmelite monk, then returned to uniform under de Gaulle, with whom he shared an absolute faith in French grandeur. He was angry, and asked if I was 'trying to sabotage what the French are doing' in Indo-China. What was the difference between what they were doing in Indo-China and what the British were doing in India?

'The British are getting out of India, Excellency,' I replied, adding that I had never encountered a worse case of censorship – it was a disgrace. In a blind rage, the little admiral stomped out, ending the audience.

The system was later overhauled and regularised. A censor was named and installed in an office where correspondents could see what he was doing to their copy.

It was while working in Indo-China that I apparently coined the phrase 'the bamboo curtain', which was to gain such wide currency. I cannot myself remember the story, but it was ascribed to me by my rival Stan Swinton, later an AP boss, in a letter to the Commonwealth Press Union, at whose conference he expected to meet me again. His letter said:

Doon is one of the really great journalists I have met during a lifetime in our profession. I will never forget in Indochina many years ago when he coined the phrase 'behind the bamboo curtain'. It was so apt and picturesque that he justifiably swept the play.

After Vietnam, I wanted to visit Phnom Penh, capital of Cambodia, a glittering wonderland wedged between Vietnam and Thailand. Robert Trumbull of the *New York Times* came along too. For 95 piastres (about £14 at the official rate) we were driven in an armed convoy from Saigon to Phnom Penh, and booked into the colonial style Le Royal Hotel for £6 a night for a shared room.

Phnom Penh, like so many cities in South-East Asia, throbbed with life, with people and bicycles, street markets with an abundance of produce, well stocked shops and restaurants doing brisk business.

Bonzes, the saffron-robed Buddhists, circulated everywhere, sometimes in jarring juxtaposition to dens where emaciated addicts, lying side-by-side on bare sloping floorboards, smoked opium and dreamed dreams.

Courting couples, the girls in dainty and colourful *ao dais*, strolled along the river bank or through scented avenues shaded by trees. With all its charm and seductive ambience, Phnom Penh was a little unreal.

We arranged an early morning meeting at the royal palace with Prince Norodom Sihanouk, who had ruled Cambodia since 1941, when the French colonial authorities pulled him out of high school and named him king.

Bouncy and bubbling with good humour, he offered us pink champagne. Girls with dazzling smiles giggled as they peeked over and round embossed lacquer screens, while Sihanouk treated us to a spellbinding dissertation on his favourite theme: Cambodia past, present and future.

Sihanouk was descended from the ancient Khmer kings who built the great temples of Angkor Wat. At that moment, nothing seemed more important to him than the 'anointment of a sacred white elephant' – a baby jumbo, more albino than white – with all the ritual and traditional trappings involved.

As Cambodia's traditional 'god-king', with magic powers and influence over the peasantry, he could do almost as he pleased. It usually pleased him at this time to practise a morally commendable but politically risky posture of neutrality.

His enemies found it easy to brand him as a vain and volatile playboy, a jazz-loving, saxophone-tootling lightweight. But few denied his shrewdness in identifying Cambodian independence and neutrality with himself, so that until the mid-60s no Cambodian foreign policy decision of any consequence was made other than by Sihanouk.

On the surface at least, Cambodia in 1947 seemed reasonably contented and stable. The peasants, tending fertile fields and rice paddies, fishing from sampans in the Mekong and working in the forests, looked well fed and comfortably clothed. The disaffected, notably the Communists, were lying low, dispersed in jungle and countryside, biding their time.

The holocaust was less than 30 years away.

8
Star of India

At the end of February, I was sent to take over in Delhi as India approached independence. India then was not just the jewel in Britain's imperial crown; it was also the star performer in Reuter accounts, producing more revenue than anywhere else.

Reuters had operated in India almost since the start. Only 14 years after Paul Julius Reuter established his first office in London in 1851, the first member of Reuters' Head-Office staff selected for foreign service, 22-year-old Henry Collins, set sail for India 'from which place I was to organise Reuters' business in the East, with my head-quarters at Bombay'. From 1919, Reuters owned outright the domestic news agency, the Associated Press of India (API), which had been launched in Madras in 1910, and became staffed entirely by Indian journalists, carefully chosen and well trained.

Cole's letter to me of 27 February said:

You have been doing a first-class job and we are extremely pleased with your work and the way you have tackled things both in China and Indochina. From your point of view the Delhi assignment, personally and to Reuters, is one of the key appointments in the organisation. When we met in India [in 1945] I told you why we were not filling it. It is very simple. There have been so many mistakes there that we were better without anyone from London than with a failure.

159

India is undoubtedly going to be the big story for a long time to come and apart from the essential news side there is a tremendous ambassadorial job to be done in Delhi, so that we can give some relief to John Turner [general manager, India, based in Bombay]. *There is no doubt, Doon, you can make a real reputation for yourself in Delhi and now it is obvious that there is going to be a new India, you can make that reputation from the ground level.*

In Duncan Hooper [news editor, also based in Bombay] *you will be working with one of the best men in the organisation, and I know it can become a really first class association . . . Hooper, playing a lone hand – in the European sense – has done wonders for us in India and I know that you have no greater admirer than Duncan and that he will be absolutely thrilled about your taking over in Delhi . . .*

Your primary job is the outgoing news file and for this you must steer clear of politics and have complete access to all the Indians on both sides in addition to getting the inside gen from the ex-Supremo [Mountbatten] *. . .*

It took me two and a half days to fly from Nanking to Delhi, and after a night there, I flew on to Bombay for a 'detailed briefing' from John Turner before I began work.

At the Bombay office I learned that Mr Turner was week-ending at his 'beach shack' at Juhu a few miles down the coast. He had left detailed instructions on how to get there by train and would expect me for lunch. A car met me off the Bombay train and took me out to the shack.

In Scotland a shack was a garden shed. John Turner's gave the word new meaning. It had carpets on the sand, linen on the tables, iced drinks, exotic fruits, servants padding about. It was an informal lunch party and Mavis Turner, a splendid hostess, introduced me to the other guests and fixed me a large gin-based drink, assuring me John would join us in a jiffy.

I was on my second drink when John surfaced from the calm sea, picked up a drink, and without a word to anyone ensconced himself behind a potter's wheel, becoming totally wrapped up in moulding his clay. Mavis several times reminded him, 'Doon's here, darling,' without response. Eventually, after lunch, I got the chance to whisper in his ear that Tony Cole was most anxious that I should be fully briefed before I took over the Delhi news report.

'How long have you been with Reuters?' he asked with an avuncular, quizzical look.

'About three years.'

'Three years covering the war in Europe, then Burma, then China and Indo-China – I know your record. What can I tell you? Just maintain the same reporting and representational standards: accuracy, detachment, no bias, sourcing, balance, honesty, that have served Reuters so well to date. Just do the same sort of job in Delhi that you did in Chungking and Nanking and we'll be well satisfied. And remember, I'm here in Bombay to help in any way I can.'

It was an extraordinary briefing, superb in its way, but leaving me dismally ignorant about the world's second most populous country, with its complex of customs, castes and dialects. Then after a visit to the API office, and a meeting with Hooper, I flew back to Delhi just three days before the Mountbattens were due to arrive.

Another letter from Cole was awaiting me, telling me that Mountbatten's Press adviser, Wing Commander Campbell-Johnson had been told about me. (Nearly four years of Campbell-Johnson's war service in the RAF had been spent on the Headquarters staff of Lord Mountbatten at Combined Operations and in South-East Asia Command, where he was officer in charge of the Inter-Allied Records Section). Campbell-Johnson could be of great help to me, though I should not become 'too blatantly close to the Viceroy's establishment', and should be just as close to Congress and Moslem League sources.

In one of my last letters home to my father I had tried to give him some flavour of my life in India:

Here in Delhi the office is a large bungalow with a garden of lawns, flower beds, badminton courts. We have three gardeners just keeping the lawns trim, pruning the trees and so on. The house belongs to us, so we are very lucky.

There is a staff of 30 — 28 Indian reporters, clerks, editors, teleprinter operators, messengers, Bill Sykes, an English engineer in charge of the wire-room and myself.

The chief is Sir Ushaneth Sen, who has been with Reuters for 40 years and has seen every Viceroy come and go since the beginning of the century. In the 'phone book he is shown as Reuters Agent in the Imperial capital. He is a fine old man of balance and discretion. He studies the papers either in his cool, shaded office or sitting under an umbrella on the lawn.

Yesterday I bought a car — a 1947 Standard 8 hp for 8,000 rupees (about £600).

In a later letter I added:

I am quite comfortable with a small suite (bed / sitting room and bathroom) at the Imperial Hotel. An excellent bearer called Ali cleans my shoes, sews on buttons, looks after laundry (at least two changes a day already necessary) brings tea and fruit at 6 am.

He also washes the car which I park outside my room or in the hotel garage . . . As a change from off-the-peg clothes, I was measured for a suit the other day by the Viceroy's tailor. A £30 job!

If this grandeur risked inflating my ego, Cole and Mason were on hand to keep my feet on the ground. Cole wrote on 25 March:

There are two things I want to impress upon you. Everything is being done to make working conditions as satisfactory as possible for you in Delhi. I do want you to be prudent and keep things in perspective. In the artificial atmosphere it is so easy to do otherwise. I do urge you to do this as you are now really on the upper rungs of the ladder and so much is going to depend in your future career on your ability to be prudent and keep both feet on the ground as you have been doing.

You will hear all sorts of fabulous stories and be an eye-witness of equally fabulous behaviour but do remember that so many of the people whom in the war years you saw behaving in this way are now either 'out' or away from the jobs that were good, but which they spoiled by expecting too much from the goose that laid the golden eggs. A steady, sane and secure job is the one that counts in the end so far as a man's career is concerned.

The other point I want you to watch is a tendency to over-write in the matter of flowery language. When you can I suggest that you re-read your cables just to see that any stray extravagance is out. Your best cable work, Doon, is always noticeable when you are being kept tight by cable restrictions. This shows that you can get all the colour that is necessary into a report when you know you have to watch wordage.

At virtually the same time, I was getting a similar message from Sid Mason:

I don't want to start in right away on the downhold business, but this is just a tip to keep a tight hand on everything particularly as we are deeply involved in costs which have to be incurred in covering UNO in New York, the big Moscow conference, the UNO mission in Greece, Palestine and so on.

On the East-Asian conference curtain-raiser I would have taken the colour right out of the story, as it is one which has no appeal here, although it is of interest to what I might call the more sober countries. Also with the Mountbatten speech from the Throne: this was good copy but outside India not a world shaker, and 350 words at urgent press wanted some justifying, particularly as Bombay always protects with highlights of anything big taking place in Delhi . . . Cable costs being what they are, a story has to be very very good to be worth more than 500 words these days as, like the British, even Continental papers are still short of newsprint.

I accepted Sid's criticism about over-filing – and tried not to feel sensitive about it. This had been a historic occasion – the swearing-in ceremony of the last Viceroy. Mountbatten, chest smothered with orders and decorations, sitting on one red-and-gold throne, and the regal Edwina on the other; the thrones flanked by leaders of the new India. What colour, what pageantry! Surely 350 words at 6d (2½p) per word wasn't going to rock Reuters? But a correspondent must always guard against overreacting, especially when every word is being weighed and costed.

Apart from giving instructions, Cole was extraordinarily kind, keeping in touch with my home, sending reassuring letters to my father, and keeping me posted about my father's deteriorating health. As a result, it was slightly less of a shock when not long afterwards, I was told of his death on 23 March in hospital in Edinburgh. Though not demonstrative, we had been very close. This was the saddest news I had ever had.

Mountbatten was a hustler – a man with a mission, in a hurry. Delhi exploded with activity.

The day after being sworn in, Mountbatten had three hours with Nehru, who was in charge of External Affairs and Commonwealth Relations in the Interim Government. The two had met before, when Nehru visited Malaya, and enjoyed each other's company. Now as Nehru was about to take his leave, Mountbatten said, 'Mr Nehru, I want you to regard me not as the last Viceroy winding up the British Raj but as the first to lead the way to the new India.'

Nehru turned, intensely moved, smiled and said, 'Now I know what they mean when they speak of your charm being so dangerous.'

Mountbatten also had two hours with Liaquat Ali Khan (General Secretary of the All India Moslem League and in charge of finance in the Interim Government), sent personal notes to Gandhi and Mohammed Ali Jinnah (President of the All-India Moslem League), inviting them to talks, and had his first staff meeting in the study of the 340-room palace called Viceroy's House.

One had to go to the corporate news sessions, or risk missing something worthwhile, but I never warmed to the herd instinct. Everything was being shared or pooled. If you were quicker off the mark in grabbing a telephone or filed faster, then maybe, possibly, you'd be first. But no initiative or enterprise was really involved. I described an average day in a letter home on 5 April:

I drive to the office – about a mile – at 7 am. I make routine daily calls at the Viceroy's House, Nehru's office or house, Jinnah's house and several other offices, Embassies and residences. Today's been a fairly full day, nothing exceptional.

In the morning I witnessed the first meeting between Mountbatten and Jinnah [Mountbatten was later quoted as saying it took most of the meeting to 'unfreeze' Jinnah], *met a couple of contacts at the American Embassy, talked to Vietnam representatives to the Pan-Asian conference, and spent some time at the French Information Bureau.*

After a hot curry lunch at the Imperial, I lay under the fan for 20 minutes listening to music relayed by the BBC on Chou En-lai's splendid little radio, bathed, attended a tea reception for Mountbatten's new Press adviser, interviewed Dr Sjahrir, the Indonesian Prime Minister. In the evening I called on Jinnah to find out what he'd discussed with Mountbatten.

Not a hectic day by Delhi standards, but in a temperature of 105 [40° C] in the shade it can leave you fair pooped. I try to make a point of getting to bed if possible by 10.30 pm because that makes all the difference to freshness next morning in this climate.

The caste system in India gave me many jolts. Once I was having a drink in my hotel bedsitter with a well endowed English-educated Indian who had taken off his jacket and hung it casually over the back of a chair. When we made a move, his jacket slipped off the chair onto the carpet.

'Ali!' he shouted to my bearer, who was in his usual posture on his haunches outside my door. Ali came in at once. Without a word, my guest pointed at his jacket. Ali picked it up and put it back on the chair. Not a 'please' or 'thank you'. I knew my young guest well and tore a strip off him, but on reflection wondered if I'd been fair.

I used to feel desperately – but impotently – sorry for the sweeper in our Parliament Street office. Bare-footed, he had a ragged khaki shirt and shorts, and wore a permanent sad and hunted expression. I was told he had a wife and children who squatted in a bare room in a garden shack.

I tried to extend a degree of human feeling to his otherwise communicationless existence, but it was inadequate and unsatisfying, and I had no wish to upset feelings in the office by more positive contact with this poor man. With the few rupees a month he had from API I suppose he was better off than millions of other Indians who begged for food and whose bed was a pavement.

Reuters' Indian staff proved to be an excellent team, headed by K. S. Ramachandran, the best news-getter in Delhi, a small wiry tough character who seemed to have near-instant access to Gandhi, Nehru, Jinnah, Deputy Prime Minister Sardar Patel, and just about every other Indian who mattered. 'We got to know each other in prison,' he joked.

He was the only newsman who could go straight from Nehru to Jinnah and then get past Patel's formidable daughter Maniben to interview Patel under his shower. He had an assertive, indeed somewhat combative attitude in news gathering, but also had charm, and made friends with equal ease among Hindus, Moslems and Sikhs.

No one could match him in sniffing out news, writing it up with great fluency and providing balanced interpretation of current politics. Although I always knew Ram as a dynamic newsman rather than administrator, he later became general manager of the Press Trust of India (PTI) which took over from API.

Underpinning the operation was the news editor, Emmy Nerurkar, a quiet sound competent responsible journalist who could run through copy, expertly lifting choice items for London. There was Mohsin Ali, Uma Bajpai (son of Sir Girja Shankar Bajpai, Nehru's External Affairs Secretary), Sastri, Rajamani, Parsuram, Bhatia, Malkani, Lazarus – each gifted, each with his own contacts and sources, each contributing to a splendid overall team effort.

After work Ram, Nerurkar, Bajpai and I liked every now and then to inquest a big story, dissect tactics and treatment over mountains of curry and Scotch. Awful fuel for the Delhi furnace, but fun. An occasional topic was the liaison between the Viceroy's House and correspondents, which was not always satisfactory because Alan Campbell-Johnson's office issued little more than bare announcements and communiqués.

Reuters/API suffered less than others because the bulk of our political news was obtained from Ramachandran's milking his contacts. I was annoyed when, in a telephone conversation, Campbell-Johnson referred to one of Ram's stories which had been the front-page lead in *The Times of India*, and said, 'A bit tendentious, don't you think? No worse, mind you, than a lot of stuff that's been appearing, but we didn't think you would go that way . . .'

I liked Alan, but for a moment I lost my cool and told him that if he made himself more available to give us one or two clues, such things would not happen. At the same time we would never allow our networks to become in effect Viceroy's channels – we would always exercise independent news judgement. I told him that if he wanted a correct version of anything involving Mountbatten, he must keep us properly informed. We wanted daily access to him, and I urged him to contact us any time he wanted to know what was happening before he read about it in the newspapers. Alan's sensitivity was of course understandable, for Delhi was a goldfish-bowl.

Meanwhile, impatient to get to grips with the main story, to have my own unmatched sources and contacts, and establish an identity, I decided to go for the top, as I'd done with Mao in China and Ho Chi

167

Minh in Vietnam. I would seek early interviews with Gandhi, Nehru and Jinnah, sending the most news-relevant questions to each.

Early in May, I addressed questions to Gandhi at his quarters among the 'untouchables' in the sanitised slum called the Bhangi Colony in Delhi. His other Delhi address was Birla House, a millionaire's mansion. Between these two dwellings in different sectors of Delhi, he helped to bridge a chasm of Himalayan proportions in the caste and class system rampant in Indian society.

Gandhi could reach out and have rapport with rich and powerful industrialists as easily as with the untouchables he called 'harijans' – Children of God. Materially it meant little to Gandhi where he was. In the mansion, he often slept on a straw pallet next to his spinning wheel. At the Colony, although on the edge of wasteland, his room was clean swept and hygienic by Indian standards.

'If only Bapu [Father] knew the cost of setting him up in poverty!' Mrs Sarojini Naidu, a leading Congress personality, once remarked.

The day after my questions went in, a telephone call said the Mahatma would be pleased to see me. It was a pleasant morning, not too hot, and Gandhi came out of the bare room where he worked and slept, on to a patio.

What should I call him? Bapu? Mahatma, meaning 'Great Soul'? Gandhiji, a term of respect and affection? I settled for Mr Gandhi.

We shook hands and he motioned me to a chair. In the background I caught a glimpse of his British disciple Miss Slade, Jagjivan Ram, leader of the untouchables and Dr Rajendra Prasad, President of the Constituent Assembly.

Gandhi gave me a notepad and pencil, and squatted right in front of me, saying, 'Right, now your questions.'

He read the first question aloud and gave his answer, starting, 'My reply . . .' I took it all down in shorthand. Clearly uncertain whether my hieroglyphics accurately conveyed what he had said, he asked me to read it back. I did.

'Good,' he said. And so through all the questions. He was most professional; hardly a pause, very articulate, never needing to revise anything. Then came the bombshell, 'Now, remind me, Mr Campbell, what is the name of the newspaper you write for?'

'I write for Reuters,' I said. 'Reuters news agency.'

'Reuters . . . Reuters . . . the imperialist agency!' exclaimed Gandhi, looking surprised, if not shocked. 'Oh, there has been some awful mistake! I thought you were from some humanitarian newspaper. I opened my mind frankly because I thought I was talking to a humanitarian. So you are not Mr Campbell of Moral Re-Armament – the Oxford Group?'

'No,' I said, 'I am Reuters' correspondent in New Delhi. I am sorry if there has been a misunderstanding. There was no attempt at deception on my part. My request for this interview and the questions were on office notepaper.'

It was an anxious moment. Gandhi might have asked me to hand over or destroy the pages of notes I had taken of his views on the British withdrawal – 'Let the British walk off right away . . . they need not wait until June 1948' – and other topics.

Gandhi reminded me that dozens of foreign correspondents, special writers and authors were now in New Delhi and many of them had sought interviews with him and were prepared to pay large sums for the exclusive type of interview he had given me. I must not 'exploit' the interview.

We came to this understanding: I should treat the interview as an 'exchange between two humanitarians', write it up and let Gandhi see it before release for publication. Then I must offer it to the Indian newspapers and All-India Radio, through the Indian domestic news agency, the API, at the same time as it would reach Reuters in London.

A prepublication sighting would never normally be an acceptable condition, but weighing everything I considered this to be a unique exception. I was convinced then – and have had no cause to change my view – that there was no misunderstanding and that Gandhi knew perfectly well that he was talking to Reuters.

I could not however make up my mind whether he also knew perfectly well that Reuters owned the Associated Press of India or genuinely believed he was wringing some concession out of me by insisting on simultaneous release to the Indian media through API and Reuters.

I typed the story in the usual way – an overall lead, then straight question and answer, and asked a young API reporter to take the copy in to Gandhi's quarters next day while I waited in the car. After half-an-hour the reporter reappeared, grinning. He handed me the copy on which one or two very minor markings, nothing of substance, had been made together with this note in Gandhi's own hand:

New Delhi 5. 5. 47
Dear Campbell,
You have certainly carried out the spirit of my remarks. I have made some relevant changes which speak for themselves.
Will you distribute copies to the Indian Press or shall I? As you know I am silent today. I made the corrections before noon but the amateur help I get here could not cope with the typing in time.
Yours sincly
M. K. Gandhi

Almost every newspaper in India published the interview, many front-paging it, and some leading with a quote. *The Times of India* (6 May 1947) headlined:

British Withdrawal One Of Noblest Acts of Nation
Mr Gandhi thinks Communal Division Is Not Inevitable

The interview brought an immediate reward in that I suddenly became known, and Indians as well as non-Indians came forward to offer information. It was something to be pleased about as I went off to visit Simla.

On 13 May, I wrote home:

Sorry no letter for a week or two but I've been to Simla, a fab hill station some 200 miles from Delhi for briefing and relaxation. The Viceroy with several senior members of his staff, and Nehru, Krishna Menon and other leading political figures have been here too. For four days I walked, even did a little riding, stuffed myself with cream cakes, read and slept . . .

Simla is far enough away from the noise, smell and heat of Delhi to give you a change, yet conveniently near not to be out on a limb if an emergency arises. The views are breathtaking – grand and austere scenery, noble yet lacking the warmth which heather gives the Scottish highlands.

I had a first-class, ice-cool compartment in the sleeper from Delhi to Kalka, where you change into a white rail observation car – like a bus on rails – to climb 5,000 feet [1,500 m] round a succession of dizzy bends and loops to Simla . . . It is a single track rail with monkeys, goats and ponies running across it every mile or so.

Simla must be one of the world's choicest beauty spots. How wise the authorities were to preserve its serenity and out-of-the-world atmosphere by banning cars in the town. Only the Viceroy and Commander-in-Chief are allowed vehicles. If you choose not to walk, you take a rickshaw since the road is very steep and sometimes deteriorates into a track.

The rickshaws are special, each with four men, two pulling and two pushing. Nehru thinks the labours of the rickshaw coolies are an affront to human dignity. From Kalka to Delhi we travelled in the Viceroy's coach with Nehru in the next compartment. The train had a corridor so we joined Panditji chatting until 1 am.

Things are happening – fast. The first draft Plan for the transfer of power has been considered at Viceroy's House and Ismay [General Lord Ismay, Chief of the Viceroy's staff] *has gone to London with a copy for Cabinet. A communiqué last Saturday said HE had invited five leaders to meet him next Saturday, i.e. 17 May, to present them with the Plan.*

Sir Eric Mieville (Principal Secretary to the Viceroy) met us at his house here last Saturday for an off-record briefing at which he made these points: need for a quick political solution; onus of choice must fall on the people themselves or their elected representatives; how the leaders were being brought through towards agreement . . .

On returning to Delhi, I went on with my 'top interviews' plan and asked my API colleagues their ideas for questions to put to the Moslem leader, Jinnah.

Ramachandran, referring to the fact that most Moslems lived in the north-east and north-west, separated by Hindustan, suggested, 'Ask him if he will demand a corridor.' Since non-Moslems would oppose such a demand, it was clearly important and I put it in as question 8.

On 21 May I was telephoned to come and pick up the answers at Jinnah's residence, 10 Aurangzeb Road, named after Emperor Aurangzeb, last of the great Moguls. It was a white house, and a golden map of India with a couple of Moslem green splashes and the words 'Our Demand' hung above the fireplace in Jinnah's study.

I noted that against question 8 was typed the word 'Yes', and asked Jinnah's secretary Khurshid if Jinnah would enlarge on that. He would not.

Once again, I gave the story a composite lead and then ran it as a straight sequence of questions and answers, but the API version led, 'Mohammed Ali Jinnah today demanded a corridor linking East and West Pakistan.'

Whereupon all hell broke loose. Every paper in India seemed to go to town on the story. One national editorialised, 'Who is this sinister agent of Reuters in our midst? . . . Is this the prelude to a trade pact between Reuters and Pakistan?' Another had a front-page cartoon captioned, 'Hottest Day of the Year', showing me, identified as Reuters' agent, asking Jinnah, 'Will you demand a corridor?' Jinnah, lying back under an ice-pack, is replying, 'Yes, yes.'

I telephoned John Turner to ask if he wanted me to beat it quick. 'Why?' asked John.

'I think it's pretty obvious from the treatment of the interview,' I said. 'Who's going to talk to me here now?'

'Forget it,' said John. 'A rattling good story – just look at the way the papers have gobbled it up.' John Turner was rock solid. You could count on him.

In London, Cole wanted to know how AP and several London newspaper correspondents 'had such early possession of your exclusive interview'. I gave him the full background:

There are few secrets about the doings and activities of foreign correspondents in Delhi these days. When it became known that Jinnah had answered the questions I submitted a few days earlier, at least a dozen correspondents bombarded his secretary who, for obvious reasons, tries to maintain good relations with all foreign correspondents.

The secretary found it hard to explain why Jinnah had chosen to reply to my questions and ignore those of others who had been pestering him over a much longer period.

Jinnah's secretary felt the easiest way out was to release all round the information in the interview with the condition that if any part of it was used by any newspaper or agency, then not only Reuters but also my name must be included. I learned he had done this an hour or two after I'd been given Jinnah's answers.

When I protested this was hardly fair, in view of the undertaking I'd been given that it was an exclusive interview, the secretary tried to recall the copies already distributed.

But the damage had been done. When filing my last take, I noticed the AP story being lodged at the Post Office. It clearly stated, 'in an interview with Reuters correspondent . . .'

I know that three London correspondents cabled their foreign editors alerting them to the story. I know that none of them, with the possible exception of the Kemsley man, tried to pirate the interview.

This is what happened in the case of the Daily Herald: *Andrew Mellor, the* Herald's *staff man in Delhi, wired Towler, his foreign editor, 'You will see Jinnah's long exclusive interview with Reuters which also outhanded correspondents here. Main features seem to be extraordinary demand for corridor ettacit admission truncated Pakistan will be accepted . . .'*

Towler to Mellor: 'Used Jinnah statement top page one under your name.'

Mellor to Towler: 'Sorry you used my name on Doon Campbell's interview. Had thought my wire made it clear interview was exclusive to Reuters and only outhanded some correspondents here for information. I will explain to Campbell if you square with Reuters.'

Towler to Mellor: 'Last night's treatment of Campbell story was subbing trick . . . Telegraph *used same material attributing to their special correspondent . . . no regrets or apologies necessary.'*

Mellor upset over what his office has done. As a gesture he made available to me Nehru's reply to Jinnah's answers. He cabled Nehru inviting reaction on all points made by Jinnah. UPA did the same.

It was an obvious follow-up which I skipped. It would have displeased Jinnah to think that as soon as I got something solid and new from him I went dashing to Nehru for counter battery fire.

Andrew Mellor, who had a room along the corridor from me at the Imperial, had given me the text of the above exchange in a personal note of apology slipped under my door.

Cole's reply to me said:

The exchange of cables between Mr Mellor and Mr Towler is noteworthy only in that it provides the supreme example of the jungle journalistic ethics of Mr Towler. Further comment would be futile . . . Your coverage from Delhi has bee.. first class.

The interview was very widely published, and Alan Campbell-Johnson, in his Viceroy's house diary *Mission with Mountbatten* (Robert Hale and Co., 1951; and, with foreword by Mountbatten, December 1972) called it 'a carefully timed and placed bombshell', adding:

The technique of releasing it seems to have been copied from Stalin. Doon Campbell of Reuters to whom the story was given told me that it was in answer to a questionnaire which he had lodged with Jinnah some days previously. No one was more surprised than he to find himself with such a scoop on his hands . . . As soon as Reuters released the story, Jinnah's secretary specially rang up foreign correspondents drawing their attention to it. Correspondents informed me privately that Jinnah offered this interview to several of them. They considered he was determined to make the statement anyhow, and merely used Reuters' request as a peg to hang it on. Reuters was, of course, a well-chosen instrument for Jinnah to exert the maximum pressure on London at this critical stage in the Viceroy's deliberations with the Government, for through the exclusive use of this source he was ensuring for himself the greatest possible coverage in the British press.

In normal circumstances, with momentous events unfolding weekly if not daily, the story would have died a natural death. But in the highly charged atmosphere of communal suspicion which pervaded Delhi I could expect an accusatory finger pointing at me in government and other quarters.

The normal free access to official and other establishment sources might become less easy, the informal, off-record talks for guidance and background, the unsourced raw material, columns of analysis and interpretation, might be less forthcoming.

A wise and typically Indian formula came to my rescue. I received an invitation to go and see Chakravarti Rajagopalachari, responsible in the Interim Government as Member for Industries and Supplies. Known as CR or Rajaji, he was hailed by Gandhi as his 'conscience-keeper', a moral giant, ardent patriot, social reformer, administrator and statesman, destined to become the country's first Indian Governor-General the following year. I had never met him but of course Ramachandran had, and was as curious as I to know what this was all about, so he came with me to the meeting.

Seated behind his desk and wearing the dark glasses which were part of his image, CR received us warmly. He wondered what was behind the interview with Jinnah, particularly the question about the corridor.

I told him in all honesty the interview was but one of a series: the first had been with Gandhi, now this one with Jinnah, and I hoped Nehru would be the subject of the third. In each case I tried to think of topical and newsworthy questions. The corridor was hardly an original topic. Jinnah had touched on it before – admittedly in a less urgent and provocative context.

CR said he imagined I realised that as a result of this interview I might now find it rather difficult to go on working in the usual way. He had been discussing the interview – and the corridor – with the Mahatma.

Gandhi had said he had met me and had formed the impression that I was 'an honest young man'. So Rajagopalachari wanted to meet me and, having done so, would like to do what he could to correct the situation and enable me to carry on working as normally as possible.

Very deliberately, and looking directly first at me and then at Ram, who had not opened his mouth and now sat staring at the floor, CR said, 'Are you sure, Mr Campbell, that you thought of that question? Or did someone else think of it and suggest it to you?'

I thought Ram blushed, but CR did not pursue the question. Instead, he started to draft a short statement about journalism being a strange craft or profession in that young men practising it, not always politically mature, could sometimes find themselves projected into headlines which were not of their seeking.

176

To any hard-nosed news-hound it was guff, waffle, gobbledegook. It did not mention the Jinnah interview, much less the Pakistan corridor, or the fact that there was no ulterior motive behind it. But most newspapers published the statement and Indians, certainly those in government, politics and the media, knew the meaning of the message. I was off the hook.

Mountbatten, who had been away in London for consultations while the Jinnah corridor uproar was raging, returned at the end of the month with the British plan for the partition of India, and the London general desk log patted me on the back, 'Delhi (Campbell) gave us a gem of an opening – "Within a quarter of an hour's flight from Palam airfield where the Viceroy's Dakota touched down, villages were burning as warfare was being fought with medieval weapons".'

On 2 June Mountbatten handed copies of the plan to the Indian Congress, Sikh and Moslem leaders, asking for their replies before midnight. Jinnah said he would come in person at 11 pm, and did, but then took refuge in the excuse that he could not decide without a meeting of the Moslem League Council, which would take several days to assemble.

'If that is your attitude, the leaders of the Congress Party and Sikhs will refuse final acceptance, chaos will follow, and you will lose your Pakistan, probably for good,' Mountbatten said.

'What must be, must be,' Jinnah shrugged.

Mountbatten asked if Jinnah considered it would be justified to advise the British Prime Minister to go ahead and announce the plan tomorrow.

'Yes,' Jinnah replied very firmly. Mountbatten felt this was as much of an acceptance as they would get before the Moslem League Council met, and said the plan seemed to represent as near to 100 per cent agreement as it was possible to get, so it would be announced officially.

None of the leaders made objection. Mountbatten then threw on the table a 34-page paper, 'The Administrative Consequences of Partition', about which he remarked afterwards, 'The severe shock this gave to everyone present would have been amusing, if it was not rather tragic.'

On the following day all the leaders broadcast on the announcement. Mountbatten was subdued, but well-balanced. Nehru's contribution was eloquent and moving, 'We are little men serving great causes, but because the cause is great, something of that greatness falls upon us also.'

Jinnah's followers thought his speech a masterpiece, 'It is for us to consider whether the plan . . . should be accepted by us as a compromise or a settlement. On this point I do not wish to pre-judge.'

The Sikh leader Baldev Singh, who was in the Interim Government as Member for Defence, called on the forces to maintain discipline, particularly against the pressures of unpleasant internal security duties.

Mountbatten gave his first public presentation of the plan to the press on 4 June; it was a scintillating performance, a 45-minute exposition of a political plan of daunting complexity, followed by fielding about 100 questions, most of them from Indian correspondents among the 300 newsmen attending.

He spoke without notes, and only twice had to refer to a member of his staff for guidance. He showed dexterity and a light touch which won some applause. When a correspondent tried to draw him on Jinnah's demand for a 'corridor', he countered, 'Which paragraph in the plan are you referring to?' – well knowing the plan contained no mention of it.

The most searching scrutiny was on Dominion status, which he insisted meant:

. . . absolute independence in every possible way, with the sole exception that the

member States of the Commonwealth are linked together voluntarily. In fact they
look for support, mutual trust and, in due course, affection.

After his *tour de force* with the press, Mountbatten that day decided
the time had come to clear the air with Gandhi. There had been
widespread fears that the Mahatma's conscience might prompt him
to extreme lengths to wreck the plan in a final effort to prevent the
vivisection of India. Mountbatten invited him round that evening
and urged him to consider the plan not as a Mountbatten but as a
Gandhi plan, incorporating all Gandhi's major concepts of non-coer-
cion, self-determination, the earliest possible date of British departure, and even his sympathetic views about Dominion status.

He succeeded. At his prayer meeting later Gandhi said, 'The
British Government is not responsible for Partition. The Viceroy had
no hand in it. In fact he is as opposed to division as Congress itself,
but if both of us – Hindus and Moslems – cannot agree on anything
else, then the Viceroy is left with no choice.'

That was that; the British plan for the partition of India was effectively accepted, and the Reuter team in Delhi, which had scored a
90-minute beat on the Indian leaders' agreement, was deluged with
praise, such as from *Yorkshire Post* editor, Sir Linton Andrews, 'Warm
congratulations outstanding news value and exclusive information in
your India crisis service past few days especially Doon Campbell
cables'; and, most important, from Tony Cole, 'Reuters supremacy
on all developments Indian story was absolute . . .Congratulations all
men concerned. Mr Chancellor asks me send his personal thanks
appreciation to you all.'

Between the plan's acceptance in June and the end of the British
Raj on 15 August, I watched and was further impressed by
Mountbatten's hustle, advancing deadlines, getting things done fast
and smoothly, giving creaky machinery a streamlined efficiency.
Working at breakneck pace himself, Mountbatten infected others

with his methods. Withal he was the freshest – and the most alert and alive – man in the capital.

On 19 June I wrote home:

What a hysterical grind work has been this last fortnight. Mountbatten sets some pace. He can be quite terrific.

During a press conference the other day he referred to himself as 'this chap'. Viceroys are traditionally addressed as 'Your Excellency', especially in Imperial Delhi – more royal than Buck House sometimes. But one bright number in the press got up and asked: 'If India wants the British to do something or other what will "this chap" do then?' Mountbatten took it in good humour.

He has a way of saying to some of his seniormost subordinates: 'If you don't have this done by such and such a date you're sacked.' They usually have it done before that date. And they see the twinkle in his eye.

I know not whence he gets his energy. He will sit through a movie (odd how these people, Marshall in China was another, get the movie habit) until midnight, then tackle a formidable pile of documents.

He scans and digests each one at speed and is very capable of ringing up one or other of his advisers at 2.30 am and saying: 'Look, old boy, I want a map of this or a detailed report of that on my desk by 8 am.'

While Mountbatten is certainly a smoothie – they used to call him Kandy Dandy – he is mentally razor sharp and tremendously resourceful. He has brains and theatrical talent.

He is an extrovert, the world's most up-market name dropper – 'my cousin the King' stuff – yet no snob, intensely human. You have a positive reaction to the man – you like him or can't stand him.

Most of the time I admire his capacity for work, his blatant self-confidence and his matchless style . . .

It is unlikely that India – as a physical and geographic unit – will disappear with partition. When the Plan has been implemented, Congress will represent that it is not a question of two Indias but of one India with areas seceding from the centre.

These areas will, of course, be known as Pakistan – a lame, truncated, bisected country. Jinnah will need to muster all the forces, talents and resources of Moslem India to make Pakistan a going concern.

Hindustan, i.e. India, with its mines, minerals, mills and human masses, will be a sound enough economic proposition, but few of the leaders will be content until the passage of time and the processes of circumstance prove the words uttered at an historic hour in the destiny of the land by Nehru: 'India's heart is broken, but her essential unity has not been destroyed.'

It was eight days after that letter that Mountbatten gave Sir Cyril Radcliffe, whom he was quoted as calling 'an upright, proud, frigid, haughty British judge', the task of dividing up 88 million people, their homes and factories, and 175,000 square miles of Bengal and the Punjab.

As Chairman of the Punjab and Bengal Boundary Commissions, Radcliffe was given the Comptroller's house on the Viceregal estate, where he could work in isolation for the duration of his stay in Delhi.

In theory, panels of four judges in each province were supposed to submit to him joint recommendations as to where boundary lines should run. In fact Radcliffe, under the terms of reference, had only to consult himself. Mountbatten wanted the Awards by 15 August – Independence Day. Radcliffe called on Nehru and Jinnah asking, 'Is it essential to have definitive lines, however defective, by 15 August?' Both insisted it was.

The partition of Bengal and the Punjab, resulting in the exclusion of mineral and power resources, was bound to weaken Pakistan's industrial economy, but it was not a total loss. The parts assigned to India were deficient in food resources. Pakistan was left with plenty of food, including a grain surplus of half-a-million tons.

The economies of India and Pakistan looked likely to be complementary at least for some time; both would be losers without close economic co-operation.

Mountbatten's other most troubled province looked likely to be the turbulent Northwest Frontier Province (NWFP). With Mohsin Ali and Andrew Mellor of the *Daily Herald*, I flew to Peshawar to cover the referendum in the NWFP, which was governed by allies of the Congress party, though the great majority of its population was Moslem.

It was apparent by this time that partition was on the cards there too. Elsewhere communal tension had erupted into violence and massacres. It had not yet come to that in Peshawar, although tension was beginning to be felt in the mediaeval walled city where Pathans strutted through the narrow streets, often armed with home-made rifles, and the women wore the *burka*, completely covering themselves, with slits for eyes and breathing.

Peshawar's picturesque bazaar was replenished regularly by camel caravans from Kabul with skins, wool, fruit, crockery, watches and weapons. Restaurants had the best kebabs I'd ever tasted, and genuine Vat 69 whisky.

We hired a car and headed for the Khyber, a brooding, God-forsaken pass through barren, forbidding hills. Along the 12-mile route into the heart of the Pathan kingdom we passed many tribesmen, all with rifles. We also passed Landi Kotal, where two months earlier Mountbatten had met a tribal Jirga of Maliks (elders) representing the once untameable, trigger-happy Afridi, Masudi and other legendary warrior tribes of the Pathans. They had presented him with gifts, including a rifle, exquisitely crafted by a man squatting on an earthen floor in a cave. We saw these weapons being made, a thriving cottage industry in arms where every imaginable sort of gun – shotgun, rifle, revolver and others of sophisticated design – was being expertly fashioned.

In this country, state laws seldom extended beyond the highway. Off the road in walled villages and on mountain tracks, tribal elders administered their own laws. The blood feud and the vendetta were an integral part of existence. The tribesmen, some of the toughest warriors in the world, now looking gnarled and wizened with age, eyed us warily.

It was an interesting trip but I was overdoing it, and the heat didn't help. Boils like desert sores started erupting, creeping up my legs, until one day I collapsed and had to be taken to the Willingdon Nursing Home, where I was given penicillin shots. A complication occurred twice when I had not enough rupees to pay for the shot. It was a case of cash on jab – no cash no jab. It took a week or two before the sores subsided.

From late July, there was a sort of partition obsession in Delhi. It covered everything from the most efficient army in the East to type-writer ribbons. There were special committees covering every aspect of the split. It was even fatuously suggested that a special committee be set up to handle the partition of 'Old Man Monsoon'.

It was 'Westward Ho' for thousands of Moslems working in Delhi's imperial redstone secretariat. Sixteen specially chartered trains were ferrying them and their files 900 miles to Karachi, already popularly identified as the capital of Pakistan and the birthplace of Jinnah, who was due to become Governor-General of Pakistan, at the same time as Mountbatten became Governor-General of India.

Jinnah's critics said that as Supreme Leader – *Quaid-e-Azam* – he would be a virtual dictator, and Pakistan might more appropriately be called Jinnahstan. Campbell-Johnson observed that his powers made him 'Pakistan's King-Emperor, Archbishop of Canterbury, Speaker and Prime Minister concentrated into one'.

A story went the rounds that 20 years before, in Bombay's plushy Taj Hotel, an Irishwoman claiming the power to tell fortunes told Jinnah, 'You will be ruler of your own State one day.' Commented the pro-Congress *National Call*, 'Who is this Irish lady? If she is found she may well claim to be appointed astrologer-general of the *Quaid-e-Azam's* Government.'

On 13 August Mountbatten left Delhi for Karachi to perform his last official duty as Viceroy of a united British India, to convey greetings to the new Dominion of Pakistan.

On the drive to Government House in Karachi, Jinnah's military secretary, Colonel Bill Birnie, told Mountbatten he had information of a plot to throw a bomb at Jinnah during next day's state procession. Jinnah had taken the view that if Mountbatten was ready to go through with the drive, then so was he.

They did, and the ceremonies took place without incident, cordiality marking both men's speeches. All was ready for the rest of the sub-continent – British India minus two provinces, two half-provinces, a residency and a district – to emerge next day as the independent Dominion of India.

9
Murder and mayhem

Out of the blue, Mountbatten had chosen 15 August for Independence Day. It had been the date of the Japanese surrender two years earlier. Nehru said many would consider it an unpropitious date, and suggested the transfer of power should take place 'just before midnight strikes'. Mountbatten thought that a marvellous, dramatic idea.

So the Legislative Assembly passed the resolution proclaiming Independence and inviting Mountbatten to become the first constitutional Governor-General. Nehru and Rajendra Prasad made their way through the huge crowds to Government House, to find Mountbatten sitting quietly at his desk, after signing the last telegrams as Viceroy, ready to hand over.

The fifteenth of August was a day of pomp and circumstance, of oaths being administered, ministers being sworn in, state drives, speeches, crowds chanting, '*Jai Hind*', the national flag unfurled on the Council House, a 31-gun salute and a state banquet for 3,000.

In the next few weeks I saw more violence and slaughter than I had seen in Europe at war. For millions of Indians, the afterbirth of independence was a nightmare of murder and mayhem. Much of the carnage was not anonymous but personal; death visited on unsuspecting neighbours by former friends – obscenely savage death, death by dagger, kitchen knife, meat cleaver, crowbars or bricks.

The first horror stories came from the Punjab: Sikhs with *kirpans* ravaging Moslem neighbourhoods; murdering men, stripping and raping women before cutting their throats.

An eight-carriage train drew into the station at Amritsar, a makeshift refugee centre for thousands of Hindus fleeing Pakistan's slice of the Punjab. It was carrying a load of corpses. The station-master found a tangled heap of human bodies, throats cut, skulls smashed, bowels eviscerated. Arms, legs, and trunks of bodies were strewn along the corridors. White-washed letters on the last carriage said, 'This train is our independence gift to Nehru and Patel.'

This and a thousand other awful atrocity stories were circulating in the capital, which was swollen by thousands of refugees – Moslem, Hindu and Sikh. Mountbatten felt that as a matter of policy he should confirm his new constitutional status by avoiding interference in the new Government's action to restore the situation. So he arranged to go to Simla on 30 August for ten days.

On 3 September Hindu fanatics and Sikhs of the Akali sect launched Delhi's wave of terror. Moslem porters at the railway station were murdered. A Hindu mob went on the rampage in Connaught Circus, commercial heart of the city, looting Moslem shops and butchering their owners. Old Delhi's Green Market, with thousands of stalls, was set ablaze. Moslem civil servants in New Delhi's Lodi Colony were victims of murderous Sikh bands.

Next day, Mountbatten received a message saying the situation was so serious that it was essential for him to come back. He duly returned and, at the request of Nehru and Patel, agreed to take the chair of an Emergency Committee. Within 48 hours of his return, Indian leaders saw the smooth and honeyed Viceroy, with royal con-nections and manners, turn into a tough and ruthless Supreme Commander coping with a crisis.

'If we go down in Delhi, the whole country will go down with us,' he said.

He ordered additional troops into the capital, assigned his own bodyguard to security duties, requisitioned civilian transport, arranged the collection and burning of the bodies littering the streets. He told the Air Force to undertake dawn-to-dusk reconnaissance flights over India's half of the Punjab, the pilots radioing hourly reports on every refugee column – its size, length, progress and apparent route.

Warned by Sikh bands that any house sheltering a Moslem would be burned, Hindu, Sikh, Parsee and Christian families turned their Moslem servants into the streets. Sikh swords beheaded some; others made it to improvised refugee camps. Ali, my faithful bearer, who asked so little to squat hours on end outside my hotel room, warned me he would have to slip away. He risked death by staying on duty.

I later took food and clothes to Ali, a tidy well-organised lad, but never did I hear him complain of conditions as one of 100,000 Moslem refugees living in filth in the Purana Qila (Old Fort), a relic of Islam's ancient grandeur. There and at Humayan's Tomb, another Mogul monument, the Delhi authorities had herded almost a quarter of a million Moslems. Too scared to leave even to bury their dead, they threw the bodies from the ramparts to the jackals.

They lacked proper food, clothing, protection from sun and rain, and sanitation. Inmates could be seen urinating, defecating and vomiting in the same water in which women were washing their cooking pots. The refugees refused to clean their latrines themselves and the Emergency Committee had to send Hindu sweepers under armed guard into the fort.

At the height of the trouble Sardar Patel, Deputy Prime Minister, had almost decided to send troops into the fort to seize Moslem arms. Mountbatten argued that such an action could be disastrous, the surest way to provoke a massacre. He suggested British troops awaiting repatriation should offer help to organise the camps. This service proved to be very helpful.

Wild rumours circulated, which could have caused still worse atrocities. Reuter staff knew they must guard against inflammatory phrases, cut out speculative writing and stick to hard and responsible sources. Twice daily, every morning and late afternoon, I drove myself round the worst affected areas, witnessing hideous scenes, calling at police stations and hospitals, counting bodies. The slaughter came right up to the hotel – that's where the corpse count began – but I never really felt afraid or insecure.

I was aware of the purple prose, against which my copy must sometimes have appeared prosaic, making tabloid headlines, but Reuters understood and supported the way I was handling the story. Then late one night, in a move without precedent, the foreign press corps was summoned to Government House.

We were assembled in the Map Room, which featured intelligence appreciations and visual aids on the disturbances and refugee movements, and was next door to the Council Chamber where the Emergency Committee met daily. Mountbatten came in with Nehru, gave us an update on the current situation in the country, then turned to Delhi.

He said it grieved him that against the reality of the previous day's violence – 26 corpses, a little looting, one or two small fires, all controlled within an hour – a news agency, 'one which prided itself on reliability and international reputation for accuracy and integrity in news', had reported to the effect that Old Delhi was a sea of flames, with blood gushing down the gutters.

I nudged the AP man, whispering a suggested name of the offending agency. He nodded. But as I was leaving, close to midnight, a senior Information Ministry official sought me out.

'You realise, Mr Campbell, that His Excellency was talking about Reuters?'

'Never . . . impossible,' I said.

'Come to my office at the Secretariat tomorrow morning.'

I tried to contain my concern with the knowledge that I could produce, for Cabinet scrutiny if necessary, every line of copy filed to London, and stand by every word.

But a nagging sense of unease persisted. For one thing, what harm could this do to the pending negotiations over a transfer of API from Reuters to Indian ownership (it having been agreed that the Indian press should be admitted to ownership of Reuters on the same terms as with Australia)?

Next morning at the Secretariat, I told the official that he and the Governor-General had made a mistake.

'No,' he said. 'You are mistaken. Here is a telex of the story as published in the *Chicago Tribune*.'

I looked at it with disbelief. There it was, signed 'Reuter', but the purple passages were unfamiliar, nothing like what I'd written. I never filed it. Nobody from Reuters or API wrote anything like it.

'It's mistaken attribution – these things do happen.'

'No, I'm sorry, Mr Campbell, but our people in the States tell us the same story was in the *Christian Science Monitor*, the *Toledo Blade* and other papers. There is no question about it being a Reuter story. We checked on that.'

I could only apologise, offer him our file copy of every news item sent to London since the start of violence, and initiate an immediate investigation. He accepted that, but said I need not bother to send him a copy of the file to London.

That made me uneasy. Did he suspect we were 'pigeoning' copy out of Delhi – sending it by some other channel than the Post Office so that the authorities could not subject it to scrutiny? I shot off an urgent press cable to Cole urging him to clear Reuters with a message proving our innocence. Alas, it was not to be.

What had happened was that a whizz kid on the North American desk in the Reuter editorial, seeing what he thought my pedestrian version, compared with the whooped-up razzamatazz in the *Daily*

Getsmuchworse, decided without reference to anyone that the Campbell despatch was for the spike, and a pick-up of the popular paper's version would be substituted, under my byline. Cole explained:

The offending version went only to North America . . . The fault was entirely that of a sub-editor who wrote into the message and did it in such a way that a slight mutilation [in transmission] *gave an astounding casualty figure. The man concerned was dismissed on the spot.*

You can be assured that we have been leaning over backwards to avoid any trouble with correspondents' copy, and this lapse, which I am quite satisfied was isolated, was caused through a new editorial layout in which we have a series of separate regional desks. It is the holiday season and several regulars are off. You can be satisfied this will not happen again . . .

Contacts, tip-offs, sources – oxygen to a foreign correspondent – need careful selection. It took about six months in Delhi for me to feel reasonably well covered, through personally forged contacts at all the obvious and more likely sources of news: Government House; offices and/or residences, secretaries and/or aides of Nehru, Patel, Jinnah, Liaquat Ali Khan, half-a-dozen princes and all the other principal news-makers; Gandhi's entourage; army, police and hospital phone numbers and tip-offs; the airport, railways, hotels, Indian editors and reporters and a host of others, including communal societies and welfare organisations.

The API provided an incomparable protective backstop. Although not the only Indian news agency, it had by far the fastest and most comprehensive coverage, and its communications network far exceeded any other domestic wire service. But a correspondent who imagines there is such a thing as total blanket cover round the clock is inexcusably complacent. There is always the unscheduled, totally unexpected news break, and no amount of effort or time is excessive in consolidating a relationship with good sources.

Very late one night in Delhi I heard the noise of aircraft. It sounded like an armada of planes. There was excited activity in the street. Sleep was impossible. I made a series of urgent enquiries, milking all my sources. Yes, aircraft were taking off. Yes, troops were on the move.

In fact, war between the world's two newest Dominions was uncomfortably close. At dawn next morning, Monday 27 October, nine DC3s unloaded 329 Sikhs and 8 tons of guns, ammunition and war material at the airfield in Srinagar, capital of Kashmir, threatened by tribesmen from over the Pakistan border. I flew there three days later.

Kashmir's population was three-quarters Moslem, but ruled by a Hindu, Maharajah Hari Singh. He had a reputation as a playboy. With his identity concealed as 'Mr A' he had hit the headlines between the wars in a sex scandal involving a gang of blackmailers who had cost him a sizeable fortune.

He had dithered over accession to India or Pakistan, and wanted to keep his state independent, but when heavily-armed Pathan tribesmen crossed the western border and got within 40 miles of Srinagar, the Maharajah took fright, and offered to accede to India. The Pathans were reported to have left a trail of rape, murder and looting across the state.

When I reached Srinagar, it showed no scars of war, not even the tension or litter of a front-line city. The war, of course, was just down the road. But it was a manageable war to cover, not like Europe or even Indo-China. You could actually take the time to look at it, assess tactics, know the terrain, capture the flavour. There was fighting all right but, by the time I caught up with it, there were few set positions or lines. Under artillery fire the Pathans seemed to evaporate.

If Srinagar had really been the objective, the big prize, then Pathan heads should have rolled. The tribesmen, unopposed, wasted so much time along the way ('giving vent to their ancient appetites for rape and pillage', according to their opponents) that the Indian army units had time to secure positions in the Vale of Kashmir, consolidate their hold on the only airfield, and eventually drive the tribesmen back in disorder.

I spent several days and nights with Indian forces around Baramullah, about 30 miles west of Srinagar. There the Pathans were said to have sacked a convent, looting the chapel and violating the nuns of the Franciscan Missionaries of Mary. We saw bodies, wounded and prisoners but after four or five days there was nothing really fresh to write about, and but for my British warm I could have become a frost casualty myself.

Fortunately there was also a political and personality story. When the Maharajah offered to accede to India, he also released from prison Sheikh Abdullah, a charismatic Moslem who led the National Congress, the strongest political party in the state. Under his leadership Kashmir successfully resisted complete absorption into the Indian Union, retaining a distinct and unique status. The Sheikh seemed to appreciate the attention of foreign newsmen. We had many meetings and talks.

In Delhi we had heard a lot about the 220 or so British residents of Kashmir. The story was, that threatened with massacre by the wild invading tribesmen, the British had declined an offer of evacuation by air because they couldn't take their dogs with them. They were too often caricatured as a Noel Cowardish breed with stiff upper lips and a yen for tiffin and gin-based sundowners. They were in fact sensible and robust men and women, usually retired army officers or Indian Civil Service officials, living more comfortably on their limited pensions in Kashmir than they could hope to do in Delhi or Dorset.

The British had a lot to do with house-boats, so much part of the Srinagar scene. Forbidden to buy land in the old days, they had house-boats built, floated on the lakes, and wedged into position with long poles. Sometimes whole families, and their animals, lived on house-boats. Flat-bottomed and broad-beamed, the boats came in varying sizes, some with three or more bedrooms, flush toilets, running hot water and carved wooden furniture.

Wood carving being an important Kashmiri craft, nearly everything was carved – ceilings in a traditional geometric pattern, chests with lilies and birds, tables with lotus blooms and chenar (oriental plane-tree) leaves.

Srinagar was in a superb setting: sprawling among mirror-surfaced lakes and criss-crossed by canals with wild duck and kingfishers, ringed by hills and forests of fir and chenar, backed by the Karakoram and Himalayan mountains. The town itself was an Aladdin's cave of bargains: silver and copperware, carpets, embroideries, papier mâché, and wood carvings – chess sets, bowls, statues of Buddha. Clothes were cheap and of limitless range – shawls, scarves, saris, kaftans, and suits: choose your cloth and have a first fitting before dinner. The suit, a two-piece – better fitting and a fraction of the price of my three-piece carrying a viceregal tailor's tag – was delivered next day.

After three or four weeks in Srinagar, churning out situationers and features, as well as filing daily on the politico-military scene, at Reuters' suggestion I moved to Jammu, the winter capital, to which the Maharajah had fled some weeks earlier. I was ensconced as solitary resident in the ruler's elegant guest-house, comfortably distanced but within sight of his palace, attended by servants, including a cook who kept stoking me with irresistible hot curry and a mouth-watering range of Kashmiri specialities.

Hari Singh showed no enthusiasm to meet me and I felt he was too mixed-up about accession to be worth chasing for an interview. I had shaken hands with him when he turned up at a local radio station reception. Jowly and pasty-faced, wrapped in a British warm, he had a lady with him, and he looked ill at ease. He struck me as a shifty character, and he showed little loyalty to Sheikh Abdullah.

Jammu was a refugee story and, since refugee stories had figured almost daily in the Delhi news file, I was hardly over the moon about going there. I wrote the occasional item about a particular refugee or refugee family, trying hard to inject fresh angles. One of the worst human problems of the Indo-Pakistan tapestry of tragedy was that of thousands of women, old and young, abducted by the rival community, Moslem, Hindu or Sikh. 'Abduction' was synonymous with humiliation, degradation and torture.

I was in a small convoy of armoured cars stopped outside Naoshera on the Jammu front by a ragged little man who pleaded hysterically to be allowed to lead just one armoured car and a few Indian infantry to a hideout in the conifers skirting the mountains where, he said, raiders were holding 500 women from neighbouring villages. It was a story I heard again and again wherever there had been Hindu–Moslem or Sikh–Moslem trouble. Often, when girls were recovered, they were unwanted by their parents and ostracised by society, though their only fault was that they had been abducted.

Despite all this feature material I languished, and suggested to London that the main story had dried up and it might be desirable to get back to Delhi where the action was. The formula reply, 'precautionarily stay put pro tem', probably meant Cole and Mason had not been consulted and desk editors did not want to risk the wrong decision. What they did not know, because I never told them, was the extent of the damage a diet of curry, morning, noon and night, was doing to my system.

Sheikh Abdullah, who seemed to like having me around and who, I suspect, contrived to get me into the guest-house, called regularly, leaving a bottle of Scotch. The effect of Scotch and curry on my metabolism became apparent; I got yellower and yellower. Convinced I would soon be a stretcher case, I took the bold step of flying back to Delhi without waiting for authorisation. It took six weeks to recover my normal colour and appetite.

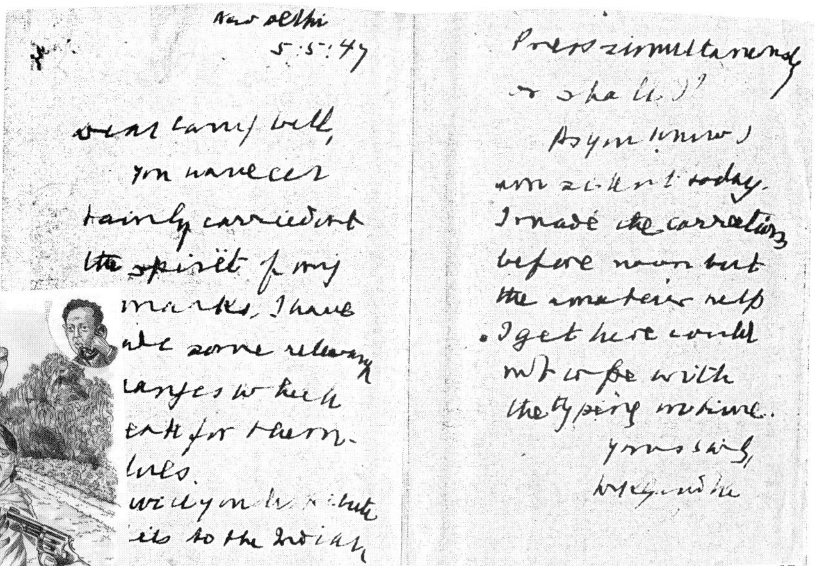

New Delhi
5.5.47

Dear Campbell,

You have certainly carried out the spirit of my remarks. I have made some relevant changes which speak for themselves. Will you distribute it to the Indian Press simultaneously or shall I?

As you know I am silent today. I made the corrections before noon but the amateur help I get here could not cope with the typing machine.

Yours sincerely,
M K Gandhi

ABOVE: Reuter montage showing Gandhi, and P. R. Roy, the reporter who witnessed the assassination (top right), telephoning me with the news (Reuters)

TOP RIGHT: Gandhi's handwritten letter to me

MIDDLE RIGHT: Recalling the assassination 27 years later (Sheffield *Morning Telegraph*, 30 January 1975)

BOTTOM RIGHT: Indian accreditation card, 1948

Martyrdom of the Mahatma

MT 30.1.75

Twenty-seven years ago today Mahatma Gandhi was assassinated in New Delhi. His murder was not just another political assassination — his non-violent creed had impinged on the conscience of mankind. DOON CAMPBELL was in New Delhi that night as Reuters correspondent. Here he recalls the news that sent shock waves round the world.

MY phone rang and a voice whispered the words that stunned the world:

"Man fired four shots at Gandhi point blank range – worst feared."

The news shattering the calm of that Friday evening in New Delhi came from a millionaire's mansion where Mahatma (Great Soul) Gandhi, apostle of non-violence and father of India's independence, lay dying from an assassin's bullets.

It came with stupefying suddenness, transforming a day of banalities into a night of tension.

Until then, nothing politically exciting had happened: items had trickled in on the printer; reporters had come back to the office with routine news items; January 30, 1948, looked like passing peacefully. Only one assignment – the Gandhi prayer meeting – had still to be covered.

There was no reason to suppose that this prayer meeting would amount to more than the customary sermon or rambling dissertation by Gandhi: perhaps a recital from Buddhist Scripture or the Koran: devotional hymn-singing and rhythmic hand-clapping.

I had attended several prayer meetings mixing with the crowd on the carefully tended

countless lives. His last major fast, with terminal possibilities because of his 78 years, had kept the country in suspense. We could not afford to miss any hint of a new fast. Undertaken at this time, it would have endangered the Mahatma's life.

The second event was that on January 20, two days after ending his 15th fast, a crude home-made bomb exploded at Gandhi's prayer meeting. He was unperturbed and told Lady Mountbatten he thought "military manoeuvres must have been taking place."

These were some thoughts in my mind when Mr P R Roy, a young trainee reporter

MAHATMA GANDHI
"Hymns of hate into songs of love . . ."

"Is he dead, is he dead?", I

professional presence of mind. When Gandhi fell, blood staining his white cotton dhoti from the neck to the abdomen, Roy bolted for the house phone. He got through quickly and shaken though astonishingly cool, dictated: "Man fired four shots at Gandhi . . ."

"Don't interfere with a CID man," he snapped at others clamouring for the phone.

We crossed the lawns and the rose and petunia beds to the spot where the shooting occurred. There Roy in clear, connected sequence described the scene. We tried to get a glimpse of the Mahatma in the room with the simple cot and the spinning wheel. Sobbing, desolate devotees blocked the way.

Back at the office everybody waited, tense and impatient. The phone rang again.

"Gandhi dead," said one message.

"A member of Gandhi's entourage announced to a silent crowd at 5.46: 'Bapu (father) is finished'," said the next.

Darkness

Then the real pressure began: Who shot Gandhi? Why? How had Nehru and Lord Mountbatten (then Governor-General) heard the news? How had they reacted? How had millions of Indians to whom he was Saint and leader taken it? What form would the funeral take? What repercussions would the assassination have on a political scene that had become a battle zone of hate and fear?

Newspapers brought out special black-edged editions and millions of people from the Himalayas to the tip of Cape Comorin prayed and

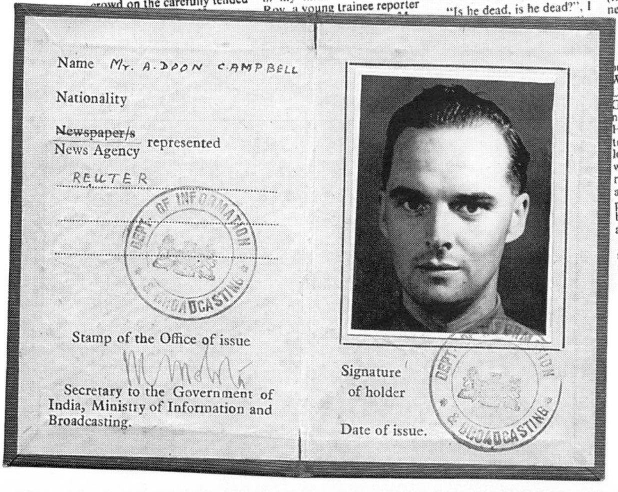

Name MR. A. DOON CAMPBELL

Nationality

~~Newspaper/s~~ News Agency represented

REUTER

DEPT. OF INFORMATION & BROADCASTING

Stamp of the Office of issue

Secretary to the Government of India, Ministry of Information and Broadcasting.

Signature of holder

Date of issue.

DEPT. OF INFORMATION & BROADCASTING

LEFT: Wearing the uniform of Jordan's Arab Legion, to which I was accredited during 1948

BELOW: With Count Bernadotte of the Palestine Conciliation Commission in Rhodes, shortly before the Count's assassination

LEFT: Inscribed portrait of King Hussein of Jordan

LIFE IN THE WORLD'S TROUBLE SPOTS

by

——— DOON CAMPBELL ———

(Reuter's Bureau Chief, New Delhi)

Palestine, Transjordan, Iran, China, Indo-China, India—the Foreign Correspondent travels them all as casually as you catch that daily train or 'bus to work. But, as Mr. Campbell tells you, he, too, is off to do a job of work,—wherever there is news and, usually, trouble.

Doon Campbell.

"WHICH newspaper do you write for?" said Gandhi, after answering all my questions.

"Reuter's," I said, "Reuter's News Agency."

"Oh, there has been some mistake," said Gandhi. "I thought you were from some humanitarian newspaper. I opened my mind frankly because I thought I was talking to a humanitarian. So you are not Mr. X of the Oxford Group?"

"No," I said, "I am Reuter's correspondent. I am sorry if there has been some misunderstanding but my request for this interview was sent in on office note-paper."

Two Years' Work

It was an anxious moment. Gandhi might have asked me to destroy the shorthand notes of his views on India, Palestine, the United Nations and world peace prospects. For two years I had been after this exclusive interview from the greatest living Indian. Something had always come in the way. Gandhi had even supplied the pad and pencil.

We came to this settlement: I should treat the interview as "an exchange between two humanitarians," write it up and submit a draft for Gandhi's approval before release.

Twenty-four hours later Gandhi returned the copy—almost unaltered, with note...

Cam...
of m...

A...
anxio...
uncon...
tation...

Cashier during the war years. Everything was laid on—transportation, accommodation, filing facilities, spokesmen, conducting officers, interpreters, handouts and censorship guidance.

During the last twelve months in Palestine, Transjordan, Iran, China, Indo-China, and India I have had more headaches coping with local conditions, currencies (pounds and piastres, rials and rupees), climates, codes, conventions, cranks and censors than with the actual business of getting ews and writing it.

Here are some random impressions of what a ewsman is up against in these countries:

China.—Correspondents in Nanking today are ther settled in their own homes or in an attractive eam-coloured, English-styled villa available—as ng as a Government subsidy lasts and the overnor of Kiangsu is prepared to let it—for

131

ABOVE: A contribution to the *Inky Way Annual* 1947–8, edited by Arthur J. Heighway (World's Press News) with Morley Richards (*Daily Express*) in aid of the Newspaper Press Fund

LEFT: French accreditation card, 1951

TOP: Best man, Tony Cole, bridesmaids and page with Mary and me on our wedding day, 11 June 1949 (PA News)

ABOVE: The wedding reception on the lawn at Whitmore, Merstham (PA News)

LEFT: Tony and Janet Cole (left) with Irene and Harold King at the wedding (PA News)

ABOVE: Having a word in a Paris hotel with Hollywood star, Ingrid Bergman, and Italian film director, Roberto Rosselini

BELOW: Press photographers crowd outside 10 Downing Street as the Prime Minister, Sir Winston Churchill, leaves to offer his resignation to the Queen on 5 April 1955, with me to the right of the policeman (PA News)

ABOVE: Sir Christopher Chancellor (left) and Kent Cooper (AP) link arms, celebrating Reuters' centenary with Prime Minister Clement Atlee (centre) and Devadas Gandhi, among other guests, 11 July 1951 (PA News)

RIGHT: Reuters' headquarters at 85 Fleet Street since July 1939, designed by Sir Edwin Lutyens (PA News)

BELOW: With Sid Mason (right), on the chief news editor's unit at the south end of the editorial department (PA News)

ABOVE: As news manager, briefing correspondents in front of the map of Reuters' worldwide interests (PA News)

ABOVE: Tony Cole mows the lawn of Burston Rectory, near Diss, Norfolk, with his wife Janet, and daughters, Mavis and Judith

ABOVE: As news manager, telephoning a contact in Hawaii via the satellite Telstar in July 1962 (PA News)

LEFT: In conversation with Ghana's first president, Kwame Nkrumah, and Fraser Wighton, with desk editor, Don Dallas and Tony Cole in the background (PA News)

LEFT: With Gerald Long (left) and Lord (Gavin) Astor (*The Times*) at the Dorchester Hotel in 1960 (PA News)

RIGHT: With Lord (Roy) Thomson of Fleet at the Dorchester in 1960 (PA News)

RIGHT: Reuters' chairman, John Burgess, greets the Queen at Charterhouse on 13 June 1963 (PA News)

ABOVE: Chatting with Shimon Peres and his wife, and Aryeh Dissentshik of *Maariv*, during a visit to Israel in the early 60s (Photo Jugend)

BELOW: The Malaysian statesman, Tunku Abdul Rahman, visits Reuters' editorial, accompanied by the chairman, John Burgess (PA News)

ABOVE: The German Chancellor, Konrad Adenauer receiving a Reuter party in Bonn (left to right) Adenauer, John Burgess, Gerald Long and Tony Cole (PA News)

BELOW: The world desk in the Reuter newsroom, 1973, at noon – subeditors busily freshening main stories for European evening papers and for dailies in the Far East

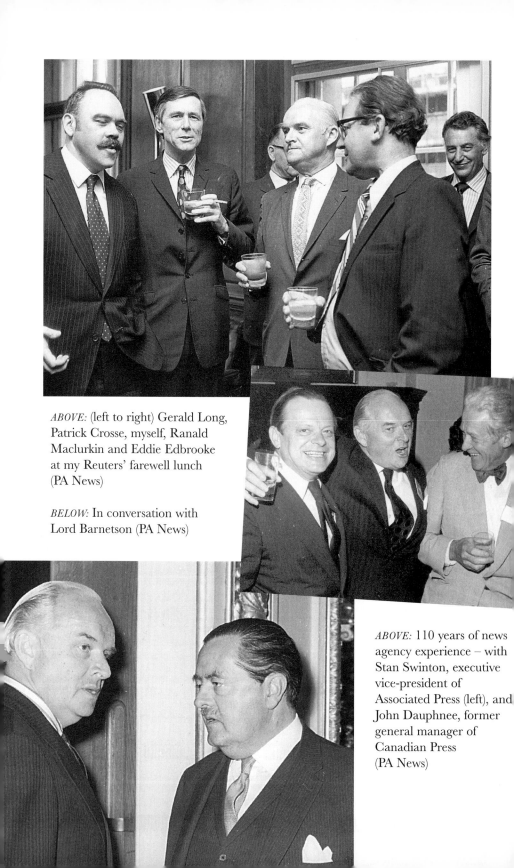

ABOVE: (left to right) Gerald Long, Patrick Crosse, myself, Ranald Maclurkin and Eddie Edbrooke at my Reuters' farewell lunch (PA News)

BELOW: In conversation with Lord Barnetson (PA News)

ABOVE: 110 years of news agency experience – with Stan Swinton, executive vice-president of Associated Press (left), and John Dauphnee, former general manager of Canadian Press (PA News)

ABOVE: Greeting Princess Alexandra at a film première in aid of the Newspaper Press Fund in 1983 (PA News)

BELOW: Meeting Indira Gandhi at a Commonwealth Press Union reception (PA News)

ABOVE: In conversation with the Archbishop of Canterbury, Dr Ramsey, at a United Newspapers lunch in 1983

BELOW: With Prime Minister Margaret Thatcher at a Guildhall reception in 1983 hosted by the Newspaper Press Fund, of which I was then chairman

ABOVE: With (left to right) Archie, Mary and Andy at Buckingham Palace after the presentation of my OBE

BELOW: Back at 85 Fleet Street in May 1994 for a recording about Reuters

LEFT: Pat Cameron in Edinburgh, 14 October 1943

BELOW: Pat 50 years on, with her much loved dog, Pip, in the garden of her home at Selkirk

Awaiting my return I found a letter from Duncan Hooper, 'Looks like you may be back in Delhi soon . . . hearty congratulations and thanks on your Kashmir trip . . . your coverage obtained exceptional play overseas and kept us right to the forefront . . . it looks as though the story is likely to fade now . . .'

The stories from my six weeks in Kashmir were widely published all over the world, and Cole's Christmas greetings were music to my ears. His letter said:

You have done a superb job of work, and your assignment in India has matured and mellowed that characteristic Campbell style without in any sense losing its refreshing enthusiasm and robustness. Anyone reading your file quickly knows that you understand India and her people . . .

I was thus back in Delhi, and still in good odour, in time for the biggest personality story of my Indian assignment: the assassination of Gandhi.

On 12 January Gandhi announced he would fast to death until the rival communities had a change of heart, and the party and community chiefs duly signed a pledge of amity five days later. Gandhi said it would revive his desire to live his full span, adding, 'That span, according to learned opinion, is at least 125 years, some say 133.'

While his fast did much for Moslem morale, Sikhs carrying black banners paraded outside Birla House chanting, 'Let Gandhi die.' Two days later, on 20 January, a crude country-made bomb exploded at Gandhi's prayer meeting in the garden there. He was uninjured, and unperturbed.

The London desk log on 24 January read: 'Campbell got a clean sweep with his story of Mountbatten to resign in June' and on 29 January I wrote home:

At 6 am on Sunday I'm off to Madras with a suitcase of clothes and a wallet of money. At 2 pm Monday I'm off to Colombo as a Government guest at Independence celebrations. I expect to be away until mid-February. An unending round of official breakfasts, lunches, teas, dinners, suppers, cocktail parties, banquets and balls is programmed . . .

Gandhi's condition and the way he's exposed and vulnerable to extremists is a continuing worry. Last weekend I airmailed to Reuters a 1,000 word updated personal closeup of the weak little bundle of bones on whom peace or communal massacre so much depends in this land of seething passions.

Friday 30 January 1948 was a routine news day. Nothing politically exciting had happened; minor news items trickled in on the domestic printer; reporters came back to the office with bits and pieces. Only one assignment, Gandhi's prayer meeting at Birla House, had still to be covered. There was no reason to think it would amount to more than the usual sermon or rambling dissertation by the Mahatma.

I had attended several prayer meetings, mixing with the crowd, watching Gandhi pass through the arboured walk from his bare room by the rose garden to the red sandstone summerhouse or a wooden platform. Small and fragile, he would be muffled up in white homespun, pocket-watch dangling from his waist, smiling or with head sunk in meditation. His two teenage grand-nieces, Manu and Abha, usually walked on each side so that he could lean on their shoulders.

The gentle shy voice seldom said anything a foreigner understood until he read next day's Indian papers. I did not expect much, if anything, from the prayers that Friday evening, but two recent events were still much in mind: the bomb incident and the fact that less than a fortnight earlier Gandhi had fasted 'for Hindu–Moslem unity'. I had a feeling he might threaten another fast, through dissatisfaction with the implementation of his last conditions.

Gandhi fasts had stopped riots, turned hymns of hate into songs of love, averted disasters, achieved miracles, saved countless lives. His

last fast, so fraught because of his 78 years, had had the country in
suspense. We could not afford to miss or be late with any hint of
another. Undertaken at this time it would seriously endanger his life.

While I was not actually anticipating anything, these thoughts
crossed my mind when P. R. Roy, a keen young reporter fairly new in
the office and always looking for jobs, came to ask me about the
prayer meeting. I told him he could go, adding, 'Watch out for any
suggestion of a new fast. Bring anything back to the office – only
phone if it's hot.'

Roy went off around 4 pm. At 5.13 pm my desk phone rang.

'A man has just fired four shots at Mr Gandhi.'

'What do you say?'

'Man fired at Mr Gandhi, Mr Gandhi – man fired at him.'

'Who's speaking?'

'Me.'

'Who's you?'

'Roy. Man fired four shots point-blank range at Mr Gandhi.'

'Is he dead? Dead? Must know, is he dead?'

'Man fired four shots. Don't know if he's dead, don't know, nobody
knows . . . worst feared.'

'Stay there, Roy, don't move. Get a story ready. Did you see the
shooting? Who did it? Don't say anything to anyone, Roy, you don't
know a thing, you haven't seen a thing. Just stay there. We're coming
right round . . .'

Roy might have been the only reporter at Birla House and I fretted lest any foreign agency might get hold of him and exploit his eyewitness account. The atmosphere in the office now became electric.
Staff crowded round as I typed, 'FLASH Double Urgent. Gandhi shot
four times point blank range worst feared.'

Roy had saved us the search for a formula to tell the story in the
first flash. No one had doubts or hesitations about 'worst feared'; a
shade less strong than 'death imminent', it was just right.

With three API reporters I drove to the Telegraph Office, less than a mile away.

Were we ahead? That's about the first thing a wire-service man needs to know. The clerk at the Post Office gave us the answer, 'Gosh, is that true?' he blurted, on reading the cable. He disappeared for a few moments (in our taut state it seemed an age), then returned to the public counter to say, 'London's got it.'

We drove at speed to Birla House, intercepting on the way a cabinet minister who turned his car round to pick up a doctor. Roy was waiting with the horror-numbed crowd. He had kept calm, showing superb initiative and presence of mind in a moment of crisis.

When Gandhi fell, blood staining his white cotton *dhoti* from neck to abdomen, Roy bolted for the house phone. Luckily he got through at once and dictated his flash. To a menacing mass clamouring for the phone, Roy snapped, 'Don't interfere . . .'

Now, quite composed, he showed Ramachandran and me exactly where the shooting had taken place. It was across the lawn and the rose and petunia beds. Roy gave us a clear, connected account:

About 500 people waited for the Mahatma to begin prayers. Gandhi walked from the house to the platform from which he speaks . . . As he approached, the crowd divided, leaving a lane for him to pass. A young man fired four shots from the hip. No one realised at first what had happened. As Gandhi fell under the assassin's bullets, he folded his hands in salute to the congregation . . .

We tried to catch a glimpse of the dying Gandhi in the room with its simple cot and spinning wheel. Sobbing desolate devotees blocked the way.

There had only been one other foreign newsman at Birla House – Bob Stimpson of the BBC – so I told Roy to keep his mouth shut if other correspondents tried to pump him and, leaving another reporter with him at Birla House, we belted back to the office. On the way we passed a car carrying AP correspondents to the scene. We already had the eyewitnesser in our notebooks.

Back at the office, the phone rang again.

'Gandhi dead,' said one message.

'A member of Gandhi's entourage announced to a silent crowd at 4.46 pm, "Bapu [Father] is finished",' said the next.

Now the real pressure began. There were dozens of questions to answer. Who shot Gandhi? Why? How had Nehru and Mountbatten heard the news, and how had they reacted? How had India – and the millions of Indians to whom he was a saint – taken it? What political repercussions would it have? When would the funeral be? What form would it take?

The entire API/Reuter organisation – editors, subs, reporters, teleprinter operators, messengers, sweepers – responded to a man. One reporter went to the police station holding the assassin; another was checking on funeral plans; another went to All-India Radio, which had a near-continuous commentary. We went all-out to blanket every conceivable angle. The entire resources of the office – reporters, editors, teleprintermen, even office boys and garden hands running copy – concentrated on the story.

Bill Sykes, the engineer, first acted as a messenger taking copy to the telegraph office. Next day I posted him in the British High Commissioner's office, across the road from Birla House, from where he phoned when the funeral procession started. So they all went on, for 36 hours with never a cheep about long hours, work intensity or status.

The profile of Gandhi which I had mailed to London a week earlier was delivered to the Fleet Street office a few hours before our flash came over the wire. It began, 'The wiry old Hindu in a loincloth who within a few days alternately threatened to kill himself by not eating and to live to be 133 is the most powerful force and human influence in Asia today . . .'

199

We needed an 'intro' confirming the bulletins on the shooting and death: 'Mahatma Gandhi, apostle of non-violence, was assassinated today. Four shots fired at close range hit him in the chest as he walked to his prayer meeting at Birla House. He collapsed and died within a few minutes . . .'

We needed an immediate reaction piece: 'Gandhi's death at an assassin's hand has hit and shocked India with an impact of atomic force. It is more than a national tragedy: to millions of Indians it is the passing of a God . . .'

A descriptive local roundup: 'Gandhi's death pulled down the blinds and closed the shutters in the capital of India tonight. The streets are dark and quiet. Cinemas closed and only essential traffic was running. Newspapers rushed out special black-edged editions and millions of Indians from the Himalayas to the tip of Cape Comorin prayed and fasted.'

Lord Mountbatten had reached Birla House not long after the murder. He knew that if the killer was a Moslem, Hindus and Sikhs might rise against the entire Moslem population of India, leading on to war with Pakistan.

So when a scaremonger told him, 'It was a Moslem who did it,' Mountbatten snapped back, 'You fool, don't you know it was a Hindu?'

You could almost feel as a tangible wave the relief when it became known that the murderer was a Brahmin. The Brahmins suddenly became 'Gandhi-killers' and the objects of riots, arson and other forms of madness.

I went to All-India Radio, its doors and corridors guarded by armed police, to hear Nehru declare, 'The light has gone out of our lives and there is darkness everywhere . . .'

Nehru also went to Birla House, where Gandhi's body, draped in a cotton sheet with his face uncovered, was carried to a terrace, with a spotlight on him as other lights were switched off. At 8 pm someone in the huge crowd shouted, 'The Mahatma is not dead. Doctors are hopeful of his recovery.'

Nehru climbed on to the gates of the residence and in a choking voice said Gandhi was dead. 'In this crisis let us not lose our balance of mind,' he said.

I was in the office from my usual 7 am on Friday until 5 am Saturday, when I slipped out for a bath and change of clothes. Then back at 6.30 am. The funeral and cremation and removal of the ashes were tremendous scenes. Then I flew to Allahabad where the holy blue waters of the Jumna and the holy grey waters of the Ganges flow together in the holiest, and filthiest, water in India.

Here was another mega-spectacle – two million people weeping, wailing, praying, silent, chanting, wading up to their necks into the river to get a closer view of the brown liquidish ash pouring out of the plain copper pitcher into the water. I can think of no story – not even D-Day, or the German surrender – which produced such spontaneous intensity.

I did get a rocket for over-use of urgent rate cables from Allahabad, but we had earlier been understandingly left alone, though a story like the assassination might have justified a stream of directives and so-called guidance notes from Head Office. At that stage they sent only one cable and it said everything, 'You ahead – keep coming.'

London's editorial report for January said:

Mr Campbell in Delhi gave news of the shooting seven minutes ahead of any other agency: his flash contained the words 'worst feared'...

Comparative [GMT] *timings were:*

	Reuters	*AP*	*UP*	*Exchange Telegraph*
Gandhi shot	*12.12*	*12.30*	*12.19*	
Gandhi dead	*12.30*	*12.47*	*12.50*	*12.46*

We lagged a little behind AP with the arrest of the assassin and his identification as a Hindu; but our Bombay and New Delhi offices were rightly cautious in view of the possible consequences of an error in identification and awaited the official announcement before filing. AP gave the man's name incorrectly.

Cole wrote on 6 February:

We do want you to know that our assessment of coverage from Delhi is that it was admirable and the file was as made-to-measure as we could hope to receive . . . Your descriptive was an example of fine reporting and your profile of Gandhi, which by coincidence arrived in this office a few minutes before your flash, was a really outstanding piece of writing. In this week's trade papers you deservedly come in for commendation.

I wrote home a week or so later:

I did not, of course, go to Ceylon. Not when the supreme news for 48 hours was in Delhi . . . I would have suffered agonising frustration and despair socialising there when the action was here . . .

Gandhi's assassination was a unique experience. It gave me the most intense 48 hours of activity, mental and physical, I'd ever known in war or peace. Agency correspondents should never allow personal feelings to intrude on copy; I fought desperately to avoid letting myself go, translating in the most articulate way I knew deep feelings threatening to spill over.

London received a shoal of congratulatory messages which in their discretion were not passed on to Delhi over an open wire. Radio stations in New York interrupted programmes to give the news from Reuters, New Delhi. Australia, South Africa, France, Egypt, Canada – from every country came the same signal: Reuters scored a double first, first on the shooting, first on the death. Cole wrote to say that not only were we first, but that I'd done 'an outstandingly fine piece of writing.' I replied that although taut as a tightrope, I'd no nervousness, no impediment in fluency because we knew from the start that we were first and when a

Reuter correspondent on a story of this magnitude knows he is leading in flashing epochal news round the world . . . well, he knows he's onto something special!

Many Indian newspapers carried nothing but Gandhi – not one line of other news in 12 pages. One was published with a completely blank leader page – only the words – 'Father Forgive Us.'

Every superpower and every little Balkan and Latin American state paid tribute to the greatness and goodness of Bapuji. Gandhi perhaps became even greater in death than in life. I do believe a new name will be added to the religions people profess because Gandhi, killed on a Friday by a man who betrayed him, has already been linked with Jesus Christ and Buddha.

Poor India . . . India without Gandhi . . . to millions and millions the two were one, part of each other. I prize the letter I have in Gandhi's own hand. Now they are vulgarising and making a mockery of the tragedy by protracted manifestations of mourning, diverting energy and labour from constructive and positive purposes to silly protestations, processions and resolutions, displaying the bloodstained clothes as at a fair or exhibition. It is getting somewhat sickening and sordid.

All this for a man Winston Churchill had contemptuously described in 1931 as 'a half-naked fakir'. I saw Gandhi quite often and on one memorable occasion spoke with him alone for about an hour. I saw in him no godlike attributes, and my profile of him did not even mention saintliness.

To many, Gandhi must seem a magnificent failure, whose teachings were largely forgotten within less than ten years of his death. He remained a father-figure to the end, but a father whose writ had almost ceased to run within the family. His followers had flouted his advice on partition and gone against his wishes not to let the Congress be actively associated with the Government.

Yet he remained in a sense the guru of Nehru, who went ahead with partition and became Prime Minister. Nehru ranked high in my bracket of Great Men. He gave towering leadership to India and to umpteen million Indians. Sensitive and gentle, he could yet explode in a flash of temper and anger, physically weighing into an ill-disciplined crowd.

Enigmatic, noble-minded, in an age of declining standards in public life, Nehru raised the sights of politics. He was immune from petty bitterness or personal jealousy. Not even his severest critics ever accused him of doing anything mean or underhand. He had total commitment to India's freedom.

He admired Mountbatten's practical dynamism, his capacity to demolish bureaucracy and get things done, his self-assured ability to reduce problems of daunting size and complexity to manageable dimensions. Mountbatten in turn was stimulated by Nehru's culture, the subtlety of his thought.

From our first meeting when I climbed through his railway compartment window in Delhi station, I encountered Nehru often, in Delhi and Simla, and in later years in London and Paris. He was an Olympian figure with human frailties. He seemed to think almost all around him had his own integrity and goodness, the same generosity of spirit and warmth of heart. He could be indulgent to old colleagues, some of whom were cutting moral and administrative corners. But in my mind, his image still glows.

10
The Near East, and no Royal Tour

I loved and loathed India – more love than loathing, but my feelings were very mixed when I was told in May to get ready to leave, at least temporarily, first to cover the possible Arab invasion of Palestine, and then sail in the battleship *Vanguard* to cover the Royal Tour of Australia and New Zealand.

This next phase of my life as a foreign correspondent was to start in Iraq. I left India on 9 May and arrived in Baghdad on 12 May, having spent a few pleasant hours in Karachi with Mohsin Ali and the head of the Pakistani news agency, Malik Tajuddin, and a few less pleasant ones in Basra on the Shatt-al-Arab.

I was met at Baghdad by our man, Mahmoud Abdul Karim. He wore elegant western dress, and had distinctive physical features and strong after-shave. Almost his first question was, 'How long are you staying?' I shrugged and told him I had no idea.

He drove me to a hotel by the River Tigris, and asked the same question again. Feeling a little less than welcome, I didn't answer until after I had been to freshen up, then met him in the foyer and showed him the cable instructing me to stay a few days in Baghdad 'being representational', and then go overland to Amman.

I could almost hear his sigh of relief. Later I learned Mahmoud suffered an anxiety complex about his job security, so must have imagined I had designs on his post. We soon became friends, and he booked into the same hotel so we could make a start next morning on my 'representational' calls at the palace and government offices.

At 8.55 am, in my Delhi government-calls uniform of newly laundered white shirt with tie and sharply creased slacks, I knocked on Mahmoud's bedroom door. He opened it, with a stocking on his head, crowning a ballooning nightshirt. But it was I who was undressed.

'Where . . . where do you think you're going?' he spluttered.

'To the palace and government offices – as we agreed,' I said.

'You can't go like that. You're not properly dressed. You *must* wear a suit.'

'Be back in a few minutes,' I said.

A short walk from the hotel I found a hole-in-the-wall tailor's shop with what looked like a grey flannel two-piece hanging inside. It was badly cut and over-padded, but it more or less fitted. So I paid the £8 17s 6d (£8.75) – failing to get a receipt, to my later embarrassment with Reuters' accounts department – and Mahmoud and I were able to go together, 'properly dressed', on the round of interviews.

Duty done, I invited Mahmoud's thoughts on the second and more difficult part of the assignment – getting 700 miles to Amman overland, years after the end of the one-time Nairn desert bus service between the two cities. Of course I could guess why London had said 'proceed overland'.

The Union Jack had just been lowered over Palestine, the British Mandate had ended, and the State of Israel had been proclaimed by a Jewish Provisional Government in Tel Aviv on Friday 14 May. Within hours of David Ben-Gurion reading out the Proclamation of Independence, the neighbouring Arab territories of Iraq, Lebanon, Syria, Jordan, Egypt, Saudi Arabia and Yemen announced plans to invade – and conquer – the new-born state.

By going overland I would have a grandstand view of Arabs swarming across the desert to join an envisaged joint command under the British-officered Arab Legion based in Jordan. That was the idea, but how? I asked Mahmoud as we sat in the hotel lounge.

'Simple, dear boy.' With a lecherous grin Mahmoud nodded in the direction of a dark feline young lady, hair cascading to her shoulders, who sat demurely concentrating on her *petit point*, with a maid squatting beside her.

'Who's she?' I asked.

'She's Carmen, daughter of the Spanish Ambassador, who's accredited jointly to Iraq and Jordan. He's here to load up with supplies – fruit juices and all sorts of things. He'll be driving back to Amman in a day or two.' It was magic, pure magic.

So, once again, I thumbed a ride – this time across a desert. His Excellency, a roly-poly, unpompous diplomat with a pawky if sparse sense of humour, drove the embassy Packard with me sitting next to him. The heavenly Carmen – who was from Seville, like her operatic namesake – sat at the wheel of a Cadillac 100 yards behind, with only her maid for company. A covered lorry with the rations brought up the rear of the convoy.

The ambassador ignored my suggestion that I change places with Carmen's maid. The drive lasted two boring days, separated by a night of generous hospitality at an oil pipeline pumping station halfway to Amman. Not a single bellicose Arab did I see. No story.

We reached Amman at dusk on 18 May to find the Philadelphia Hotel very full, mostly with war correspondents in Arab Legion regalia. The ambassador rated a small suite. Carmen had a room to herself immediately above him on the next floor.

I was squeezed into a basement bedroom with two or three others, including Seaghan Maynes, one of my closest war correspondent mates from D-Day to the German surrender in Europe. Seaghan had been handling this front single-handed and winning bouquets from London for speed and quality of cover, but if he felt any resentment over me getting in on his act it was well disguised.

Seaghan had a valuable advantage over other correspondents. Most of them hired cars or took taxis to the scene of fighting. Reuters owned an open two-seater MG Midget, and every day the gutsy little green sports car could be seen whizzing along the 50 miles of hard-surfaced road to Jerusalem, where most media attention was focussed.

It became a routine drive over Jordan's hills and through green valleys, past the Mount of Olives and the Garden of Gethsemane, though the last mile or two before Jerusalem could be hairy because the road was exposed to Israeli sharpshooters who regarded almost anything moving on it as a target. The drill was to accelerate hard until you reached the city walls. Never once did the mighty Midget let us down.

Seaghan and I used the MG on alternate days, without friction. The Arab Legion, to which we were both accredited and whose uniform we wore, allowed us to fill up at their military petrol pumps. We sometimes took sandwiches for lunch, and usually tried to get back to Amman before dark to file our stories.

Although troops from several countries were said to have gone to the aid of irregular bands of Arabs fighting against the Israelis, and sporadic fighting certainly took place over a wide area, one saw little evidence of co-ordinated strategy or tactics; the campaign depended mainly on the Arab Legion and the Egyptian army.

The situation of the Jews in the Old City had been getting steadily worse since late 1947, when an estimated 1,800 faced 20,000 Arabs. The Arab numbers were then swollen by refugees from the New City, while some of the Jews escaped the Old City. By the time I saw it, the Holy City was an unholy mess. Soldiers and sandbags occupied streets and buildings. Artillery, mortar and rifle fire went on incessantly. Military scout cars gingerly negotiated the narrow cobble-stoned Via Dolorosa.

At noon on 28 May, the Jewish quarter of the Old City surrendered to the Arab Legion.

I myself suffered a gentler ambush and invasion in the dimly-lit corridor outside the Hotel Philadelphia's basement dining-room. Exhausted after a day covering events in Jerusalem, I had had a late dinner, and was last to leave the room.

Just outside the door was the demure Carmen, with whom I had never been alone or even had a conversation. 'I want to take your mind off war,' she whispered, and propelled me along the corridor to the room where I slept, explaining that she dare not go to her own room because it was right over that of her father, who was sensitive to noise.

We had just got into the room when a colleague who shared sleeping space there, having decided on an early night, burst in without knocking.

There was no light on and he had no cause to think anyone might be in the room. With diplomatic discretion, Carmen beat a hasty retreat, and never returned.

On 10 June London cabled me to go to Rhodes, where Count Folke Bernadotte and a small team of American, French and Swedish experts were trying to work out a formula that would lead to an Arab–Jewish settlement in Palestine. Next day, the United Nations secured a ceasefire in Israel, which lasted until 9 July.

I left Amman for Cairo, for another snatched interlude with my old friends Marjorie and Haig Nicholson, who opened new vistas in style of living and looking after visiting Reuter colleagues.

In two days we lunched or dined at the Turf, Gezeira, Mohammed Ali and Sphinx clubs, among others; saw the Nile, the pyramids and the sphinx; and compared notes on the enlightened news agency for which we had the good fortune to work.

Then on to Athens, though not before the Egyptian customs men at Cairo airport had relieved me of files, papers and a tiny pistol and five bullets, which I had hoped would pass unnoticed in a pile of socks at the bottom of my grip bag.

In Athens I was to meet for the first time another Reuter corre-
spondent/manager whose byline lent lustre to so many despatches
from the area: Sam Modiano. Sam, near blind, had uncanny anten-
nae and sources, especially in political and commercial circles. I
relieved him of a few million drachmae and headed for Rhodes.

Almost the first person I met at the airport there was Mr Papadakis
who, before I left, was to become Reuters' representative in Rhodes.
He was a little man who seemed to have every conceivable agency –
tyres, fuel, the lot – and also owned a car, then comparatively rare on
the island.

I had no difficulty getting into the Hôtel des Roses where Count
Bernadotte and his secretariat had their headquarters. The press
room adjoined a large sunny room marked 'United Nations
Secretariat'. There were no troops, no barbed wire and fewer armed
guards than bathing beauties and grey-uniformed porters.

About a dozen foreign correspondents were already established at
the hotel. They included Clare Hollingworth (*The Daily Telegraph*),
Sam Souki (UP), Ed Curtis (AP), and Jack Flower (*The Sydney Morning
Herald*). Bill Stoneman, whom I knew as a *Chicago Daily News* war correspondent in Europe, was now a UN official handling press releases
and background information on Bernadotte's mission. Scope for
scoops hardly existed, since the only real story was Bernadotte. Half
the time or more he was away in his white-painted Dakota pursuing
his mediation in Cairo, Tel Aviv, Damascus or Beirut. On his return
he would brief the dozen or so correspondents. We all had the same
primary source, the same information, the same communications.
We might make slight differences of emphasis, nuance or interpretation, but in essence we were all filing the same story.

This meant a relaxation, if not total rest from 'call backs' from
Head Office ('X saying so-and-so unsighted anything yet from you')
and I'm not sure whether this made for a more congenial press camp
atmosphere than in, say, the Chungking Press Hostel, where tooth

and claw and bare knuckle attitudes had more often been the order of the day.

For relaxation I hired a bike or borrowed Papadakis's car to visit beauty spots like Butterfly Valley or dig for local stories. London's clamour to cut cable costs and send mailers could become strident, so I used every idle moment to pursue features, which London lapped up insatiably.

One was on the fairytale romance of former hotel porter, Anastasio Caralampis, and Princess Azza, daughter of King Feisal I of Iraq. Others were on the ancient history of Rhodes, the 2,000 crew of 150 small fishing caiques from which dozens of divers daily risked their lives on the bed of the Mediterranean to gather sponges, and the UN observers supervising the Palestine Truce.

The four key men at Bernadotte's headquarters were: Ralph J. Bunche, a 44-year-old black American who was the personal representative of the UN Secretary-General, Trygve Lie; Paul Mohn, a 50-year-old Swede who drew up the Palestine partition plan; Henri Vigier, a 62-year-old French former official of the League of Nations; and John H. Reedman, 43-year-old Yorkshire-born South African who was an economic expert on Palestine.

We had daily contact with these four and could discuss generalities, but they never really yielded hard news. Four Arab 'experts' could not or would not say anything, and the four Jewish 'experts' – who always sat at different dining-room tables from the Arabs and had separate meetings with the Count – said they were not in Rhodes on a political level.

As a news source, that left the Count himself, and I found him a likeable man, accessible and helpful. With his wife and two sons, Ockie and Bertil, he would usually have a swim before lunching in the main dining-room. He had high standards and principles without being priggish or prudish.

Sitting on a leather-bound sofa in the bar one day he told us, 'If I

211

represented a newspaper I would certainly not come here just now to try to find something interesting to tell the world. You may have noticed I am a rather silent mediator. Perhaps a little disappointing so far as journalists are concerned.'

One major concern at this time was the attitude of the Israelis to Arabs who had fled their homes and who wished to return. At a meeting with Israeli Foreign Minister Moshe Sharett on 17 June the UN mediator asked about the policy of the Israeli government with regard to the 300,000 Arabs who had left the Jewish areas: would they be allowed to return after the war and would their property rights be respected?

Sharett said the question could not be discussed while the war was going on, but told Bernadotte that property rights would be respected. However, the Foreign Minister later approved a plan to relocate the refugees permanently in neighbouring Arab countries, and at a meeting on 10 August Bernadotte again pressed him about their return.

Sharett would not agree to any repatriation, saying it would create a problem and a constant source of friction. It was in the interest of all concerned that the Arab minority in Israel should be small; Syria and Iraq could easily absorb the refugees.

Within a week of this meeting, I accepted Count Bernadotte's invitation to join him on a flight back to Stockholm. I did not return to Rhodes, but felt I could not quit without letting Bernadotte know the respect I felt for his efforts. I wrote to him on 16 August:

I am not returning to Rhodes, as I am going to England for some leave before covering the tour our King and Queen are making to Australia and New Zealand next year. I cannot leave Stockholm without expressing sincere thanks for all you have done to make the task of a correspondent assigned to a complicated situation like Palestine so much easier.

The great thing about Rhodes was that the material from that source – and

more than 90% of it was direct quotes from you – was factual and objective, com-
pared with the half-truths, partisan items, and even deliberate distortions emanat-
ing from certain Arab and Jewish centres . . .

I am speaking for every correspondent at your HQ when I say that your open
and co-operative attitude made a great impression. It was a model of the relations
that should obtain if the world is to understand and appreciate the nature and com-
plexity of problems with which it is faced.

Back in England, I once again opted to stay at Gatton Point in Surrey, a decision that was to change my life.

John and Mavis Turner from Bombay were in London on a brief business trip, and Harold and Betty Carter gave a dinner party for them. The house at that time had four or five male guests and to help balance the party Harold invited two young ladies he knew from amateur dramatic occasions at the neighbouring village of Merstham.

One of them was Mary Elizabeth Toms. We met that night for the first time, became engaged before the end of the year, and married the following June. It was the best – and easiest and most important – decision of my life. Mary was a wonderful wife and mother – loving, caring, understanding, tolerant, generous and sensible.

This was all in the future when I flew in from Stockholm, to find awaiting me a letter from Cole, saying:

I do not want you to spend any unnecessary time in London, on duty at any rate,
and the only call I think you should make is to report to Colville at the Palace in
connection with the Royal Tour.

Commander Richard Colville was the royal Press Secretary. He was a navy man and when King George VI appointed him to create the press job in 1947, *Time* magazine punned that it was a mix-up between Fleet and Fleet Street. There was some truth in this, in that the choice was made because the King had served in the navy under Colville's father, Admiral Sir Stanley Colville. The Commander had to learn about journalists the hard way and made himself, at times, unpopular. He did, however, represent the royal family's point of view, which was that they should enjoy 'as much privacy as was compatible with their public duties'.

After talking to Colville, the PA Court correspondent and others who knew the protocol for royal tours, I drew up my wardrobe list:

1 Suit of tails; 1 Dinner suit – white and black jackets; 2 Lounge suits; 2 Summer weight suits; 1 Sports outfit; 2 Pairs of white shorts and 2 of khaki; 3 Pairs of shoes – black, brown and white; 8 Ties; 12 White shirts; 6 Dress shirts; 6 Miscellaneous shirts; 12 Pairs of socks and 4 pairs of white and khaki stockings; 1 Black hat; 2 Grip bags or suit cases.

I already had most of these, and found the list could be completed with 188 clothing coupons and an estimated outlay of £116 at Austin Reed of Regent Street.

Then came a series of palace meetings to discuss press arrangements. It was stressed that it would be impossible for everybody to transmit messages from *Vanguard* at the same time, so it was decided to ask the Admiralty for three transmission periods in every 24 hours, the first and second to allow for approximately 200 words from each press representative, the third to allow for 100 words each. It was also agreed that a roster should be prepared, so each representative would have a turn in sending his message first. Well, what a doddle! With all sources contained in this one battleship, this limited wordage and this transmission drill it looked like being a holiday cruise.

I spent a memorably liquid night at a 'familiarisation' visit to *Vanguard* and retrieved a Plymouth gin bottle whose label I kept.

On 28 October an invitation arrived to a sherry party to be held on 19 November at Buckingham Palace to meet members of the

Royal Household who would be accompanying the King and Queen on the tour. At this unstuffy party I met and chatted with the Master of the Household, the Keeper of the Privy Purse, equerries and extra equerries, private secretaries and aides, including Princess Margaret's lady-in-waiting, Jennifer Bevan, and Group-Captain Peter Townsend, later famous as the Princess's sweetheart.

I wrote home later:

It was more a Scotch party than a sherry party. One Townsend, a Group-Captain who accompanies the Queen a lot, grabbed me first and poured a large VAT 69.

Then a Commander Ashmore recharged my glass. Then Captain Lord Sempill – one of Margaret's favourites – loaded it again.

And as I was leaving one Ulick Alexander stopped me to have 'one for the road'. But my road out of Buck House was quite wobbly enough by this time.

Spent last Thursday night on Vanguard *as guest of the Captain and officers. Interesting but little known item: when he cruises on* Vanguard, *the King brings aboard his own food, his own cook, servants, waiters, etc.*

And just to make sure the ship's company does not get a whiff or a sight of what's being prepared in the royal kitchen, the King has ordered the sealing up of all portholes in the royal kitchen. I could not, of course, write that.

But while all this jollity was going on, and unknown to us, the Queen was becoming increasingly concerned about the King's health. At Balmoral in the summer he had been easily tired and had pain in his left foot. On 12 November the doctors told the Queen he was suffering from arteriosclerosis, with a danger that gangrene might set in, raising the possibility of amputation of his right leg.

Less than 72 hours after my Buckingham Palace sherry party, the Royal Tour was off. Like my great eyewitnesser of the Arab warriors gathering in the Jordanian desert, and my night of passion with the sinuous Carmen, it wasn't going to happen. And I was left without a clue about where I was to go next.

11
Paris: King for three years

I drifted round the London editorial, volunteering for one-off reporting or subbing jobs, never quite sure what I was meant to be doing or
even to whom I should report. Then Cole told me he had decided to
send me to Paris as news editor, in effect number two to the legendary bureau chief, Harold King.

In government and diplomatic circles, Harold King was probably
the best known and most influential foreign newsman in postwar
Paris. I had never met him, but in my first days on the London desk
had been involved in subbing his Moscow despatches on the drive to
the Dniester.

I also knew of his reputation as a bit of a tyrant, given to barrack-
square language and discipline. Youth and inexperience seemed most
vulnerable. One man had resigned, another gave notice, a third had
been sacked. Had so many staff really been useless or just incompetent? Could some of the fault reside with the imperious autocratic
Harold King?

The son of a German psychiatrist called Koenig, King had lived in
Paris from 1931 until the Germans arrived. He was with Reuters in
London in 1940 – already showing an interest in General Charles de
Gaulle – and two years later went to Moscow as a war correspondent.
In 1944, he restarted Reuters in France and built up business from a

216

one-bedroom office at the Scribe Hotel to Reuters' largest European bureau with about 50 staff.

On one level, he was the hard-nosed bare-knuckle newsman who set high standards on the editorial coal-face and made no concessions. On another, he took pride in holding a high French decoration, knew everyone worth knowing in France and had his finger on the political and commercial pulse.

King knew de Gaulle and, maybe even more important, de Gaulle knew Harold King – '*mon ami, Monsieur King*'. It was said that King was the only correspondent whom de Gaulle addressed using the intimate *tu* form of speech. He even delayed starting one of his elaborately staged press conferences until King was seated. King was, undoubtedly, a Reuter star.

I told Cole it was a wonderful assignment, but I was concerned that shunting aside the existing news editor just to accommodate me could have an appalling effect on morale. It did not make sense, as my French was only classroom standard, and my knowledge of Paris amounted to one night trying to sleep in an enamel bath in the overcrowded Scribe Hotel while waiting to cross the Rhine with the American airborne troops.

Cole listened, but seemed unimpressed. When he became fixated with an editorial idea, he didn't budge easily. But finally he agreed: I'd go to Paris simply as another reporter, but as soon as I felt ready to assume authority and take control, I should signal Head Office and be designated news editor.

I arrived in Paris on New Year's Day 1949. London arranged for me to start off by staying with a French family, hoping this would make me fluent more quickly in French. It never did. It took me only two minutes in my new home to learn that Madame taught English, and with her that was what I always spoke.

She didn't need to work because her husband was a well established medical doctor. The children, two boys and a girl, were well into senior school. They were a delightful family and I did converse in French over family meals and at weekends.

The apartment at 59 rue de Spontini, in a classy quarter close to the Bois de Boulogne, offered an easy bus ride or healthy walk to the office at place de la Bourse. Once installed, I straightaway telephoned Harold King to clock in and tell him I would be at his place in the fashionable 7th *arrondissement* within an hour.

When I got to their small apartment, up 80 steps at 128 rue de Grenelle, I warmed at once to Harold and his wife, Irene, a Rumanian-born sculptor of international repute. Our relationship, which waxed and waned, endured stormy buffeting and withstood all manner of moods and vicissitudes, was to survive close on 40 years.

At the office next morning, King treated me with extreme formality, as if we had just met. That suited me. We would have to work out a *modus operandi*, but I was in no hurry. I wanted to watch and weigh the Paris set-up. King was suspicious and, like the news desk, uncertain how to handle me.

The Paris editorial staff reporting France to the rest of the world then consisted of: Harry White, news editor; Robert Boulay, a political correspondent worth at least two reporters to any news organisation in Paris; Odette Laguerre, sister of André Laguerre, the *Time/Life* bureau chief in Paris; Camille Lemercier, the talented wife of a distinguished French journalist and author; Robert Yoakum, a young American who went on to become a well-known columnist; Russell Howe, a bright young man, inclined to be impulsive; Sam Hooker, a quiet solid deskman and gifted composer of clerihews; Bill Latham and Sandy Sandford, experienced sub-editors.

All had fluent French: I had not. After a week or so, I decided that in view of this the only satisfactory way for me to operate was to assume responsibility for all main non-French news serials.

These included a number of then-new organisations: the Marshall Plan offices of Averell Harriman and Paul Hoffman; the OEEC

(Organisation for European Economic Co-operation), a 16-nation group to co-ordinate the economic affairs of European countries receiving recovery aid; UNESCO, (the UN Educational, Scientific and Cultural Organisation); and the ICFTU (International Confederation of Free Trade Unions), claiming to represent 51 million workers in 60 non-Communist countries.

I also took responsibility for the British, American, Canadian, Indian and several other more newsworthy embassies and missions; for coverage of important arrivals and departures at Le Bourget and Orly airfields; and for a regular supply of mailers, situationers and human interest and off-beat items – or 'brighteners' – plus frothy interviews with visiting personalities, film stars and the like.

Harold King accepted without reservation my proposed allocation of duties. I felt he was relieved that I had no aspiration to interfere with his beat, the political story, on which he had the best contacts and sources and on which his news instinct and strength was completely undisputed.

He and Boulay instantly and instinctively recognised French political news and its significance. They understood what lay behind a nuance, a raised eyebrow, an inflection in briefing tone, or just the manner in which a spokesman or parliamentarian fielded a question.

In broad terms, the separation of duties worked well. Early on, King and I stalked each other at a distance. He worked in his own room. Alone. I worked in a doorless cubbyhole off the cramped newsroom, shared by the London desk, French desk, operators and teleprinters. Logs written by the London desk editors percolated from King's office only when he chose to release them. Twice he addressed these to me when they recorded that we had been 'pipped' by one of the American news agencies.

'Why?' he wrote.

'Because we had superior cover,' I replied. 'Why sacrifice quality or completeness, for a purely notional edge on time, on such an item?'

He would grunt. He had fulfilled his main purpose: he had registered reaction to London's implied criticism that I'd been late.

Harold King drove himself hard, and showed shoot-from-the-hip intolerance of what he considered sub-standard work. Loafing, assumed carelessness, or weak sourcing caused an explosion, which I repeatedly told him was self-destructive. On one occasion he called me at 1.30 am to complain about the gentle hard-working Sam Hooker, 'That b***** Hooker has just hung up on me!'

'What d'you mean?'

'What I've just said. He put down the phone. Slammed it down.'

'Why? What did you say to him?'

'I just asked him what he'd done about an item in *Figaro*. He told me and I said he was a stupid f****** idiot. Imbecile.'

'When did you tell him that?'

'About five minutes ago.'

'Well, Harold, if you said that to Sam Hooker at 1.30 this morning, I think I understand why he hung up. Think I'd have done so, too.'

He rang off, and never mentioned the matter again, to me or Sam. Nor did Sam Hooker ever mention it, though I heard he had told Harold, 'Rinse your mouth.'

This side of King was heavily criticised by Edward Behr in his book, *Anyone Here Been Raped and Speaks English?* but I thought Behr went over the top. King did not have a bad relationship with all young recruits and trainees – he got on well with many, including Freddie Forsyth, Gerald Long and John Bush, to name but three.

I always ranked Harold King among the top Reuter journalists – not as a writer in the class, say, of Vincent Buist of Moscow, Warsaw and Vienna fame, nor as a journalistic technician like John (Pat) Heffernan of Washington, nor as an outstanding all-rounder like Ian Macdowall, the best editor Reuters never had, who was equally gifted at subbing, reporting, news editing, editing, handling and understanding communications and administration.

But without possessing unmatched skills, King had competence in each of these sectors, plus a robust overriding commitment to news. He was a newsman's newsman. He sensed news, felt news, got excited about it, treated it with enthusiasm, detachment, respect, verve. He knew the Reuter rules backwards, he had incomparable sources, and he knew how to reach them, by the back-alleys as well as the boulevards.

King delivered the goods. He could sniff out – and pocket – bureaucratically classified 'confidential' documents while the opposition still scratched round for them. If economical on elegance and style, his writing never lacked substance. He was best at picking up news and getting it down fast on paper, not at polished essays.

Discerning Paris desk staff often saw a need to tighten King's copy, to break up and shorten a meandering sentence with a maze of subordinate clauses. But they seldom touched it. Why risk King's wrath (something to behold!) when London could carry the can?

Surprisingly, London seldom did. King usually accepted, indeed once or twice even applauded, minor changes or improving rewrites by London desk subs. They handled his copy with great care, guarding against distortion even of emphasis, let alone substance. One of the most meaningful compliments that he ever paid me was in saying he would be glad if I would 'process' his copy if I happened to be around.

It took Harold King about a month to make his first gesture indicating a change in the cool correct regimental sort of relationship we had in the office. About seven one night, clearly leaving the office with nowhere to go, trilby on the back of his head and wagging an umbrella, he asked if I would care to join him. We drank whisky, two or three large ones, before moving on to a bistro to eat. We talked shop the whole time. That was the start of what became almost a nightly ritual, and the invitation became somewhat peremptory – you had to satisfy him with a good reason to decline.

221

King was a workaholic. He and Irene, though a devoted couple, went their separate working ways: she to her studio, he to his office.

He did not seem to have a wide circle of close friends, although several times I joined him in the company of André Laguerre, Stephen Coulter, Kemsley's man in Paris (*Sunday Times*), and Noel Barber, editor of the *Continental Daily Mail*. He had an aged mother living in London, and a son with whom he seemed to have lost contact. He never wanted to speak about him except to tell me, usually late at night after a jar or two, 'You remind me of my son, just about his age.' (I was, too. I later looked up his son at Cambridge.)

His favourite theme at interminable talks was the office, with clinical dissections of every member of staff. He was forever thinking, dreaming, even fantasising about making Reuters Paris the ultimate in company offices, setting new business targets, winning scoops and beats, a model of efficiency.

He seemed to envisage me being with him indefinitely, and nightly we would discuss changes, improvements, plans, tactics to deal with Head Office.

One night, as we were crossing the place de la Concorde in a taxi, he started talking about a time-schedule for physical office and staff developments, and I said something like, 'Fine, but that will have to be after the wedding.'

'Wedding, wedding, what wedding?' said King.

'My wedding.'

'What?' he exploded. The taxi driver turned round anxiously. 'Does London know?'

'Yes. Cole will be my best man. We hope both of you will be there.'

King hardly spoke to me for two days. I had upset him. He had a very possessive streak. In his view I had no right to be getting married. I should have been thinking only and totally of furthering his great aspiration and dream: a Paris office that would be a model for all offices in the Reuter domain.

Or was it all just an act? He was known for histrionics and he could strike theatrical postures – what Cole called 'unorthodoxy'.

When it came to it, Harold and Irene were both at Merstham Parish Church for our wedding on 11 June. The life and soul of the party was Tony Cole, his arm in a sling ('I fell off the Taj Mahal,' he said), accompanied by his wife Janet and their two young daughters, Mavis and Judith. Others at the very Reuter event included Sid Mason, Julian Bates from New York, Fraser Wighton, the political correspondent and Ranald Maclurkin, UK chief correspondent.

By the end of June Mary and I were back in Paris, in temporary quarters at the small Hôtel d'Albion in the rue de Penthièvre, a short walk from the British Embassy in the Faubourg St Honoré. The Kings were kind, having us to the rue de Grenelle every week, sometimes two or three times. We played canasta most nights. Irene called Harold 'Mickey', which suited him in that ambience, far removed from the autocratic regime of place de la Bourse.

All the time I was becoming better organised, widening the circle of contacts, sources, tip-offs. As a news centre, Paris had just about everything, from philosophy to street riots.

On my entertainment beat I tracked down an old film favourite, Deanna Durbin, by then married to a Frenchman and living quietly outside Paris; had drinks in their hotel suite with Ingrid Bergman and Roberto Rossellini; bumped into Elizabeth Taylor and her newly acquired second husband, Michael Wilding, in the Champs Elysées, and sat next to Simone Simon at the Le Touquet première of *La Ronde*.

I had my first stab at reporting a title fight, featuring the stylish and flamboyant Sugar Ray Robinson, who used to drive round Paris in a lavender-coloured Cadillac, and my first horse race, the Prix de l'Arc de Triomphe, at Longchamps, where I thought the fillies fussing round Aly Khan in the paddock more fascinating than the equine thoroughbreds.

I never felt comfortable among the pretty people at the Paris fashion shows, but that didn't matter as the experienced Peggy Massin was always there with her expert technical descriptions – not always appreciated (or even understood) by the news desk.

In the ever-newsworthy department of political 'sleaze', I interviewed a five-minutes-of-fame character named Sydney Stanley, who turned up in Paris after nearly bringing down the British Labour Government by showering gifts and hospitality on a junior minister. Stanley belonged to musical comedy. To let me in on his far-fetched plans, he always sought the anonymity of dark streets as if he feared an assassin or the KGB.

When I got back to the office he rang to say, 'You never saw me tonight, see, and I've not said nothing. Between ourselves, of course, I did talk to you, but as a friend. Don't you write anything. I've given my lawyer an undertaking that I'll not see nobody nor say nothing till my complaint is lodged.'

But the most newsworthy, co-operative and prolific sources were ambassadors, officials and offices handling Marshall Aid – the greatest, most successful, most humanitarian aid programme the world had ever seen.

It made the name of the man I had known as a mediator in China forever synonymous with American munificence on a colossal scale. In four years the United States spent $13 billion, most of it in free grants. Marshall Aid saved Western Europe. It provided the economic underpinning of the North Atlantic Treaty Organisation (NATO) and was the prelude to the Common Market.

The Americans had high-level representation in Paris. Besides Averell Harriman and Paul Hoffman, their ambassador, David Bruce had quite exceptional qualities of intellect, culture and lineage. Born into the full American purple, Bruce volunteered as a private in the First World War, headed the US Office of Strategic Studies (OSS) in London in 1942, became chief administrator of Marshall Aid in Paris

in 1947 and ambassador in 1949. He epitomised a breed of leadership the United States produces from time to time, adding to wisdom,
charm, gravitas, humour, taste and manners the capacity to view
day-to-day events with the eye of a historian.

I spent many magical moments talking – or mainly listening – to
another of the all-time greats: India's man at UNESCO, Dr Sarvapalli
Radhakrishnan, the philosopher who became President of India. At
UNESCO and in his modest quarters, I used to sit spellbound at
the pure poetry of words pouring forth from this gentle intellectual
giant. Although I was never very late, on some evenings I would find
him lying stretched out on top of the bed covers in his long johns,
reflecting quietly on the state of the world, India, UNESCO, prelates
and presidents.

He was courtly, compassionate, had a delightful sense of humour,
and possessed that rare gift of making you feel completely at ease,
demolishing all barriers of cultural, religious and mental distance.

Another reminder in Paris of my time in India was a visit by
Devadas Gandhi, son of the Mahatma. An editorial executive of the
Hindustan *Times*, he had been chosen by Indian newspaper publishers as their first director of Reuters. He cabled me that he would be
passing through Paris on his way to a Reuter Board meeting in
London, asking me to meet him at the airport and arrange overnight
hotel accommodation.

I knew Devadas's home in New Delhi. He lived in a modest
upstairs flat, with a fair amount of graffiti and litter, certainly not a
pretentious place though perfectly acceptable in Delhi. I thought he
might be uncomfortable in the opulence of the Ritz or Crillon, so
instead chose a good four-star hotel.

Gandhi arrived late at night. My wife and I met him with the office
car and drove with him to the hotel. It was high summer, warm but
not uncomfortable, nothing like as hot as Delhi at that time of year.
Devadas put one foot in his room and decided it was far too hot and

stuffy. He needed a good night's sleep to be completely fit for the
Reuter board meeting.

It was about midnight. In vain we telephoned the George V, the
Bristol, the Meurice – every hotel said the same: full up, too late.
Eventually the Grand Hôtel on the place de l'Opéra said it had a
'cool' room. When we got there, Devadas was dismissive about the
room, but reckoned that one bend in the corridor had a draught
which was just what he wanted. If the management could find a sofa
or something and put it at the strategic point in the corridor, he
would be happy.

It was now nearing 1.30 am, but Devadas insisted on us joining
him for a drink on the boulevard. He ordered three orange squashes.
We were back at the hotel at 7 am to take him to the airport, but he
wrote an appreciative thank-you letter later.

Another important Indian visitor, A. D. Mani of *The Hitavada*, the
English daily of the Servants of India Society, paid me a useful com-
pliment by writing to Chancellor:

*I met Doon Campbell in Paris, and he is one of the most enterprising newspaper-
men I met on the Continent. The Indian Embassy in Paris was thinking of suggesting that an Indian should be appointed by the Press Trust of India in Paris,
but I told them that they could have no better friend than Mr Campbell, who was
going out of the way to help the Indian Embassy . . .*

*I have been telling Indian friends in the newspaper world that as far as the
Continent is concerned the Press Trust of India should rely wholly on the Reuter
staff, who are extremely alive to the interests of the Indian press . . . and that the
PTI should concentrate on strengthening their London staff instead of trying to go
about opening bureaus in countries where language difficulties stand in the way of
proper appreciation of the political situation on the Continent.*

Our reconnaissance for possible places to live after marriage had
not been fruitful. My original landlady at rue de Spontini had an

elderly friend, a titled lady now feeling the financial pinch, who had a spare room with bathroom, four floors up in the boulevard de Strasbourg. But this was hardly the most salubrious place for a young English girl – the ladies of the night were thick on the ground, prowling the pavements and propositioning every likely male.

So Mary took over the search and quickly found the upstairs of a little house, or 'pavilion' as the French called it, at 1 rue Jean Bleuzon, in the middle of the suburb of Vanves, a few miles south of Paris. It cost less than the room-under-the-roof in boulevard de Strasbourg, and we had far more space.

There was a double bedroom with connecting doors to a living-room and to a passage wide enough to take another bed, a bathroom, a kitchen, a tiny garden and street access to a garage, though there was an excellent train service to the office.

We became integrated into a suburban village community, occasionally affording oysters from a street vendor on Sundays, rum and Coke tipples, strolls to the local park, and luxuries in the form of embassy receptions, official lunches, trips on the Bateaux-Mouches. We never missed or felt any inclination to explore 'Gay Paree' at the night clubs of Montmartre.

In October 1949 Harry White resigned as Paris news editor. So far as I know, he was not pushed or even eased out. I never had any friction with Harry, a competent newsman but not one to whom I could ever feel close. The title Reuters had wanted to impose on me ten months earlier was again offered. This time I felt no reservation about acceptance.

Harold King – signing himself as Reuters' chief representative in France – gazetted my promotion in an editorial memo dated 18 November: 'I take this opportunity of recording officially Mr Doon Campbell's appointment last month as News Editor of the Paris Bureau. Mr Campbell's appointment involves his being in full charge of all Departments of the Paris Bureau in my absence.'

Every year, King took off for a week or two at the Privat-Klinic Bircher-Benner at Zurich, also favoured by the British Chancellor of the Exchequer, Sir Stafford Cripps. While not averse to indulgence – some might even say occasional over-indulgence – at the table, when in Zurich King went on a Spartan, mainly if not wholly vegetarian, diet, scaled some of the smaller mountains and 'cleansed the system of impurities'.

His return would be signalled by a call to lunch at rue de Grenelle, forsaking the bistros and restaurants that had a bottle on the table before he'd shed his coat. Chez King at such times meant vegetable soup and cheese washed down with Evian water or Perrier. Irene coped, knowing it was just a matter of days before he would revert to normal living.

During one such absence of King at his Swiss retreat, I had a cable from Cole that led me into real trouble. It told me: 'Rupert Henderson, important director of Reuters, arriving Paris with wife for first holiday in years. Make sure they enjoy it. Book hotel and roll out red carpet. Rely you.'

Rupert Albert Geary (Rags) Henderson, was managing director of *The Sydney Morning Herald* and with Sir Keith Murdoch (father of Rupert Murdoch), was largely responsible for the partnership between Reuters and the Australian Associated Press (AAP).

I met Rupert and Hazel Henderson off their plane, drove them to their five-star hotel, and asked what they'd like to do.

'Campbell, I think you're married,' said Henderson. 'We'd like you and your wife to pick us up about seven tonight and lay on dinner and a good show afterwards.'

So started thirteen consecutive nights of gastronomic indulgence and entertainment, ranging from the Lido on the Champs Elysées to the pits of Pigalle.

Knowing nothing of Paris nightlife, I tapped the pool of editorial knowledge, and enlisted the help of everyone from the office driver to the head of Reuters' administrative unit, Max Bouckalter, to suggest where to go.

Rupert and Hazel (like most Aussies, they dispensed with formalities) seemed good sports and had extraordinary resilience and stamina. They never tired, never drooped. Even when their cabaret tolerance threshold sagged ('Christ, Campbell, can't we do better – or worse – than this?'), we had to plumb the depths with two or more so-called revue bars a night, one or two real dumps among them.

We started (where else?) at Maxim's, but being unsophisticated – indeed, untutored – in such matters, made the *faux pas* of taking the Hendersons there for dinner at 7.30 pm.

Instead of tables crowded with titles, the literati and cultural elite, personalities like Aly Khan and Coco Chanel, Chevalier and Mistinguett or Josephine Baker, we had the Edwardian splendour of the famous restaurant all to ourselves.

Without spectator sport Maxim's hadn't the same appeal, but Albert, the famed and portly head waiter, never batted an eyelid, and the loneliness of our foursome in the fashionable rue Royale restaurant was more than compensated afterwards at the Lido's superlatively spectacular revue, with its gorgeous dancers scantily clad in not much more than feathers and sequins. Towards 2 am we dropped the Hendersons at their hotel.

'Same time, same form tomorrow, but change the scenes,' said Rupert. 'And we'll have Percy Spender with us.' Sir Percy Spender was then Australian Minister for External Affairs, later Ambassador to Washington and from 1964–7 President of the International Court of Justice at The Hague.

I wanted no repeat of the Maxim's experience, so King's secretary telephoned the Tour d'Argent to tell them a distinguished Australian cabinet minister would be with us, and ensure that we had the right table, next to a panoramic window overlooking floodlit Notre Dame, and the best service for the speciality, pressed duck.

The restaurant was a hit, and at the Bal Tabarin afterwards Percy Spender danced alternately with Hazel and Mary while Rupert and I talked shop. Spender, a small man like Henderson, was good company, with terrier-like qualities of mind and character, industry, application and independence.

When we dropped him at 3 am, Rupert Henderson said we would be dining that night with Sir Keith Officer, Australian Ambassador in Paris, then going on to the Lido. And that was how it went on. In Harold King's absence, my work load had anyway increased. I was getting to the office before 8 am, working until about 5.30 pm, then dashing back to Vanves to change.

There were two respites from this excruciating routine. For the first, we took the Hendersons in my new company car, a Hillman Minx, to Chartres cathedral, the presidential palace at Rambouillet, and Versailles. For the second, we offered them English Sunday lunch at our modest pad in Vanves.

When I fetched them from their hotel, Rupert complained of a pain in his knee. I took him to a pharmacist who gave us some pills, but the pain persisted. However, a young doctor lived right next door to us and I remembered seeing him in his short shorts tinkering with his old banger.

'Not to worry,' I said. 'A doctor is laid on.'

Rupert was impressed. Five minutes later, grease still smudging his face, the breezy young French doctor rang our bell. He ushered Rupert into the adjoining bedroom, and insisted Rupert should drop his trousers, though the connecting door to the room where the girls were sipping drinks kept swinging open.

'Tell the silly bugger it's me knee that hurts, not me guts,' he protested. But not understanding English the doctor just pushed the debagged media tycoon unceremoniously back on the bed.

Either he cured the pain or Rupert decided he had suffered enough indignity for one day. We thanked the doctor, had lunch and went on to Fontainebleau and Barbizon, before having dinner at the Berlioz.

Rupert Henderson asked many questions about Reuters and the men who ran it. He wanted to know how much I was paid, and whether I would be interested to move at more than twice my current salary to his paper at Newcastle, New South Wales. I told him I saw myself as a Reuter fixture.

On several days, Mary escorted Hazel on shopping expeditions and to the leading couture houses. But despite their continuous demands on our time, and our increasing exhaustion, the Hendersons grew on us. Almost invariably he picked up the tab at restaurants and night clubs.

Those 13 days must have cost the Hendersons well over £1,000, in addition to their hotel charges. I tried to keep the Reuter end up by insisting on paying for the final drink before leaving each establishment, but my expenses came to less than £100. At London's request I sent an itemised account, in French francs:

Friday, 18 August	Dinner at Maxim's then Lido	11,800
Saturday, 19	Dinner at La Tour d'Argent then Bal Tabarin	6,100
Sunday, 20	Dinner with Sir Keith Officer then Lido	500
Monday, 21	Dinner at Périgourdine then Dinarazade Club	6,000
Tuesday, 22	Dinner at Alsatian rest., Folies-Bergères	6,300
Wednesday, 23	Chartres, Rambouillet, Versailles	1,900
Thursday, 24	Dinner at L'Ermitage des Loges, St Germain; then La Montagne Ste Geneviève and Nouvelle Rose Rouge night clubs	8,200
Friday, 25	Dinner at Eiffel Tower then Venus and Eve night clubs	6,000
Saturday, 26	Dinner at Café de la Paix, then opera	4,500
Sunday, 27	Lunch at Vanves, drive to Fontainebleau and Barbizon then dinner at Berlioz	1,600
Monday, 28	Lunch at Cazeau with G. Parthasarathi, evening Casino de Paris	4,850

Tuesday, 29	Dinner at L'Auberge du Fruit Defendu,	
	Le Monocle and Naturalistes night clubs	8,300
Wednesday, 30	Dinner at Berlioz, Pigalle night club	3,700
Thursday, 31	Farewell Dinner at Berlioz	3,000

Harold King, who had to visit London on business, took the list with him. It produced a mini-crisis, for he returned to Paris with the news that Christopher Chancellor would not allow the expenses. Now fiddled expenses – hired aircraft, launches, sherpas, camels and other even more hallucinatory items – are legendary among foreign correspondents, but I had always been scrupulous with Reuters, kept all relevant receipts, separated personal items and so on.

The only explanation I could get of the general manager's decision was that he thought this an 'exorbitant amount' of Reuters' money to spend on the Hendersons. I was in a quandary. Presumably Chancellor was unaware of Cole's cable telling me 'roll out red carpet'. I would not shop Cole, but having legitimate expenses challenged and rejected came as a jolt. Momentarily – just momentarily – resignation crossed my mind. King saw my mood. In the end Chancellor agreed that the company would meet half the total of these fringe expenses and King told me the balance would be more than covered by an adjustment of my allowances. I accepted, but the episode left a nasty taste.

Two Paris news desk subs and I, together with Pamela Matthews of the London diplomatic desk, reinforced Serge Nabokoff in Brussels for the conference at which General Eisenhower was appointed Supreme Commander of NATO in 1951. We formed a compact compatible team and won both play and plaudits, being an hour and 38 minutes ahead of all competition with the appointment.

Even before his arrival in France, I decided that General Eisenhower and his headquarters belonged to general news as distinct from politics, King's preserve.

During the war I had often seen Eisenhower at close quarters, had spoken to him and had been in his company many times, but I never knew him, and he certainly did not know me. He gave occasional press conferences, very seldom interviews. I never tried to interview him, partly because he had an efficient PR set-up which issued releases on anything significant, and partly because I was never impressed by his articulation. He was given to long convoluted sentences which didn't always have an ending, so you couldn't always be sure what he was saying, or even trying to say.

With his wife Mamie he lived quietly in a 40-room, white-painted villa among the 850 residents of Marne-La-Coquette, a village 10 miles west of Paris in the Seine valley. A fifteen-minute drive from there took him to his office in the vast sprawl of prefabs called SHAPE (Supreme Headquarters, Allied Powers, Europe). Socially the Eisenhowers were rarely seen, except at French presidential receptions. Near neighbours included their good friends the Guenthers. General Al Guenther, his Chief of Staff, eventually succeeded Ike as Supreme Commander.

SHAPE became a useful news source, the British there including Field-Marshal Montgomery, the Deputy Supreme Commander; Brigadier Bernard Fergusson, a monocled Scot who had led Orde Wingate's chindits in the Burmese jungle; Brigadier Lionel Cross, the PR Chief, later Secretary of the Commonwealth Press Union, and his kilted young deputy, Lieutenant-Colonel Stuart Chant, for whose company Mamie Eisenhower showed an innocent liking.

As a soldier, I never rated Eisenhower in the same battle-winning class as Monty or Alexander. As a statesman, he never measured up to George Marshall in gravitas or stature. But everyone liked honest, amiable Ike with his infectious grin, friendly presence and his air of mastery of the complex technicalities of wars.

Although guarded in everything he said in public, and discreet in private conversation, Eisenhower was seen by many Europeans as a future US President. Did he have such aspirations when he returned to France?

Less than five years earlier he had firmly disclaimed them, but he felt no American had the right to refuse 'any duty that his country might demand of him'. From his arrival in Paris until he gave up the Supreme Command to seek the Republican nomination, Eisenhower's greatest difficulty lay in phrasing his statements so that they could not be interpreted as a refusal of a national duty, or a criticism of political life.

Early in 1952 it became apparent that I would soon be returning to London. We had mixed feelings about that. Paris had been our home for nearly three years. We liked France and many of the French. But Mary was pregnant with our first child, and was staying with her newly-widowed mother in Surrey. I fretted to join them, but King was ill and went off to his Swiss clinic, while the French government underwent a series of crises.

And what would I be doing in London? Cole wrote on 25 January that I would get a basic £1,400 a year plus expenses. His letter did not specify my duties but said:

I have told Mason that I want you to have at least two weeks, probably longer, wandering round the desks and seeing how the thing ticks.

What is important is getting to know various people – keep out of the tittle-tattle, and if you feel you want longer on the loose to really get the feel of things, then tell Mason. I think it is quite probable you will make such a request – I think I would if I were in your position, because once you are on a regular duty it is very difficult to break clear.

A few days later another letter, this time from his London apartment, in his own hand and customary extravagant style, told me:

You are where you are because the 'great divide' between the ordinary existence and that involving leadership in the wider representational spheres necessitates a knowl-edge that is primarily psychological.

In the past one thing has always stood you in good stead – a mind that never ceased to seek a second opinion if in doubt. In the new sphere, with snags that must inevitably crop up in the administrative context, never hesitate to exercise the query-ing instinct and specially towards me, as always you can count on receiving all I can give. You know that. There is much that I can pass on and I am only too happy to do so.

And bear this in mind always – you are doing extraordinarily well in the role assigned you, the record is splendid, and when you are under the personal scrutiny of the top you should rejoice. It is when one is not that it is time to worry.

I was still in Paris when our first child, Mary Catherine, was born on 5 February and did not finally get away until the end of the month, carrying with me a parting gift from Irene King, a bronze bust of my wife which was to take pride of place in our Surrey home. I was no longer news editor, Paris, but – as had happened in France – it was again to be nine months before I had any new job title.

12

Campbell's Kremlin

In some ways the move from place de la Bourse to Fleet Street left me uncomfortable, almost ill-at-ease; certainly not euphoric, as I'd felt moving from Scotland to Reuters nine years earlier. In terms of quality of life, London in 1952 seemed grey compared with Paris, and a salary of £1,400 before British income tax would not provide luxury. In terms of job satisfaction, Paris seemed to offer more sharp-end journalism.

I couldn't shed a feeling of sadness if this move meant the end of being a Reuter correspondent, a proud breed which were profiled by *The Observer* on 8 July 1951:

Anyone who has gone abroad for a newspaper will have met those harassed, alert men, the Reuter correspondents. It is usual for the employee of a newspaper to thank God that he is not as these others, that his own life is more leisurely, his stories more richly coloured by chosen idiosyncrasies of style and opinion. Yet it must be said that Reuter correspondents seldom seem to regret the puritanical limitations which are imposed on them. They are the true and proud devotees of news for its own sake, unadulterated by personal quirks, and free, too, from any imposition of opinion by their employer. Their lives are hard, because anything which is news for anyone is fit news for Reuters Agency (whereas even the hungriest news hound of an individual paper has a diet which is limited to one class of news or another). And theirs is a vocation without much public glory, for usually their monochromatic writings are attributed simply to 'Reuter'.

I had qualms about putting all that behind me and becoming a cog in the nerve centre of a worldwide machine. Without really knowing much about it, I felt ill-equipped to become a Head Office institutional fixture. For one thing, I loathed committees.

But I was now 32, an experienced correspondent, in a sense established, married, a father. Outweighing everything else, this move represented promotion, and I had to think of my long-term career. I had no real wish to look the other way.

The first thing I had to do was to get to know more about the corporate body of my 'magic mistress'. At the head was the board of directors representing the various agencies and media organisations that were our owners; but 'Mr Reuter', the general manager (chief executive) solely responsible to them for its activities from 1944 to 1959 was Christopher Chancellor.

Like Cole, he was a Scot with Edinburgh connections, but Chancellor had been educated at Eton and Cambridge, where he got a first in history. He had joined Reuters as a trainee in 1930, but within a few years became a minor *taipan* as one of the international band of 'old China hands', and a friend of the China trading princes, the Keswicks. It was largely due to Chancellor that Reuters survived the war intact.

Despite his workload, he was a member of the Fleet Street Home Guard and also took part in fire-watching. On one occasion the then PA night editor stopped to pick up a rifle that Home Guard Private C. J. Chancellor dropped outside 85 Fleet Street while lacing up his oversize boots. Another was at 2 am on 17 April 1941, when according to Tom Stockwell, a senior Reuter desk editor, Cole and Chancellor (who was on fire-watching duty) took part in an emergency meeting about a landmine that had come down outside the front door, but miraculously was prevented by an overhead lighting cable from hitting the ground and exploding.

Cole, while still PA night editor, had been active in establishing a Dutch-language newspaper, *Vrij Nederland* or *Free Netherlands*, of which the profits went to Dutch war charities, and he had edited and produced a weekly pamphlet called *Voice of the Netherlands*. He had also provided the world media with scores of stories about the Dutch resistance to Nazi occupation, and was regarded as one of Holland's best friends in Britain, later becoming a Commander of the Order of Orange Nassau.

In 1942 Chancellor had taken Cole from the PA, bringing him into Reuters with the title 'News Manager', though from the first moment he was effectively the editor and Chancellor's number two in a five-man administration. Cole then practically lived on the job, working 15 hours a day, immersed in detail, handling copy on the desk, lunching on sandwiches, sleeping in the building.

But no one did more than Chancellor to re-establish the agency's authority in the postwar period. He was an accomplished man of the world, internationally known and respected, primarily an administrator, part diplomat, part businessman, less practised in chasing and handling raw news than in marketing a packaged product.

In speeches and lectures he tirelessly preached Reuters' integrity, and had new contracts with other agencies governed by this widely welcomed preamble:

Both parties to this present agreement declare that they are news agencies serving no other purpose than the dissemination of truthful, unbiased news, that they are free from any Government or tendentious control, and that the news which they supply to each other shall be compiled and selected purely on its news merit as news, and that editorial discretion on each side is free from outside dictation or pressure . . .

He could sometimes be testy and dismissive, but Chancellor had presence, stature, authority, and although my personal contact with him was limited, I felt reassured by his presence. Somehow, up there in his large superbly proportioned corner room on the seventh floor, he epitomised Reuters' competitive standards, high principles and ethics in global news gathering, and stood for much that made it 'the leading world news agency'.

He and Cole shared a total commitment to Reuters, but were opposites in many ways. Chancellor belonged to the boardroom, Cole to the news coal-face. Chancellor was clever, cultivated, soigné, an intellectual aesthete with a probing mind; Cole was extrovert, intuitive, instinctively clever and clued-up.

Chancellor had a youthful, almost boyish freshness, with a dangerously disarming smile and a quiet clipped way of speaking – it would be the same, you felt, if he were sentencing you to death as when he was asking the time, remarked one obituarist. Cole was larger than life, back-slapping, pressing the flesh, talking fast – some might say gabbling – in a hybrid Scots/mid-Atlantic drawl.

Chancellor was slight and sparing in food and drink; Cole (all 18 stone – 115 kg – or more) ever in need of refuelling. On European business trips together it was not uncommon for Cole to be up at first light, stealthily tucking into an English breakfast with all the trimmings at a modest bistro, before joining Chancellor in their hotel dining-room for a croissant and coffee.

Chancellor was knighted in 1951, Reuters' centenary year. In 1952, the administration comprised, apart from Chancellor and Cole, Cecil Fleetwood-May, European manager; A. H. L. Walters, chief accountant; and Harold B. Carter, company secretary.

I had an easy relationship with Carter, found Walters prim but quite human, and liked and respected the round and balding Fleetwood-May, who first built up the commercial services and the reception of news by radio.

The administration occupied the seventh floor of 85 Fleet Street, the editorial the fourth, and the commercial department most of the fifth, though it later moved to the second.

On the editorial floor, Cole's chief assistants were Geoffrey Imeson, who had joined as a sub in 1930 and been news manager and assistant editor, and Sid Mason, whom Cole had brought in from British United Press as night editor in 1942, and then made chief news editor until he retired in 1965.

Broadly, Imeson had charge of the Head Office editorial, while Mason had operational responsibility for the correspondents in the field around the world. They did not always see eye to eye, but though Imeson and Mason factions did surface from time to time, few sought to exacerbate their rivalry because both were held in regard on merit.

When I reported to Sid on my return from Paris, I found him sitting at one end of the east side of the big open editorial floor, with his back to a window looking out on St Bride's and St Paul's, at a T-formation of desks also occupied by one or two assistants and his faithful and highly-protective secretary, Ena Buckle.

The main editing unit, the central desk and the sports desk were at the other end. Between the chief news editor's unit and the central desk were the units reporting British news, the diplomatic correspondents and the telephone typists.

The whole of the west side was occupied by editing desks for the regions – Europe, Asia, Africa and so on.

'Ullo, cock, how's it going?'

After his usual greeting, Sid gave me an instant fill-in on the state of the world, Fleet Street, Paris and Harold King, women in journalism, Reuters and his new car. What did he want me to do? Sid shrugged. 'Suit yourself, son. Pick up all you can, but don't get involved. Don't stay long in one place.'

It was sound guidance. Sid knew Cole had decided to bring me back to London, but he didn't know what was in Cole's mind. Who did? The fourth floor Kremlinologists had their theories: Campbell had been brought back from the field to head an editing desk, to join the bosses upstairs, to take charge of a new service.

Emollient to all, I sat unobtrusively in the background at editorial conferences, attached myself briefly to several specialist and regional desks – feeling quite inadequate but gradually piecing together the bits of their jigsaw – talked to every editor and news editor in sight, assessed their knowledge of the markets they were serving, read all the books and documents I could find and gradually built up an over-all picture.

The economic service, Comtelburo, was then something of a poor relation to the general news service. The important man there seemed to be Alfred Geiringer, who had begun before the war as assistant to the chief correspondent in Austria, then moved up from head of radio listening station to European editor, and assistant European manager.

As Fleetwood-May's number two, Geiringer had been involved in rebuilding the company's offices, communications network and busi-ness relationships in postwar Europe. Then he had become chief of Commercial Services and manager of Comtelburo, in which role he recruited Glen Renfrew and Michael Nelson, two of the triumvirate of managers whose specialist skills were to transform Reuters from a proud prestigious, but chronically impoverished, international wire service into a lucrative electronic information industry.

Renfrew, taken on trial by Geiringer at half the normal rate, told his boss he couldn't live on his pay. 'All right,' said Geiringer in his guttural English, 'I can give you a few more pounds a year.' The increase turned out to be 11s 6d (57½p) a week. But Renfrew and Nelson both eventually became millionaires.

After a month or two, Sid Mason asked me to join his unit. Reuters had always been exemplary over keeping correspondents informed about competition and the use made of stories, and they valued this 'feed-back'. At Sid's elbow I developed 'impact' messages, sent quickly to active centres on our own communication lines, telling correspondents whether they were ahead or behind, where they had been published and so on.

From Frankfurt, chief correspondent Jack Henry wrote to Mason:

The considerably expanded impacts are of tremendous value especially when we see a nice array of credits for German items. Everybody feels bucked to read this sort of thing and I really believe it encourages that extra effort often needed to make a good story. One or two chaps have said in the office here recently 'Ah, that ought to get a mention in the play reports.'

On 5 November Cole got back to London from an extensive tour and sent this note to Mason and Imeson:

Everywhere I went there was the most enthusiastic praise for the impacts from London. Men in the field find them most useful and the fact that they do make a very genuine attempt to spotlight the fate of stories the overseas offices have been working on makes them of tremendous value. They are first-class.

But impacts represented only a fraction of my time and effort. I was into everything: traffic, costs, liaising with the Press Association, getting to know representatives of the unions: the National Union of Journalists (NUJ); the National Graphical Association (NGA – the teleprinter operators); the National Society of Printing and Allied Trades (NATSOPA – clerical and other staff). I also made contact with associates accommodated as Reuter tenants at 85 Fleet Street, including Tass (the Soviet news agency), the South African Argus newspaper group and the South African Press Association, the *Chicago Tribune, France Soir* and DPA (the West German news agency), and with the bosses of PA-Reuter Photos and PA-Reuter Features.

In November 1952 I at last got a job description. At Mason's request, Cole appointed me deputy chief news editor, to work under Sid's direction and deputise in his absence. Next month I had a note, one of the first, from Sir Christopher praising my 'splendid work' and raising my salary by £250 to £1,650. I was to be 'the DCNE' for the next five and a half years. Standing in for Sid when he went on holiday, helping to choose correspondents for overseas jobs, briefing them, analysing their news files, checking expenses, monitoring cable tolls, coping with communications and other problems, I was progressively learning how to be chief news editor.

I formed an easy working relationship with Henry Martin, the PA's editor-in-chief from 1928 to 1954. According to *Reporter Anonymous – The Story of the Press Association*, for a time in the 1930s Martin's mind was deeply engaged by Frank Buchman's controversial Oxford Group or Moral Re-Armament movement. This helped explain Cole's uncharacteristic interest in the MRA, for it was Martin who had originally engaged Cole as a reporter and promoted him to deputy news editor, assistant day supervising editor and finally night editor. Cole regarded Martin as the 'best news editor in Fleet Street'.

To my delight I did, while DCNE, get the chance of the occasional return to being a correspondent, often on royal stories for some reason. On 2 June 1953 I gave a hand in covering the coronation of Queen Elizabeth, sitting on one of thousands of hard inflexible seats perched on scaffolding erected along the Mall. The tedium of the wait was relieved by the presence and animated chatter of Peter Ustinov on the seat in front.

Inside Westminster Abbey was Ranald Maclurkin, for years the leader of the team reporting Britain for overseas. He watched from a gallery in the Abbey, sending live copy down a tube to a tin hut where Eddie Edbrooke, a newsroom assistant, telephoned it to Fleet Street. Afterwards Maclurkin came back to the office to write a considered piece, the definitive Reuter report of the coronation.

Now, to produce the best copy on a descriptive story like this a reporter needs total concentration, and it was with horror that I saw the large figure of Tony Cole looming over Mac, breathing down his neck and suggesting alternative leads. Maclurkin began tearing the paper out of his typewriter, completely put off his stroke.

I produced my most valuable contribution to the Reuter coverage of the coronation by diverting Cole's attention, as diplomatically as I could, to some other pressing matter, thus allowing Mac to collect his thoughts and finish the story.

The administration also put several 'freebies' my way, including a celebrity cruise on a new Greek liner, a Lufthansa flight to the Lebanon, and a KLM flight to Japan over the North Pole. In 1953 I got a £1 a week rise ('finance is pretty tight at the moment', said the note of thanks from Chancellor), and in 1954 a more substantial £150 a year with praise for my 'excellent work' and 'great contribution'.

In 1956, the Anglo–French invasion of Egypt over the nationalisation of the Suez Canal, coinciding with the Soviet invasion of Hungary for its attempt at 'Communism with a human face', dominated world headlines, seemed to balance history on a knife-edge, and surprised Reuter editorial staff by bringing a note from Chancellor reminding everyone that Reuters did not take sides. Coming from him gave it special significance. He seldom offered guidance, much less direction, on editorial matters, considering that our reporters and subs knew their business and Reuter standards.

Like all good newsmen, Chancellor held personal opinions on major issues, sometimes passionate convictions covered by discretion. As a good Reuterian he never allowed such views to intrude on the agency's honest and balanced news services. His son Alexander wrote in *The Spectator* 30 years later that British Prime Minister Anthony Eden's television appearances at the time justifying the invasion 'infuriated my father, who on one occasion threw a glass of whisky at the screen and stamped out of the room'.

For the editorial, it was a heavy year. Chancellor estimated that AP outnumbered Reuters by three to one in reporting the Suez crisis. My contact with him remained minimal and formal, but towards the end of the year he wrote to me:

I would like you to know how very much impressed I am by the way in which you have worked during this critical time. You have been a splendid lieutenant to Mr Cole and I know how much he has relied upon you. You have not spared yourself and your devotion to the news service has been unstinted. I shall make a point of seeing that the Reuter Board knows what you have done.

In 1957 I covered the Queen and Duke of Edinburgh's tour of Canada and the United States. I remember one crowded day in New York when my role in the team was to sit in one of the royal motorcade's limousines with American Bob Considine and keep the Queen in my sights in case of a security incident.

I never wrote a word. Any bouquets belonged to our New York reporters. But the Press Association's summing up to Cole, somewhat surprisingly, said:

Easily the best reporting came from Doon Campbell, whose despatches were always colourful and well done without the more jarring Americanisms which occasionally cropped up in another service . . . [His] work was remarkable both for speed of clearance and felicity of treatment.

Nearly as remarkable as the desk's rewrite skills!

It was not however, until the spring of 1958, when I was returning from holiday, that Chancellor's intimation of greater things to come was made manifest. I received at home a personal and confidential message asking me to report to the general manager's office before showing my face in the editorial. I did so and found Cole already there, unusually edgy.

'What's up?' I asked.

'The GM will be here in a moment,' was all he would say.

Chancellor came in, shook hands, motioned me to sit down, and got straight to the point.

'Campbell, we would like to appoint you news manager.'

'How will that affect my relationship with Mason?'

'You will be Mason's boss. You will be the senior executive in the editorial.'

'I asked because since joining Reuters I've always worked to Mason, under Mr Cole.'

'That's up to you, Campbell.'

'Thank you, sir. I accept.'

Downstairs on the fourth floor, Sid was dictating to Ena Buckle when I borrowed his wastepaper bin to squat next to him.

'Sid, I've just been offered and have accepted the position of news manager.'

Turning round on his swivel chair to face me, Sid stuck out his hand for mine. 'Right, son. Somebody had to do the f****** job and I'd sooner it was you than anyone else. Chancellor offered it to me and I told him to stuff it up his arse.'

I later learned this was substantially correct. Looking to the future, Cole had wanted to clear the editorial deck. Sid, aged 58 and not in robust health, was too entrenched. Cole's idea was to promote him to be news manager working on the administration floor. Sid had seen this as being a diabolical plot to ease him out of his niche on the editorial floor.

I told Sid what I had said to Chancellor, and that I expected and would need his loyalty and co-operation. He said I could count on it.

Chancellor confirmed my new appointment in a letter on 14 May, in which he said that 'it is hoped by the Board that you will play an increasingly important part in the day to day running of the Reuter news services' and 'as a token of its confidence in you, the Reuter

Board has authorised me to increase your basic salary to £2,250 a year from 1 June and we all look forward to the increasingly important part that you are to play in the Reuter organisation'.

Of the members of the newly-constituted administration, George Cromarty Bloom, 48, had joined Reuters in Shanghai in 1934, went to Comtel in 1954, and succeeded to its managership in 1958 when Alfred Geiringer left to form his own company-information agency, Universal News Services.

Patrick Crosse, 41, had joined Reuters in 1935 when he was 18. A correspondent in India, France, Malaya and Czechoslovakia, he had later become a war correspondent in Eritrea, Iran and North Africa, and was taken prisoner in the Western Desert. After the war he was successively chief correspondent in Belgium, Switzerland and Italy, and from his Rome base masterminded Cole's major venture to take Reuters into the newly independent African states. Later, under Gerry Long, he took overall respnsibility for Reuter affairs in Latin America.

Stuart Underhill, 44, had joined Reuters as North American desk editor in 1950, in which role he had made a special study of commercial services in North America, and had been supervising editor since 1957. He had previously been with Canadian Press, the Canadian national news cooperative, for 13 years, becoming bureau chief first in CP's London office, then New York. Under Gerry Long, he was to be named managing editor in 1965, and general manager in charge of North American affairs in 1968.

Staff below the administrative level had little contact with members of the Reuter board, apart from sometimes seeing them in the building on their way to or from board meetings, held monthly on the seventh floor. An exception had been in 1953 when the head of the *Mirror* group of newspapers, the craggy Cecil Harmsworth King, had joined the board and invited about a score of us senior deskmen and reporters to a Christmas feast at *Mirror* headquarters.

For several weeks after becoming news manager, I stayed on in what was known as the chief news editor's unit. Besides Sid and myself, it had several experienced staff, including Brian Stockwell, until his appointment as South-East Asia manager (followed by many top roles, including that of general manager, after Gerry Long became managing director).

Others on whom we relied were L. P. (Jack) Allen, one of the fastest newsmen in Reuters, an authority on the Sudan, and one-time Reuter manager in South-East Asia and West Africa; Leslie Haynes, a former parliamentary gallery reporter, political correspondent and sub; Sydney Taylor, one-time Commonwealth correspondent; Donald Wright, a senior editor and overseas manager, involved in the planning or setting up of six African national news agencies; and Eddie Edbrooke, who joined Reuters as a messenger in 1936 and retired as assistant staff manager in 1981.

They were a hard-working, resourceful and loyal team. I felt protected by them, and by keeping close contact with editors of the strength and ability of Ranald Maclurkin, Derek Peebles, Clifford Wakefield, Jack Henry, Gordon Ditchfield, Ron Cooper, Nick Carter, Ian Macdowall, Arthur Mulcock and Harry Kerly, who knew where news pressures were building up, what union chapels were thinking, and where embers of discontent were smouldering.

Cole kept pressing me to break away from the unit and establish a separate physical and working identity. This I did by moving a few paces away into a glass-walled office with 'news manager' on the door, but quickly known as 'Campbell's Kremlin'. For the first time I had a degree of editorial privacy, necessary because it was there that staff were promoted, told of bonuses, praised, carpeted or even sacked.

However, a summons to the Kremlin or a visit there by Cole or another administration member could spark wild and sometimes mischievous speculation throughout the open-floor newsroom, so I soon had to have the glass wall obscured by roller blinds.

The year I became news manager proved one of the heaviest and costliest yet for Reuters. Top stories included a crisis in France with de Gaulle returning to power; the death of Pope Pius XII; insurrection in the Lebanon; the assassination of King Feisal of Iraq, the Crown Prince and General Nuri al-Said and the subsequent landing of British and American troops in Jordan and the Lebanon; the Fuchs–Hillary crossing of Antarctica; Nikita Khrushchev succeeding Bulganin as Soviet Prime Minister; and the Manchester United football team being virtually wiped out in the Munich air crash.

On weekdays, I lived in the office, using one of a half-dozen 'bedrooms' – mere cells with a basic bed and chair – on the eighth floor of the building. The intensive work did neither me nor my career any harm. Chancellor wrote on 7 August:

I feel that I must write and tell you how impressed I have been by the splendid effort that you have put forward during this extraordinary news period. You always rise to crises and I have the Hungarian story particularly in mind. You show real qualities of leadership and your concentration upon the job in hand and your steady good humour combine to make you a really first-class news editor.

That same month the American magazine *Newsweek* led its Press section with a long plug for Reuters, praising exclusives by Vincent Buist in Moscow, Abdul Karim in Baghdad, John Anthony Halabi in Amman, and Alex Valentine in Beirut, and declaring that the agency had regained the prestige of its early days and was being published in major American papers.

Six months later I received my next boost up the hierarchy. Chancellor and Cole had been pressing me to come up with an editorial command structure which would more clearly define operational control, tighten liaison with the unions and administration and try to bridge the gap – sometimes a yawning chasm – between the seventh and fourth floors, the familiar 'them and us' syndrome.

I had an impression that at least a few of the more militant union members were giving Chancellor an uncomfortable time. There was even talk of them trying to bypass the administration and go direct to the board. So I was promoted to be a member of the administration, and the established liaison point for the NUJ.

Sir Christopher wrote to me on 12 February 1959:

I reported yesterday to the Reuter Board about my talks with you and about my talks with the NUJ Chapel. The Board were delighted to hear the good things I told them about your work and they cordially approved your appointment as a member of the Reuter Administration.

This means that you are now fully responsible for the Editorial Department and you will henceforth receive all the information that is available to the Assistant General Managers. This information includes my regular monthly reports to the Board and the monthly estimates which go before the Board . . .

I am writing to Mr Cleaver [Terry Cleaver, Father of the NUJ Chapel] telling him that your appointment to the Administration has been confirmed . . . I do congratulate you upon this development which I regard as an important pro-motion and a very definite and well earned step in your Reuter career.

In his letter to Terry Cleaver, Sir Christopher made the point, 'Mr Campbell will thus be fully conversant with all matters relating to the company and he will now be the established and recognised head of the Editorial Department and the liaison between your Chapel and the Management . . .'

Only about a month after signing these letters, Sir Christopher was approving embargoed drafts I'd prepared for release to PA and Reuters about his own resignation, to become a director and vice-chairman of Odhams Press Ltd, one of Europe's largest publishing houses. Why did he go? His unexpected decision had the rumour mills at Reuters and in Fleet Street working overtime. Much of the speculation was wide of the mark.

One far-fetched piece of scuttle-but claimed that Cecil King had advised Chancellor against his intention to assign a woman, Elizabeth Bower, as Reuters' correspondent to Ghana. Bower, a capable hard-working journalist, herself became the story when after a four-day search she was found unconscious and badly-bitten on a roadside 53 miles from Accra. It was believed she had suffered from sunstroke. King was said to have huffed, 'I told you so, Christopher.'

Another unlikely tale was that Chancellor was angry that a permanent chairman was to be appointed who would actually have an office on the seventh floor.

The monthly board meetings had always been chaired by directors in rotation, and Chancellor knew the nuances, the detail which directors could not always be expected to absorb or fully understand. It might have been different if the board had planned to impose its own permanent guardian to keep an eye on things and safeguard their own interests.

The official Reuter history, *The Power of News*, says Chancellor was dissatisfied with the lack of interest shown by board members, especially when his proposal that Reuters and PA should go into television news for the new British commercial network was vetoed by *The Daily Telegraph*'s Lord Burnham.

I felt that after 29 years at Reuters, 15 of them as general manager, he wanted a change. His prestigious title carried more clout than cash. Chronic shortage of funds often frustrated his plans to strengthen services and expand into new technology and new markets.

Since the end of the war, Reuters had built strong relationships with West European agencies, doubled revenue from North America, trebled Comtel revenue, and had the edge over the American agencies in Africa and parts of Asia. But its home market produced less than a fifth of its revenue and in 1957 Chancellor found it necessary to warn the board that editorially Reuters was 'down to bedrock – perhaps below'.

If really big news broke, Reuters would have to go into the red. Editorial staff levels were dangerously low and could not be further reduced. Trying to match the editorial resources of AP was 'like David and Goliath, a great struggle'. To a live wire like Chancellor, it must have been a depressing prospect of holding or cutting costs, and 'limping along in decorous poverty'.

At the Annual General Meeting on 11 June 1959 it was announced that the board had appointed Cole to succeed him as general manager, and elected John L. Burgess of the Cumberland *Evening News* as non-executive chairman.

13
Reuters' Cole-face

In 13 years of unswerving loyalty and readiness to acknowledge his debt to Chancellor, Cole had found himself increasingly shouldering the responsibility for company policy and taking corporate decisions, and must occasionally have cast a covetous eye on the general managership. Now he fitted easily into the general manager's seventh-floor suite.

The leading world news agency had at the helm a man who was first and foremost a newsman. For years he had made his living from going out and looking for news. He had an uncanny nose for it. To him, news was an all-embracing enthusiasm which left little room for anything else.

But those critics who contended he was too much of a newsman for a post requiring other qualities didn't know the man. He had formidable powers of leadership, initiative and drive. He had already proved himself in organisation, administration and salesmanship, and he had an inspired approach to public relations. His strengths far outnumbered and outweighed his weaknesses, though he did have weaknesses.

He drove himself too hard for his own good, and he was too easily touched by deprivation or a sob story, real or simulated. Wilfred Taylor, diarist of *The Scotsman*, never forgot what happened after he allowed himself a tailpiece recording completion of tending 'this cabbage patch on the leader page'. He wrote:

Nobody paid any attention to this act of self-indulgence, this piece of narcissism, except a few faithful readers and Mr Walton A. Cole in London, with whom we had had no contacts whatsoever in our life. A few days later, one of the reporters told us that a large package was awaiting us on our desk . . . The contents proved to be a bottle of champagne with a note signed 'Tony Cole'. The message was so friendly, and so absurdly flowery: 'After 21 years of doing one of the roughest jobs in the trade, you are entitled to celebrate. Take your wife out and go on the town.'

Cole could be tough, and tongue-lash a man for sloppy or irresponsible work, even sack him; but before the wretched man left his office, Cole might be offering him £100 or more from his own pocket.

One of his first acts on becoming general manager was to get my salary raised to £2,750, and on the big story his attitude was 'spend what it takes', but he had a Scottish canniness with company money which caused him unnecessary worry over the bottom line. Checks and controls on expenses and expenditure generally were rigidly applied and he would not tolerate 'fiddling' in any form.

However, when he saw genuine hardship hitting a conscientious worker needing relief from grinding routine, he might say, 'Send old Fred to West Africa for a couple of weeks on expenses.' He just assumed 'old Fred' was dying to be asked to go to West Africa. Also he knew the expenses would be modest and that 'old Fred' would turn in a weightily acceptable file of news and feature material.

He could also be brutal when he thought he was being kind. I recall another 'old Fred', a specialist of enough status to entertain at the Savoy, on company account, guests like Lords Shawcross and Soames. This old Fred had asked the chief accountant if he could borrow £100 from the company. The chief accountant told Cole, who said he would handle it.

'What do you think, old Fred wanting to borrow £100?' Cole asked me. 'He had more than £100 last year. This can't go on.'

'You know old Fred as well as I do,' I said. 'He's pretty hopeless at looking after his personal affairs. What's £100? There's plenty of collateral security; his pension fund contributions must be many times that amount.'

'That's not the point. What does he take us for? Reuters isn't a milch-cow, there for anybody who runs out of cash. It's just not good enough. I'm going to have him up here. You stay.'

'This is very personal. He asked the chief accountant and now you're in on the act. Surely it would be better if I left.'

'Stay.'

Cole telephoned, and soon an uncomfortable old Fred appeared, hands knotted.

'Hello, old man. What's this request you've made for a £100 loan?'

'Well, I'm sorry; can't say how sorry I am, Mr Cole, but you know how it is . . . a lot of bills coming in recently, and the money just seems to run out.'

'But we're all in that situation. What right have you to think Reuters will bail you out when you get yourself in a mess like this? What do you do with your money? How much do you give your wife for housekeeping? What about your kids? They've done well by you, what contribution do they now make?'

And so it went on. Old Fred's lips were quivering, he clenched his fists and crossed his legs. I was embarrassed to be there. In the end, of course, he got the £100, but when he had shuffled out of the office, I said to Cole, 'I think that was bloody awful. Fancy speaking to any employee like that. What an inquisition!'

'No, no, no. You don't understand. Old Fred was flattered that I showed that amount of interest in his finances and well-being.'

And maybe he was.

On 12 November 1959 Cole signed a notice listing members of his administration – and unlike Sir Christopher's 18 months earlier, it did not say anything about the board having authorised it.

Kim Rogers, Nigel Judah and I had thus been elevated to the administration. Kim Rogers had joined in 1930 and had headed North American activities as long as most of us could remember. Nigel Judah, only 28, had joined Reuters in 1955 as a management accountant with Comtelburo, and risen like a rocket.

I had unhindered access to Cole, both formal and spontaneous, and saw him several times a day when he was in London. Our relationship must have seemed strange to others, for while other and subordinate executives addressed him as 'Tony', in public I always respectfully called him 'Mr Cole,' 'GM' or 'WAC'. To me he was not just head of Reuters, but the wire-service journalist *sans pareil*.

In the early 1960s, I doubt if Fleet Street had anything more exciting to offer than being on the end of a hot line from Tony Cole. When the buzzer went and that drawling voice asked, 'Spare a sec, old son?' I would drop everything and hare upstairs – no crystal ball could foretell what I would hear or discuss in the next couple of minutes or hours, but it would be fascinating.

I would hear his latest piece of oral shorthand or slang, such as 'tell old Fred to get on his bicycle and drop some birdseed' (get off his seat and into action), or the latest on talks to increase subscriptions, our success in getting our service or reporter back into a country from which we had been excluded, new communications links being set up, inside information about what was going on elsewhere in the media world, or about our own staff.

Cole was genuinely concerned with the details of his staff's lives. A case in point was Ronald Farquhar, a Glaswegian who had joined in 1952 and was to work for us in every Communist country in Europe. While in Prague he had fallen in love with Vera Svobodova, a translator/assistant in the office there, but the Czechoslovak authorities refused them permission to marry.

In 1958 Farquhar was moved to Peking, but Cole told the Czechoslovak authorities their refusal to allow the marriage was inexplicable and inhuman, and on a visit to Prague he secured the support of the head of the national news agency, Ceteka. In 1960, Farquhar's return from Peking was via Prague, where he and Vera were married on 11 August. Cole derived immense pleasure from this, and from the terms of a letter from Ronnie:

I am sure you will be glad to know that your intervention has been instrumental in bringing about the happy result . . . We hope it may be some satisfaction and reward to you to know that you have helped to give us the chance to find happiness together . . .

A favourite ploy of Cole's, after inducing a matey mood, would be to ask me, 'What do you think of So-and-so?' And the 'So-and-so' would not be a correspondent, desk editor or even manager, but might well be a member of the administration. After this had happened several times, I told him, 'You know, you're a so-and-so yourself. You ask me what I think of A and B and C and D, and as soon as I'm out of your sight you're probably asking them, "What do you think of Campbell?" '

'OK, what's wrong with that?' he'd say. 'Just checking.'

Though I was a member of the administration, and responsible for news, I was not the editor, and never expected to be. Cole was too attached to that proud title. He told me when I first became news manager:

Look, son, as long as I'm around you'll never be Editor – I'm holding on to that. You can act Editor, have the authority, take the decisions. I'll back you all the way, but I'll keep the title.

Sid Mason still did most of the forward planning, for set-piece events like conferences, elections and major sporting events on which detailed staff and communications briefings were needed.

My day as news manager would start with the incoming service messages, many of which dealt with the differing roles of overseas bureaux and London editing desks. Correspondents, often working long hours under pressure, could lose their cool and blow their tops when they saw distortions, errors of fact or emphasis, or sloppy rewriting in London's version of their copy. Angry exchanges were not unknown and could be quite healthy, the parties quickly realising each other's problems. Some examples of opening shots:

Proeditor appreciate compare Kissinger series as moved from London with my original copy. This kind of pedestrian rewrite is always demoralising and like to know whether company insists on it. [Simple answer: the company would like to ban it forever.]

Must protest heartily at crucifixion of daylead Nasser. Clumsy insertion of Leila Khaled angle into second take puts quote in third para completely out of context and makes nonsense of the original. Khaled story being absurdly upplayed in context today's events in Cairo and can we please relegate her henceforth to nominal role deserved? Most disappointed last night's work results in hotchpotch like that this morning. Informatively no one's face in Cairo is streaked with two days of endless weeping.

I quoted 'usually reliable sources' in my Soviets series of November 2 and this was changed to 'informed sources'. View sourcing so important in stories from Peking grateful deskmen do not alter original sourcing. On previous day's Walkout series the words 'social imperialism', which Chinese jargon for Soviet Union, changed to 'socialist imperialism.' Grateful deskmen fully understand use of words 'social imperialism.'

Sometimes the tendency to rewriting could be traced to one of a number of different regional desks all trying to tailor the torrent of words to a news service most acceptable in speed, content and length to a particular market. This regionalisation was, however, also a source of strength.

Instead of shovelling out words, sub-editors concentrated on selection and treatment, giving Africa a predominantly African news file, cutting a UN debate on Kashmir shorter for Europe than for the sub-continent. It might mean a Norwegian heading the European desk, a Frenchman the French desk, Indians and Pakistanis on the Asian desk, and North American services subbed by Americans, Canadians – and occasionally a Briton like Derek Jameson, who could write in American idiom and spellings.

Sometimes an overseas bureau would ask for a style ruling in advance. I recall Madrid noting that words like 'dictator' and 'partisan' could be considered subjective judgements, and therefore taboo, and asking what epithet would be acceptable for references to Hitler and Mussolini. Here the desk editor replied that 'partisan' did not have emotional overtones and was acceptable, while 'dictator' could be used in cases where it was the generally accepted verdict of history, as in the case of Hitler and Mussolini.

Now and then desk and correspondent found it necessary to remind each other to keep a sense of proportion. Cairo told London, '. . . don't panic. An air raid doesn't make a war.' London told Bonn, '. . . bank robbery may be top story for Germany but it's not supreme story of night for rest of world so don't trip over your feet trying to rush it out'.

Fundamental Reuter principles were always being reinforced, as in:

Just reminder that we would rather lose out on a timing than risk going into print with a potentially misleading story. Both sides beginning to get a bit trigger-happy and think you should raise your sights from now on when deciding whether story rates snap treatment.

Service messages needed care in wording, and not only to avoid angering the recipient. A message of congratulations for a beat on an assassination could be misconstrued by other readers as congratulations on the success of the murder. An offer of reinforcement could take on military meaning to a paranoid dictator.

One example of misunderstanding occurred just before a royal visit to Ghana when the desk tipped off the Accra correspondent about what rival agencies were saying in these words, 'Opposition have Ghana *Evening News* telling Roman Catholic Church it must toe line and set up CPP branches within church.'

A Ghanaian newspaper saw this message, took 'Opposition' to mean the Ghanaian political opposition, and accused Reuters of 'very wicked . . . almost Satanic' mendacity.

Warnings to correspondents took many forms – government warnings of 'nasty consequences', blunt threats of expulsion; and this chilling call to one correspondent's wife from a senior Information Ministry official, 'Your husband must remember he has a wife and children. He is not going to be expelled. He will get a stray bullet in the back.'

Contrary to my experience as a war correspondent, we were repeatedly telling reporters, 'Personal safety is more important than any story. Reuter reporters must not venture into any situation where they feel there is undue risk.'

Ranald Maclurkin, respected by those on the desk and in the field, did most of the 'inquests'. He was a craftsman with words who practised and preached simplicity in writing. Universally known as 'Mac', he had a generous and compassionate nature, masked when it suited him by a dour Scottish demeanour, and he gave working and moral strength to the newsroom.

He had graduated in journalism at D. C. Thomson in Dundee, and was my colleague and friend for 40 years, becoming head of Reuters'

UK news bureau, assistant news manager, chief news editor and final-ly editor general news. For more than four years he contributed to my editorial newsletter a feature called Style Notes, which set standards for a generation of Reuter correspondents.

I felt closer to Mac than to many of the others in editorial, and regarded him as a sort of chief of staff. At this time his tasks included studying the contents of the spike, on which incoming stories were often discarded, looking into regional treatment of some stories, and investigating complaints, including those from correspondents.

For example, one correspondent disagreed with the deletion of parts of his report of a trial and asked for an assurance that his views were formally put on record. Maclurkin replied with what I thought a good letter, in just the right tone:

Your disagreement will be placed on record. So will this reply which asks you to acquaint yourself more thoroughly, as a journalist, with libel dangers and also to think more deeply before you accuse colleagues in London of lack of courage, fair-ness and objectivity.

British law does not easily grant licence to the media to publish material which maligns the character of an individual, whether he be a humble citizen or Prime Minister. This applies to reporting of proceedings in foreign courts.

To confirm it in this particular instance we had the guidance of three lawyers, including a barrister specialising in libel, and the advice of all was that there was a strong libel risk . . .

For your information and future guidance the authoritative case on the subject of defaming British nationals in the reporting of foreign judicial proceedings is Webb v. Times Publishing Company in 1960. The judge in this case ruled that there was no qualified privilege of a general or blanket character for fair and accurate reports of foreign judicial proceedings in any courts in any country . . .

After disposing of the service messages, including the restricted-circulation ones to and from members of the administration, I would move on to the mail, already opened and sorted, apart from letters marked 'Personal'. I would deal with about a dozen letters a day myself and distribute twice as many to colleagues, including specialists, for appropriate action.

One letter in March 1960 was an unusual acknowledgement of one of our reporters, my namesake Finlay Campbell, based in Paris. He was one of the first on the scene of the earthquake which killed around 12,000 people in the Moroccan port of Agadir. One of the survivors, rescued from his flattened hotel after being trapped for 22 hours, was an Englishman, Philip Allard. He wrote to us:

Of all the Press representatives who approached me while I was on a stretcher in an aircraft of the USAF at the airport, Mr Campbell was the only one to carry out his promise to notify my brother at Guildford. I was dug out . . . in the very early hours of March 2, and by the afternoon of the same day my brother was notified, through the good offices of your agency, of my safety. This was the first intimation my family had . . .

Though Sid Mason remained chief news editor, I was also involved in planning coverage of events, such as the 1960 East–West Summit conference, intended to be the first for five years. It was always exciting and professionally satisfying to be in on the ground floor of such exercises, but this one turned out the most challenging postwar assignment of its type.

Eisenhower, well into his second term as US President, went back to Paris to meet Nikita Khrushchev in May, just as an American U2 spy plane was shot down over the Ural mountains, and its pilot captured. Khrushchev said he would take part only if Eisenhower cancelled all future U2 flights, apologised and promised to punish those responsible. Eisenhower refused, so the summit collapsed before it began.

Khrushchev then staged a mammoth press conference in the Palais de Chaillot. For more than two hours he ranted and clowned, a hysterical performance, at times pure pantomime, burlesque, bitter and banal, menacing and fearsome. James Cameron of the *News Chronicle* judged it unmatched 'in terms of size, scale, implications and universal news impact'.

I spent two days in Paris appraising our operation and heard a number of spontaneous tributes to the accuracy, balance and speed of the Reuter report from American, Indian, European and Japanese journalists and diplomats. The London correspondent of the Japanese news agency, Kyodo, said our file maintained the highest objective standard in contrast with the 'emotional' approach of the American services.

I was able to report to the Reuter board that we alone among the news agencies supplied a full running report of the questions and answers, done largely by correspondents taking in turn the Russian, French and English versions, and the full 6,000 word text. The *New York Times* displayed our copy over 11 columns; *Asahi*, the leading Japanese daily, filled 70 inches a day with Reuter copy.

It was a sweat all right, a physical and mental feat for correspondents. I squirmed when Clifton Daniel, Margaret Truman's husband and then assistant managing editor of the *New York Times*, strolled into the Reuter office, looked at his watch and remarked, 'You're running four minutes behind . . .' But he meant four minutes behind Khrushchev's voice, not our rivals.

Although still desperately strapped for cash, Reuters somehow always managed to show strength where it really mattered. The AP had 21 staff correspondents, UPI 31, including photographers, whereas Reuters had only 14 – but they were the best, they worked 18 hours a day, and we had our own special circuit direct from the Palais de Chaillot to London. The efficiency, and the long hours worked without complaint by telegraphic operating staff contributed materially to our success.

Though we could call on some of the best professionals in the world, in 1960 the alarm bells were ringing over the rate at which we were losing editorial staff. The London editorial establishment was only 133, yet in the last five years 141 skilled journalists had gone to other jobs – mostly at newspapers and the BBC – and the loss rate was rising: 16 in 1957; 20 in 1958; 28 in 1959; 20 in the first half of 1960.

Cole told the board that losses among foreign correspondents and non-journalists were negligible, although we had lost 23 of the 44 graduates recruited under the graduate training scheme since it began in 1947. The main trend was to lose sub-editors after two or three years service, i.e. when they were of most use. Discontent over salary was the most important single factor, followed by the frequency of night work.

The NUJ chapel was urging a graded wage scheme like the BBC's. Up to then, we had never tried to fix basic rates, or ceilings for the top positions, as everybody else did. Staff joining, usually on the union minimum rate, had no assurance of financial advancement. There were no automatic increments, as at the BBC and PA.

Cole named me to head 'a small continuing study committee' to see what could be done. The other members were Nigel Judah, Ranald Maclurkin, Brian Stockwell, Clifford Wakefield and Donald Ferguson, a highly capable young Canadian who became Cole's personal assistant.

Committees were anathema to me, but I got more pleasure and satisfaction from this 'Staff Wastage Committee' than from any other administration-type assignment. It meant talking to and dealing with colleagues for whose ability, commitment and loyalty I had respect, and it enabled me to do a little to project their role at Reuters to the higher echelons.

The full committee met only four times. Alone or with Brian Stockwell, a man whose character, integrity and inability to dissemble certainly enriched my life at Reuters, I conducted confidential interviews in depth with a representative cross-section of 20 subs. On 17 January 1961 I gave Cole my report, which did not mince words:

The common thread running through all interviews concerned salary level. Everyone felt the high standard of work, the pressure, the degree of responsibility and specialisation involved deserved higher rates of pay. Some said pride kept them from requesting increases – 'it should be up to the company to know an employee's worth and reward him accordingly'.

There were divided opinions on a graded pay scheme. The majority recognised its advantages but feared it might become too rigid, too like the Civil Service, reducing the scope for merit awards. There was enthusiasm for an annual or even twice-yearly salary review.

A common complaint was over frustrated ambition and lack of prospects. The system of choosing people for overseas was felt to be unfair and haphazard. Staff were put in senior positions without adequate recognition or means to enforce discipline. Management were too remote from staff.

So why did they stay at Reuters? The consensus answer was: because of the integrity of the news services, the principles of accuracy, honesty and balance, the excitement of dealing with world news, and the job security – editorial staff were seldom sacked.

Cole put my report to the board in full, saying he believed it to be 'the first study of its kind ever attempted in a news agency', and that it exposed the failure of management liaison with union executives to reach the actual staff.

The board accepted the recommendations and I was told to get on with the next phase: producing a comprehensive editorial salary structure. This I did with a new-look salary structure providing for automatic increases, recognition of long service, and ceilings – to be reached in a fixed number of years for top positions like copytasters, file editors, splash subs and so on.

I put the final version of this to Cole on 9 June 1961 and one week later he wrote to me, 'The Board, in giving an unqualified go-ahead to the proposals . . . asked me to say how tremendously impressed they were with the way this subject had been tackled.'

Eight months later, he was able to tell them:

In 1960, we lost 32 fully trained editorial staff, 18 of them with three or more years service. In 1961 the comparable figure was 10, and only three of them were employees with more than two years of service; one of those left journalism altogether, another started up in business, and the third, a Canadian, went home mainly for family reasons.

Apart from money prospects, there was also the problem of frustration. If I saw a good man becoming restless and casting around for another job because no posting had materialised, I would ring Cole. He would always see the man, usually right away, and – provided his record was satisfactory – guarantee him a move either within a few weeks or by a fixed date.

I recall one case where a first-class man called at my office, to say goodbye. I had had no idea things had reached this stage with him. As soon as he went out of the door, I buzzed Cole and told him an excellent man was leaving because he had been left languishing on a regional desk instead of going overseas, as some executive had promised but failed to implement.

Cole immediately got the front-door commissionaire on his intercom, told him to intercept the departing journalist and send him up immediately. There was no shilly-shallying now; Cole saved a good journalist for Reuters.

I had authority to send and move correspondents all over the world, and did so regularly, but usually on a 'fireman' (quick in and out) basis, or as temporary reinforcement on a big story. I would never add to or reduce a bureau's establishment or transfer a senior man without consulting Cole, unless it was urgent and he was not readily available.

Hiring and assigning editorial staff was relatively uncomplicated then. We had no personnel experts, no psychiatrists' couches – real or metaphorical – no induction dossiers, much less induction videos. We did demand references, evidence of educational level and knowledge of languages (if any), state of health and marital status. That was about it.

It did not matter if the candidate spoke cockney, Yorkshire, Scottish or Oxbridge English. It did matter that he was clean and reasonably turned out for interview – no tee-shirts, jeans or trainers. Skinheads and the long-haired would scarcely get past the commissionaire.

Graduates usually offered languages and since it became company policy to assign correspondents who were fluent in the language of the country where they would be based (with some exceptions), we had an annual university intake of about six, but languages alone never ensured jobs. They had to take a written test of journalistic aptitude.

Because recruits with the benefit of a few years of provincial paper experience usually recognised news, needed less basic training and could more quickly assimilate Reuter techniques and standards, the inclination in those days was to prefer them. Derek Jameson was a one-off, joining as an outdoor messenger, being spotted by Cole and made an 'apprentice reporter' at 16, and becoming a senior Reuter journalist before going on to fame as a Fleet Street tabloid editor and television personality.

More often, if we liked what we heard or saw of a reporter or sub we might try stalking and even poaching him – not always easy because Reuters could not match national newspapers in salaries and allowances, but recruits knew the comparative security and job satisfaction. The prospect of a foreign posting was often the bait to attract young reporters and subs to Reuters.

One unofficial unpaid Reuter head-hunter was Stanley Bagshaw, the editor of the *Eastern Daily Press* in Norwich. In 1961, he brought us Frederick Forsyth and, in 1963, Anthony Grey, both of whom made their Reuter mark in East Berlin and went on to use their Reuter experience later as best-selling novelists.

The recruitment of Donald Wright and David Reid, two senior journalists who deserved well of Reuters, was fairly typical. Wright ended the war as a major, returned to his job at *The Daily Telegraph* in his early 40s, but could not settle easily in the postwar editorial atmosphere. A chance meeting in Fleet Street in 1946 with his old friend Tony Cole led to lunch and to Wright joining Reuters as European desk editor. He stayed with us for 22 years.

David Reid I first met in 1953, when Ernest Atkinson, London editor of the *Birmingham Post*, invited me to his office one evening to sample a new sherry. He had with him a smart-looking young man in the uniform of a British army captain, introduced as David Reid of the *Glasgow Herald*, returning home from some training course. In ten minutes I learned enough about Reid to conclude he was a natural, nipped next door to Reuters and asked Cole to give five minutes right away to meet him. Reid spent the next 34 years working for us in senior journalistic jobs all over the world, and teaching the craft to many others.

Before the end of 1960 George Cromarty Bloom left to become general manager of the PA, and Gerald Long was gazetted as assistant general manager, based in London 'specialising in European affairs'. Stuart Underhill was made responsible for Comtelburo, and Alan Hammond and Michael Nelson were named its joint managers.

Alan Hammond, 49, had been with Reuters commercial services since 1928. Nelson, then 32, had joined Comtelburo in London only in 1952 but, Cole told the board, he had been certain since they met in Bangkok in 1955 that Nelson would develop into a first-class executive for our commercial service.

The question of Comtelburo's future name and policy control was the subject of a 'mini-summit', attended by the administration members, overseas assistant general managers and other senior executives, which went on almost continuously from the night of Thursday 13 October till the morning of Sunday 16 October. The conclusion was unanimous: it was the Reuter name which really sold the services, and future trading should be as 'Reuters Commercial Services'.

Cole chaired the marathon, at which projects such as a new European ticker service to 'exploit the Common Market', and an improved sales organisation were decided.

At the 1960 annual lunch the chairman, John Burgess, marked the end of Cole's first year as head of Reuters by praising him as one of the 'few men to become legendary while still at their prime', and particularly for his plans for a news service to and from Africa, set up after a tour he had made of the continent.

14

'Comic Cuts'

It was amazing how, when out of London – and he girdled the globe untiringly for several months every year – Cole contrived never to be out of touch for more than a few hours. He clocked up a million miles by air but reported in with the regularity of an airliner from whatever capital he'd reached.

Though communications were far less sophisticated then, policy matters could be referred to him as easily in New York or New Delhi, Moscow or Melbourne, as at his desk in London. Editorial logs, service messages, letters covering routine matters, as well as corrections and complaints, were constantly being air freighted or otherwise ferried to him.

Cole had an insatiable appetite to know what was going on, and never became so immersed in what he was doing that he couldn't find time to shoot off a cable or letter, be it rocket or bouquet. Like this, handwritten to me on Waldorf Astoria letterhead during New York talks with AP and the *New York Times*:

Simply magnificent! The atmosphere for negotiations was admirably created by the news service. As always I am so grateful . . . There's a frightful rumpus here over AP. The lesson is the old one: sourcing . . .

Again and again the lesson should be driven home that our future is dependent

on accuracy, sourcing and unreservedly adhering to Reuter standards. Do your stuff
everywhere on this . . .

His globe-trotting widened his circle of friends and contacts to
include most of the world's chief news executives and many of the
news makers, like President Kennedy – 'clinically calculating and
charming' – and South African Prime Minister Dr Hendrik
Verwoerd – 'who has a fanatical belief in divine approval of his cause'
– as well as Dr Konrad Adenauer of West Germany, Colonel Gamal
Abdel Nasser of Egypt and Dr Kwame Nkrumah of Ghana.

Cole saw it as part of his job to ensure that such national figures no
less than media moguls were accurately informed about Reuters'
operations, its objectives, its role. And because he was always a
reporter at heart, he invariably had an urge to tell the Reuter board
of directors about the people he met and the impressions he formed.
His monthly reports, often more than 50 pages long, were described
by the then chairman of the Reuter Trustees, James Henderson of
Belfast, as 'a constant joy to read. They are full of humour and sound
common sense, practical to a degree and exceptionally informative'.

Here is just the opening paragraph of a note by Cole on an interview with President Kennedy in April 1961:

Pedestalled in the washroom, bog, john or by whatever nomenclature a lavatory in
the executive suite of the White House is currently identified, a Reuter teleprinter
has been clattering forth our complete North American service since 6 am on
April 13. The site was the only tolerably soundproofed sanctum available for
delivery of the REUTER report for President Kennedy's use and the story of how
Reuters arrived at the White House is witness to the unorthodoxy, initiative, imag-
ination and impetus that I found, on this 'in the sixties' pilgrimage to the American
capital, to be the keynote of the first phase of the Kennedy era. 'Whoosh' was the
tempo everywhere of the administration in April, against 'waffle' that I sensed on
the last Springtime visit just two years ago. Surging and bursting out all over was

the atmosphere, and there is surely significant relevance in the waggish appraisal that the Kennedys are doing for sex at the White House what Eisenhower did for golf! The President, a democrat distilled from the crucible of privilege, is clinically calculating and charming. At 43 he is the supreme American organisational man spawned by Harvard. The discreet neckwear; the sober grey-toned suitings with their cut spelling out Savile Row; the sandy mane of brittle hair; the teeth and smile meriting a TV commercial; the strong, manly, delicately moulded hands; the pallid complexion. Such was the cameo that was mine when President Kennedy rose from his desk in the Oval Room at the White House to greet me: and as, stooping slightly, he came towards me, his surprising height, length of arm, breadth of shoulder and extraordinary lightness of foot accentuated an impression of buoyancy and resilience.

At about this time, I had received one of Cole's 'spare a sec?' summonses, and went up to be told in his usual oral shorthand, 'Look after IPI in Israel, old son; usual stuff but importantest get to know Swinton and Bob Brown of *E and P*. And Shik – get a real relationship going with him, too. And do the routine rounds, ITIM, representation, you know.'

It needed filling out like a cable: go to Tel Aviv for the general assembly of the International Press Institute at the end of May; get on matey terms with Stanley Swinton, AP's recently-appointed director of World Services; Robert U. Brown, the editor of the leading US trade journal *Editor and Publisher*; and Aryeh Dissentshik, the editor-in-chief of *Maariv*, Israel's leading evening newspaper, make contact with our customers such as ITIM, the Israeli news agency, and work at being a good representative for us with all the other media bosses who will be there.

The first part was easy enough, thanks to Arye Wallenstein, our chief representative in Israel since the early 50s, a great journalist, loyal friend and good companion. He booked us a table at the best restaurant in town, Swinton and Brown had brought their wives, and we had quite a party. It was easy going with Stan and Bob for most of 20 years after that.

Wally Wallenstein also fixed up a breakfast with Dissentshik, a leading figure in Israeli journalism for 40 years, which was the start of a warm personal friendship that lasted until Shik's death in 1978.

I twice called on the chief editor of ITIM, Hayim Baltsan, and told him we needed more than the derisory sterling fee he was paying for exclusive rights to the Globereuter service, but saw there was little hope for early improvement. Of the 25 daily newspapers, only three – all Hebrew – made money; many published in European languages for new arrivals folded as the immigrants learned Hebrew.

Knowing the American agencies used self-promotional techniques at IPI meetings, we arranged for ITIM to multilith copies of a digest of world and special interest Reuter news, updated three times a day, and distribute them to delegates. I was able to report to Cole:

The tactics of the American agencies proved exactly as you forecast: they played it loud, with extravagant displays of their photo and press services. The UPI, at heavy rental, plastered a panoramic glass plate outside the main dining room with a scroll boasting that whenever news broke anywhere in the world, a UPI man was there. Its printer was fouled up much of the time by appalling reception.

AP was even less smart, if more ambitious, in the area it booked for its printer and photo display. We had by far the best reception. The appeal of our special news digest was widely remarked, and its value was seen in the number of copies read while the conference was in session.

This was my third or fourth visit to Israel, and I was beginning to like the place, as indeed I liked several of the Arab countries. The Middle East, with all its violence and intrigue, had almost as much appeal as the Asian countries where I had worked and enjoyed myself.

I was finding that despite being brought up in a Scottish manse, I had no religious favourites – Presbyterians, Moslems, Methodists,

Hindus, Baptists, Sikhs, Quakers, Buddhists, Jews, Arabs and the various kinds of Roman Catholic and Orthodox Christians were all people, some good, some bad.

Two personalities in Israel fascinated me: Golda Meir and Abba Eban. I saw something of the Old Testament in Mrs Meir: her creased and craggy features with that occasional 'wrath of God' expression; her solid frame and drab dress; her austere lifestyle, uncompromising morality and honesty; the fire and brimstone with which she defended her beliefs.

It was said that after a disagreement President Nixon once told her, in a reference to Secretary of State Henry Kissinger, 'Well, at least, Mrs Meir, we have one thing in common: we both have Jewish Foreign Ministers.' To which Golda Meir replied, 'Yes, but mine speaks better English than yours does.'

Which was true, for Abba Eban was educated in London, took a Cambridge Triple First in Classics and Oriental Languages, and was a dazzling speaker. I first met him when he was ambassador in Washington. Our bureau chief Pat Heffernan, inviting me to see him giving correspondents a background briefing, said, 'Come and hear the most lucid, exciting exposition of the situation in the Middle East; you'll never hear anything like it again.'

I once asked Wally Wallenstein why Eban never became Prime Minister. 'Maybe he's too clever, maybe the people don't trust him,' said Wally.

Later in 1961, Cole was delighted at two big communications developments: the Russians at last agreed to allow us a teleprinter circuit between our Moscow office and Helsinki and, even more important, we got our own private continuous two-way transatlantic cable link connecting our European and American networks.

He was in New York on 18 September to throw the switch inaugurating the link, and we almost immediately had a 42-minute world beat on the death in a plane crash of the UN Secretary-General Dag

Hammarskjoeld while trying to arrange a ceasefire in the civil war in the Congo.

Our massive showing with this story, capping consistent success in coverage of the 14-month Congo crisis, was enhanced by a long lead the previous day in establishing that Hammarskjoeld's plane had not in fact turned up at the airport where he had been expected.

Customs officials at Ndola in Northern Rhodesia (now Zambia), where Hammarskjoeld was to confer with the Katanga leader Moise Tshombe, said he had arrived, and like everyone else we carried this. But our man in Leopoldville (now Kinshasa), Friedl Ungeheur, cabled that the plane could not possibly be in Ndola yet.

I put a phone call in to Ndola, which got through, and confirmed that in fact Hammarskjoeld was not there. We immediately put this round the world, leaving our American rivals badly burned, as they went on reporting that the Hammarskjoeld–Tshombe meeting had actually taken place until forced to retract many hours later.

Don Maxwell, editor of our pioneer US subscriber, the *Chicago Tribune*, was at Chicago airport in person at the weekend to welcome Cole there, and later told him our Congo coverage alone justified the *Tribune*'s Reuter subscription, having 'completely outclassed' AP and UPI.

Among those who gave us our superiority on the Congo were Vincent Buist, Gerald Ratzin, Horace Castell, James Wolfe, Gordon Martin and two who were to become celebrities later in the world of television – Nigel Ryan and Henderson 'Sandy' Gall. Sandy has written in his book, *Don't Worry About the Money Now*, of his terrifying Reuter experiences, including being beaten up and threatened with shooting by Congolese soldiers, dark hours in Idi Amin's execution cell and warfare in Israel, Suez, Biafra and Hungary.

Nigel, a first-class reporter who went from Reuters to a glittering career at ITN, said he never forgot one Congo cable from me, 'Coverage spectacularest costs transcendental.'

He wrote of some of the difficulties in October 1960, 'Heat, hostility and hopeless inefficiency have been piled on top of all the more conventional frustrations to make the Congo story a nightmare for the working reporter . . . He is faced with airplanes which don't take off . . . cables which take longer than letters . . . telephone delays of from 30 minutes to three days . . . teleprinter connections that go dead just as you are getting through.'

Some time later, in a phone call to Cole, Nigel said that since leaving us he had been impressed by 'just what a professional organisation Reuters is'. He had been to Algiers for ITN and while he and 200 other newsmen there were failing to get phonecalls out to London, the Reuter correspondent Basil Chapman was filing through inward calls, booked to him by Reuters' offices in London, Rome and Paris, a technique we practised widely at the time.

This kind of thing was a major part of the content of one of my most enjoyable jobs: producing the *News Manager's Review*. Cole promoted this, after detailed discussion with managers and correspondents during a 15-nation tour in 1961. It was the second to have the *Review* title.

The *Reuter Service Bulletin* had been issued in 1917 to 'promote a sense of fellowship among our scattered people' after Reuters Limited superseded the former Reuters Telegram Company.

The idea was revived by Sir Roderick Jones in 1938 with the *Reuter Review*. During and after the war, there was only the plainly typed monthly editorial report, which I had helped to edit when I returned from Paris. Then as news manager I provided a Note on the Editorial Report, which Cole now wanted amplified to cover 'our main successes, defeats, major dispositionings and other highlights'.

The first issue of the *News Manager's Review*, 11 pages – still plain typescript – appeared on 3 January 1962, and continued fortnightly through 1962, metamorphosing into *The Editor's Review* in February 1963, dying in 1964 and reviving in 1969 as the *Newsletter*, jazzed up with photographs and facsimiles. It was widely known as 'Comic Cuts', and went to all editorial staff, highlighting not only Reuter successes and defeats but quirky communications, brushes with censors, the story behind the story, noteworthy reporting skills and techniques. It contained rockets for loose or excessive writing and weak sourcing, and bouquets for attractive 'brighteners'.

I also encouraged retired correspondents to rack their memories, producing items like Allen Bettany's recollection that Hitler had a 'podgy, warm hand . . . rather vague and protruding eyes . . . and I understand from medical friends that such are a symptom of hyperthyroidism . . . PS: Hitler also had flat feet and walked like a duck.'

Another memory was from Harry Harrison, of being thrown out of pre-Communist Yugoslavia in 1937 for reporting the big queues for a cartoon film in which Mickey Mouse had the same motoring and sporting hobbies as Prince Paul.

To a great extent, the *Reviews* and Reports are my diary of the early 60s, for the stories they celebrate were the centre of my working life. There really was never a dull moment, for the whole spectrum of life cascaded into the newsroom around the clock – erupting volcanoes, earthquakes, typhoons, Yeti footprints in the Himalayan snow, Nazi war criminals in South America, apartheid and assassinations, crooks, cranks, follies and foibles.

Reviews from the first half of 1962, for example, show:

[February] *Julian Bates, Ronald Batchelor, John Bulbeck and Mary Bubb combined in a great team operation on Colonel Glenn's spaceflight from Cape Canaveral, flashing the launch round the world in one minute and dictating copy straight to the printer for two hours. The PA said, 'A triumph for Reuters'.*

[March] *We had a two-hour beat with the news that the seven and a half years of war in Algeria had ended with a ceasefire pact. Harold King told us, 'We had the news at the same time as it was telephoned to General de Gaulle.' I began the*

Review *with the cable Cole received from the General Manager of* France Soir, 'Bravo pour formidable scoop près de deux heures. Une fois de plus Reuter triomphe . . .'

[April] *John Miller in Moscow scored us dozens of front-page credits, facsimiled in the* Review, *by getting personal interviews with both Donald Maclean and Guy Burgess at their Moscow homes, to check reports that the two diplomat-spies might return to England.*

[June] *Arye Wallenstein was elected by the world press in Israel as one of two to represent them all at the hanging of Adolf Eichmann after his 577-day trial for his leading role in the Holocaust. Wally's flash was 41 minutes ahead of any other wire service and his eyewitness account was published worldwide.*

Every day was different; anything could happen. I seldom knew what to expect, or what further good or bad incursion might happen into the semblance of private life to which I tried to cling.

This was the year when Cole, wanting me on hand around the clock, provided for my personal use a proper 'bedroom' on the eighth floor of 85 Fleet Street.

Thus I was in the office from Monday to Friday, eating and sleeping as well as working there. At weekends I had routine morning and evening calls, plus frequent *ad hoc* telephone contact, and on Sunday night went to the local station to collect a bulky package sent from Reuters by train so I could 'read myself in' before Monday morning.

In August, we had planned a holiday on a British beach for Mary and me, and our children, Kate, 10, Archie, 9 and Andy, 7, but the central desk news log recorded that we had lagged a minute or two on coverage of a plane crash near Barcelona. Cole sent me his copy of the log with the scrawled annotation, 'Too bad. OK with me if you want to shoot over to Spain.'

I had never been to Spain, and it sounded better than 'Old Fred's' trip to West Africa, so I got an air ticket to Barcelona and told Mary to pigeonhole the idea of a British beach and instead organise a family motoring expedition to the Costa Brava, where I planned to join them later.

Henry Buckley, our chief correspondent in Spain, was waiting for me in Barcelona. I had a lot of time for Henry, and used to think he was knocked more often than he deserved by the younger louder types at Head Office who mistook his quiet rational manner for weakness. Though slight and gentle, he was tough as steel. A friend of Ernest Hemingway since the Spanish Civil War, he had distinguished himself as a war correspondent at Anzio and Monte Cassino, and later in Berlin and Rome, before heading the Madrid bureau.

We went over the details of the crash coverage, and decided how most effectively and economically to strengthen the arrangements with our part-time stringer correspondents. At this time, Spain had started to experience an invasion of British tourists, and of beach-combing freelancers who concentrated on covering holiday stories which could score in UK provincial papers.

I authorised Henry to double stringer fees if necessary, offer a bonus of up to £25 for good stories that stood up, and to establish an effective stringer network in another coastal area where it was reported the Duke of Windsor was going to buy a house. All this would be much cheaper and more effective than sending a staff correspondent to Barcelona to try to cover the *Costas* in the peak holiday months.

Buckley and I then went to Madrid, where the most significant event was to make my first contact with Franco's new Information Minister, Manuel Fraga Iribarne. Napoleonically small, balding, dynamic and capable of scissoring through a phone line if the call irritated him, the cigar-smoking Fraga was a combination of bad temper and high intelligence.

He was also preoccupied with a new Press Law, after years of rigid government control, and one of his first acts had been to agree with

Michael Nelson a contract for Reuters to provide its English-language news service to the Spanish Foreign Ministry.

Iribarne gave me a 45-minute interview, from which I concluded that his new Press Law could mean the unshackling of the Spanish media from many stifling controls, and filed a story on it which was widely displayed under my byline in several European countries. As a result of this piece, I found the Spanish media pursuing me, and I shared the entire front page of *Madrid* with Rita Hayworth, with pictures of us both.

After that, I beat it to the Hotel Mar Sol at Rosas on the Costa Brava, to find my family and a telegram from Cole, 'Saludos to my favourite front page story. Thought Madrid piece terrific. Happy hols and love to Mary.'

We had a week of sun, sea and sand, of paella, shrimps and garlic, of fish soup and Spanish flies and then, with stomachs protesting, decided to drive straight home, right through the night, to Boulogne. At a hotel on the front there, we were told night-watchmen would look after the car, parked right outside the main entrance. Pooped as we were, we awoke in good time to catch the ferry home, but found the car had been stripped. Everything was gone – clothes, dolls, papers, even an artificial arm.

I got home to find a letter from Cole, thanking me for the set-up I had left in London with Ranald Maclurkin and Jack Allen covering the bases and 'no worries on any front'. I wrote back summing up my thoughts about Henry Buckley:

His integrity, loyalty and character are exemplary – and following this visit I am even prepared to make allowance for those defects in his copy which can cause minor exasperation on the desk . . .

At a time when sensitivities are particularly acute as the Spanish authorities experiment with relaxed controls, I can think of no one more responsible than Buckley to represent our interests . . .

He will continue to be late, even to miss, the occasional story. Without effective backstop, and with up to 500,000 British tourists annually descending on Spain, each a potential source of income to the beachcombers, I cannot see how, short of paying disproportionately for stringers, we can competitively dragnet everything . . .

We have more aggressive reporters than Henry Buckley but, all things considered, he does a first-class job for us in Spain and I recommend that he should be allowed to stay there.

Which he did, until he retired.

Another enjoyable outing came in October, with a ceremony in Aachen to mark the fixing of a commemorative plaque on the house where Paul Julius Reuter's first pigeons arrived in 1850 with the closing prices on the Brussels Bourse, to start his agency.

A salient consideration underlying the commemoration was the fact that continental Europe then, just as now, represented Reuters' most important single overseas market. It was good for Reuters, born in Europe, to be seen going back as a potent force in European journalism, to honour its founder.

Before a large crowd of media publishers, editors and executives, diplomats, officials and local citizens, Cole tossed a single white pigeon into the air, a signal for the traps on a mass of pigeon cages to be released so that the birds took flight in wave after wave of beating wings – and droppings!

At a luncheon the chairman, John Burgess, praised Cole as a worthy successor of the Baron, and Cole spoke of the importance of harnessing communications, forecasting, 'In the lifetime of many here today, a Reuter correspondent could file a despatch from the Moon; outer space, the Moon or Mars will become part of "assignment Reuter".'

In fact, the previous day I had exchanged greetings with the *New York Times*, using the new communications satellite, Telstar, then on its 914th orbit, and the public celebrations ended with a demonstration of our worldwide network, displaying messages from offices in far-away countries on a visual screen for viewing by a large audience.

Over a drink later that night, two Reuter directors were telling me of their admiration for Cole – a giant in every way, a superb journal-ist-administrator but, they wondered, was there not a little improvi-dence in that nobody was being groomed for the succession?

'But Cole is only 50,' I said. Well, yes, they knew that, but it's a big job, a very demanding job, and maybe it's not before time the next man should be in sight.

I was sufficiently surprised to feel that, late though it was, I should put Cole in the picture. He did not fail to respond.

At breakfast in Bonn next morning I was sitting in a partitioned area of the room when Cole and his old friend Gavin Astor came down. Cole was talking about people worrying over his succession.

'Absolute nonsense,' he said. 'Why there's so-and-so and so-and-so, several young men, able and qualified to take over. And there's Gerry Long, absolutely first-class in Europe, brilliant linguist . . .'

I was to remember this three months later.

Meanwhile Cole continued with his unique lifestyle and his globe-trotting. Towards the end of 1962 he produced an eight-page report on a visit to Moscow, noting the big changes under Khrushchev and describing a meeting with him arranged by Mr Adzhubei, the editor of *Izvestia*, married to Khrushchev's daughter. It took place at a big Kremlin reception.

I was summoned to a corner of the room where Mr Adzhubei and his wife were waiting. Placing themselves on either side of me, they escorted me past the security guard, through the phalanx formed by the diplomatic corps to a clearing in the front of a platform where Mr Khrushchev stood quite alone except for his interpreter.

He was expecting me and put aside a small glass of champagne he carried, before we were introduced. Then he stepped back two paces, his podgy, pallid face alight with laughter, he surveyed me from head to foot and exclaimed:

'Ah, I know why they called you the big man of the Western news agencies. You are in every way. You are big like Reuters. Actually I saw you in the crowd earlier and realised that you must be a capitalist commissar, or a Director General. I would like our people of authority to look like you.'

Cole's size was clearly connected with his legendary food intake, though Laurence Scott of the *Manchester Guardian* had a theory:

Perhaps Cole's most unusual ability was that like a small child he could immediately convert a steak into energy. After a full day's work or a long tiring train journey he would demand food, preferably beef, and rising refreshed from the table would start another bout of work into the small hours.

I knew Cole liked food, quantity as well as quality. When he came to our house for dinner and we had a joint, it was not just folklore that on being invited to carve he would count the heads round the table, then slice the beef into that number of portions. I'd watch the exercise, praying that he'd leave enough for second helpings.

But until one evening when we went out with Dr Jolle Jolles, head of the Dutch news agency, Gerald Long and Don Ferguson, I had never experienced the torture of being out on the town with such a legendary trencherman.

We started in the GM's office with champagne and mock caviar, smoked salmon and other canapés. Then to Sheekeys for king-sized portions of dressed crab washed down with Guinness or Black Velvet. Then on to Boulestin, a multi-star restaurant in the Covent Garden area, where Cole embraced his friend Malcolm Muggeridge before the serious business of studying the menu.

Starters – melon, pâté, avocado, whitebait? Then Cole opted for some roast duck – who would share his choice? We all did. Enough? Never. Cole's knee nudged mine under the table, 'Did you say savoury, Doon?'

I hadn't mentioned savoury; the last thing I wanted was a savoury.

'Okay. I'll join you. Angels on horseback for two. Are there any more takers?'

By this time I couldn't look at cheese or trifle before we came to coffee, with chocolate mints, and brandy.

The wine too was memorable. Cole was fond of drink – spirits, beer, or wine – but only socially and never to excess. He found it easy to cut out alcohol, and did so when his wife gave it up for health reasons. Even without alcohol, however, his capacity was gargantuan. A whole tumblerful of soda water would go down in one gulp. A wise host always had several syphons at hand.

Chancellor thought Cole looked like King Farouk or Hilaire Belloc, but he was also often likened to G. K. Chesterton, who used to say that if ever he felt like taking exercise, he would lie down until he got over it. Cole, too, seemed to have an aversion to organised exercise, though I seldom knew him to lie down.

In bracing weather, he enjoyed the 15-minute walk to the office from his home at Charterhouse, near Smithfield meat-market. From his country home, Burston Rectory near Diss, in Norfolk, he sent a Christmas card showing the family working in the garden, with Cole himself manipulating a motor mower.

But even when weekending in rural Norfolk, his thoughts never strayed far from Reuters. He had a private teleprinter line from the Rectory to 85 Fleet Street so he could stay in touch.

Though he did not go in for tycoon trappings, and had no holiday home or boat on the Mediterranean, Cole enjoyed his increasingly comfortable lifestyle. He got a kick out of switching from his well worn old Wolseley to a new Jaguar in which he could whizz overseas visitors along scenic roads to the Reuter radio listening station in Hertfordshire, or some rustic five-star restaurant.

Cole had such a zest for life; by his example, his presence, his voice, his very being, he dominated Reuters. He seemed somehow too big and strong to let routine ailments like colds bother him. But in December he had a severe and lingering bronchial attack, and his absence was felt throughout 85 Fleet Street, indeed throughout the whole Reuter world.

My last messages from him contained his usual extravagant praise. Handwritten annotations on my fortnightly *Review*, 'Not first-class but brilliant . . . The best reading I get and done superbly well.' And a letter, written on 17 December:

Understandably the Board has been tremendously impressed by the consistent and outstanding Reuter achievement in news coverage in recent months . . .

I told them of the key part played by yourself in achieving these magnificent successes through your imaginative and diligent direction.

It is appropriate therefore that in informing you of the Board's reactions, I should ask you suitably to convey their congratulations to all concerned, at the same time associating me with them in fullest measure. Certainly nothing could afford me more pride and satisfaction than our recent editorial record.

Unusually, I replied to this 'herogram', saying:

We now have a machine of which we can be proud. It is so heartening to find the mood of the whole Editorial responding to our successes – and defeats. Again, best thanks for your tremendous support and example without which this job I am doing would mean so much less.

Warmest wishes for your complete recovery – to quote words you so often address to others: 'Don't think of coming back until you are completely fit!'

But of course, he did. The current concern was negotiations with the Belgian news agency, Belga. Cole had told the board in November that these would be a 'significant showdown', because they suspected Belga's director-general, Daniel Ryelandt, of being 'in the pocket' of the French news agency AFP and if the outcome was for Reuters to go it alone in Belgium, it could have repercussions with the other European news agencies.

The negotiations were conducted in Brussels by Gerald Long, Glen Renfrew and James Wolfe. The first round found Ryelandt conciliatory and anxious to assure Reuters that his agency's bias in favour of AFP was a thing of the past. By the end of December, however, the scene had changed and Ryelandt decided to seek a personal meeting with Cole, hoping no doubt that he might squeeze a more advantageous deal for Belga.

As a courtesy Cole, though not yet recovered, agreed to see Ryelandt at his office on Friday 25 January. My office phone rang about 3 o'clock. It was Nigel Judah. His tone was agitated, peremptory – not the usual quiet calm way Nigel spoke.

'Come at once to the GM's office, at once, urgently.'

I raced up the stairs to find Nigel and Cole's faithful assistant Maggie Alliston outside Cole's room. They said he had collapsed. We opened the door, and found Tony sitting in a big leather chair, which he found more comfortable for dozing off than the one at his desk.

At first glance it looked a fairly normal posture. He could have been asleep. His expression was peaceful, in no way contorted by pain. His shoelaces were undone.

Then I saw his lips were purple. I held his wrist, trying to feel his pulse. There was none.

'He's dead,' I said.

The ambulance men arrived with a stretcher, and wheeled him to the lift. I came down the stairs and, in the small group forming in the entrance lobby to watch the stretcher being eased out of the lift, I saw the tall figure of Daniel Ryelandt, waiting for his appointment.

With Eddie Edbrooke, I got into the waiting ambulance, where desperate efforts were made with oxygen and artificial respiration, to no avail. When we arrived at St Bartholomew's Hospital the company doctor, Dr Hugh Richards, was waiting.

'Too late, Hugh,' I said. 'Tony's gone.'

Later I went to Charterhouse to tell Janet Cole. She had been seriously ill herself but had borne it all without fuss or complaint. I will never forget the composure with which she carried the awful pain and anguish she must have felt at my news. She died within the year.

That night I set up a desk and with a relay of colleagues and typists worked until dawn, handling an avalanche of tributes, from palaces, presidents and prime ministers, from press barons, publishers, news executives, journalists and non-journalists, from people in all walks of life.

For Cole's funeral on 30 January there was a personal message from the Queen, the Reuter house flag flew at half-mast and staff observed a minute's silence. More than 1,000 people attended a memorial service at St Paul's Cathedral on 13 February, and at the same time representatives of the Japanese press met in the London office of the Japanese news agency, Kyodo, to honour his memory.

There was a footnote a year later when 200 clerks at 85 Fleet Street presented a lectern as a memorial to Cole on the 25th anniversary of the founding of their chapel of the National Society of Operative Printers and Assistants (NATSOPA). The Chapel Father, or branch chairman, George Holden, said they wanted to commemorate 'the man who had come to mean so much to us all'.

'He was one with us,' he said. 'A man of this age, intent on keeping Reuters, as it is, the greatest news-reporting organisation in the world. He put his finger on the most vital factor: concord between staff and management.'

15

A wise old hand in London

On 12 February 1963, the day before the St Paul's memorial service for Cole, John Burgess came to my glass box in the corner of the newsroom to say the board would be interviewing senior staff next day, myself included.

He mentioned the sort of questions he would be asking: how was the mood and morale in editorial and among correspondents overseas; the strength of the editorial structure; provision to cope with contingencies; staff wastage? None of the questions gave me the slightest worry.

He did not say the interviews were for the post of general manager (i.e. chief executive), and at this stage I had no idea, not even the vaguest hint what was likely to be on offer to me. At most, I supposed, it might amount to retaining the title of news manager, but probably that was wishful thinking. Might it be news editor at Head Office, or maybe an overseas bureau?

Only after lunch next day, in a small eighth-floor ante-room, usually occupied by the nurse, did I get the picture: already assembled there were Pat Crosse, Stu Underhill and Gerry Long, and then Harold King drifted in. Long got the first summons, and I was next.

It was off-putting. I had a distinct impression that the director sitting opposite me at the board-room table was quietly snoring, but the questions were as rehearsed: straightforward and easy.

In fact five candidates were interviewed. The fifth was Michael King, son of Cecil King, chairman of the *Daily Mirror* group of newspapers and a former Reuter director. Michael had previously worked for Reuters, on the diplomatic desk.

That evening John Burgess called me to his room.

'Well, Doon,' he said. 'I'm sorry you've not got it, but you are one of three deputies and additionally you are the editor.'

The full announcement listed: 'General Manager: Mr G. Long; Deputy General Managers: Mr D. Campbell, Mr A. P. Crosse, Mr H. S. Underhill; Mr Campbell carries the additional title of Editor.'

I was stunned. And nervous at the thought of my new role: Cole had been a giant, professionally, in global experience and stature.

By contrast, there was no surprise at Long's upgrading to general manager at the age of 39. I had overheard Cole mention him as a potential successor to Lord Astor of *The Times* only a few weeks earlier and guessed, correctly, that John Burgess had consulted Sir Christopher Chancellor.

But what a gesture to foist three deputies on him, without his knowledge or consultation! It took him ten years to shed us three unasked for, unwanted and, to him, operationally irrelevant deputies. I was the last to go. We were strong individual characters, but incapable of coalescing.

Failure to reach an effective or even comfortable working relationship with Gerald Long was a personal disappointment of my last decade at Reuters. It was my fault as much as his. We were totally different characters.

But Long was the right choice to succeed Cole. Nobody else fell into quite the same league. He had a formidable brain, commitment, vision, maybe even a touch of genius. In 17 years as chief executive, he took Reuters' total revenue from £3 million to £90 million, with the economic services revolutionised by computers accounting for 86 per cent of it.

Outside the office I often enjoyed his company – if occasionally quirky, he could be fun. I recall the boyish boisterousness with which he hurled himself into the snow after a Helsinki sauna with the head of the Finnish news agency. He loved cooking; it was not unusual to go to his Highgate house for dinner and find him in the kitchen preparing the meal, or in the cellar choosing the wine.

Though considered fierce, he was not vindictive, and could be tolerant of human inadequacies. I remember a loutish Scottish sub asking, at a formal dinner hosted by the head of the West German news agency, 'Has anyone ever told you of your resemblance to Colonel Blimp?' Long carried on as if nothing had been said.

Having joined the army as a private in 1943, when he was 20, he had trained as an army parachutist but, with his fluent German and French, ended his military career as a major helping to establish the postwar German press. He then returned to Cambridge until 1948, when he joined Reuters, working in Turkey, France and Germany, including as news editor in Paris under Harold King, and chief representative in Germany.

He represented Reuters well, and was much in demand for lectures, and at seminars and conferences, for his positive thinking and forthright expression. He was well read, cultured, and his interest in design (he was a member of the British Design Council from 1973–8) led to the widely-praised Reuter 'dots' logo and the flowing lines of the Reuters data access television monitor.

This interest led to a lengthy and on the whole favourable article about him in the *Financial Times*, but he refused to allow it to be reproduced in the Reuters staff newsletter. He gave no reason, just the order, 'Don't use'.

Long was ready to take risks, but never rash; willing to be an intellectual bully to get his own way, well able to 'flannel' if that seemed more likely to work. But he could be arrogant, easily bored and impatient; his moods could be mercurial. One moment he would be guffawing loudly with his whole frame heaving, the next morose and sulky. During our rare confessionals, he told me both that he and I had worked well together, and also that we had never worked well together even before he became general manager. He was to my mind an unusually complicated, even tortured personality weakened mostly by his flawed judgement of character.

As soon as he was appointed, Long moved into the general manager's spacious seventh-floor suite, and asked me if I wanted to move up with the other deputy GMs. I thought that as editor I should stay where I was, in close operational contact with the newsroom.

There was, in fact, little difference between being news manager and being editor, though there was a difference in doing it under Long instead of Cole. Cole had seldom left me uninterrupted for more than an hour at a time, morning, noon or night, and every issue of my fortnightly review came back to me with his comments all over it, critical or congratulatory. Long left me undisturbed, with minimal interference and no valid comment on the reviews.

I had succeeded Cole as editor of a news service whose standards were now widely recognised. In October 1962, when the commemorative plaque was unveiled on the house in Aachen, West Germany, where Paul Julius Reuter launched his original pigeon post service, one British newspaper had paid a glowing tribute to the agency by saying that in an age of often conflicting mass communications, Reuters was read and trusted by Capitalist and Communist alike, by East and West, by Arab and Jew and by Hindu and Muslim. Even Hitler, the article added, never thought twice about believing Reuters, and when he intercepted a Reuter cable in his Berlin bunker giving the news of Himmler's betrayal, he immediately made his plans for suicide. Around that time a Hong Kong racehorse owner had also apparently named one of his best horses 'Reuters' and, when asked why, had explained, 'Because it's fast and true.'

A few months after Cole's death, I attended a reception at

Charterhouse in the City of London, the first time Queen Elizabeth and the Duke of Edinburgh had been entertained by Reuters. The Queen, hearing my proud title, asked me the typically simple and direct question, 'How do you edit Reuters?'

Well, how do you? Reuters then had at least a score of editors at Head Office: desk editors selecting from a flood of up to 500,000 words a day to meet the needs of individual countries or whole continents; political, diplomatic, commonwealth, financial, commodities and sports editors. New York, Paris, Singapore and other main centres had more, but there was only one Editor of Reuters, one person ultimately answerable for all incoming and outgoing copy.

The Editor is expected to have the right man in the right place, at the right time, with the best available communications and 'backup', that essential of contingency planning. He is expected to keep an eye on costs. Yet the Editor is still an editor, expected on certain stories to monitor and compare original cables with edited versions, forever guarding against hold-ups in handling, slanting, or sloppy rewriting, passing the death sentence on dubious stories.

These may be despatches from correspondents over-reacting to ominous manoeuvres or shows of military strength, like the 24-year-old Freddie Forsyth, returning home in East Berlin one night, who found his path impeded by Soviet armoured divisions rumbling along the Karl Marx Allee. A Russian assault on West Berlin looked imminent. What a story! He filed about 300 words, but the sceptical night editor in London was rushing his copy only to my desk, page by page.

'Hold everything,' I instructed, placing a priority phone call to Berlin. Years later, now a best-selling novelist, Forsyth recalled the oucome, 'Then a wise old hand in London suggested a check if it was a Russian rehearsal for May Day parade. It was.'

Something like this lay behind my hasty answer to the Queen's question. I replied, 'Easier to do than describe, Ma'am. Accuracy comes first, transcends everything. If Reuters says so, it's true; it had better be! Then balance and speed. We try to be first. Usually are. The chances are, if you're first, newspapers and radio will use your copy.'

As often before in my career, I should have cut my wordage, and left my reply as, 'Easier to do magic than describe it, Ma'am.'

An event in that first year as editor was a curtain-raiser to what was to prove one of the great worries of my final years: the way we ended Reuters' relationship with Tom Little, general manager of Regional News Services, which distributed news in the Middle East and Latin America. Towards the end of the year I did a two-week business tour of ten Islamic capitals, meeting national news agency chiefs and RNS (formerly Arab News Agency) staff, accompanied throughout by Little.

I had first met him a year or two earlier, when I had to interrupt a lunch Cole was having with Little at Simpsons in the Strand. I suggested to Cole that he might slip out for a moment for the consultation I needed, but he replied, 'Fire ahead, Doon. Tom is one of the family.' Then and at later meetings, Cole indicated implicit trust in Little.

An obituary on Little in *The Times* on 28 February 1975 applauded him as 'one of the best informed writers on Egypt and the Middle East in the 1950s and 60s', and went on:

It was largely through his efforts that the Arab States have today access to world and regional news received by teleprinter in their own language . . .

The Arab News Agency, which he headed for 20 years, was British owned, and it was Little's achievement to transform it from its wartime propaganda role into a professional purveyor of news, collected with accuracy and transmitted with urgency . . .

This would not have been possible without the help, both journalistic and on the communications side, of Reuters, with whom he made arrangements lasting for 14 years to act as the distributor of their service.

My tour with Little went well. We called at Khartoum, Aden,

Bahrain, Kuwait, Baghdad, Teheran, Beirut, Amman, Jerusalem and Cairo, and I did interviews for publication with the Shah of Persia and King Hussein of Jordan.

I enjoyed being editor of Reuters, but it lasted less than two years. After a board meeting on 10 December 1964, Long called me to his room and said the directors had authorised 'a redistribution of responsibility among members of the Reuter administration'.

He wanted me to become European manager. He said our European associates felt the lack of liaison through a top executive, and he considered I was 'well qualified' to handle Europe.

I was reluctant to leave the editorial, making the point that I had only fractured French, with which to take over a beat that had for years been his special preserve, with his fluent French and German.

That did not worry him, he said. He was sure I would make a great success of the job. Cole had 'made a fetish of the language problem'.

I said another member of the administration seemed largely to be doing the work listed.

'He is not doing it at all to my satisfaction,' said Long. 'I want you to take it and make the maximum personal contact with our associates. You can travel as much as you like.'

Underhill would take over the editorial position, but with the 'more appropriate' title of managing editor. 'Remember, he's 50 now, and does not want this intensive travel,' said Long. 'His wife will not take it.'

Next day John Burgess called. I told him I realised I had very limited administrative experience, but the transfer had come as a jolt. Resignation had crossed my mind.

'Don't you dare think of resigning,' said Burgess. 'Reuters is in your blood. Cole killed himself by overwork and we appointed three deputies so that the workload would be shared in future. Crosse and Underhill have both concentrated on admin duties in recent years, and you have done none. Europe will be good for your future, and will give you some ease-up from a round-the-clock news schedule. I have noticed from service messages how often you are on duty at all hours.'

So I left my glass box and instead took responsibility for what was, after all, Reuters' most important and profitable trading region, since European revenue in 1960 was more than twice that of any other continent's. It was also the most competitive, with the leading American agencies distributing direct to subscribers, while we and AFP operated mostly through the national news agencies.

My first sortie was to Germany to tackle the fast-developing television and radio stations. I had not a word of German, but had not missed it when I covered the surrender of Hamburg, and found its absence no handicap now. Most senior officials and media executives spoke fluent English and our excellent chief correspondents in Germany, first Peter Johnson and then Lionel Walsh, were on hand for translation if necessary, as well as setting up meetings.

The tour was a success: it brought new contracts with Deutsche Welle and Deutschland Rundfunk in Cologne, and a new six-year contract in Hamburg with First German Network TV (ARD) worth almost half a million sterling between us and our TV associate, Visnews (later taken over and renamed Reuters Television). ARD became Visnews's second biggest subscriber after the BBC.

It was smooth going after that, and non-stop – Moscow, Scandinavia, and every Western and Eastern European country, except of course Albania.

(Our failure to penetrate Albania had always bothered Cole, and he would have been delighted if he could have known that Ronnie Farquhar got in to cover a football match there in 1965, and that Reuters' services started to be distributed there in 1989.)

After two years, I asked Long if he would like me to cover the Middle East as well as Europe and, in July 1996, he asked me to do so, adding, 'You know the area, and your authority is accepted by the Arab staff in a way no one else's is.' More flannel, of course!

A week later he called me to his office to tell me of 'an intriguing proposal' by Tom Little: that I might succeed him.

I am not going to duplicate here the detail on the relationship between Reuters and RNS given in the official Reuter history, The *Power of News*, which says that when Reuters handed over distribution of its services in the Middle East in 1954, making the Arab News Agency (later RNS) its fourth biggest subscriber, it knew ANA was covertly subsidised by the British government.

I asked Long if he felt it would be in Reuters' interest to have someone like me in Little's job; would he say Reuters would like me to take it? He said he would not do that; it was entirely up to me. He could not say the projected RNS job was more important than Europe, where I had done 'remarkably well', but I might feel it offered scope, reward and the satisfaction of being my own boss.

He said he did not have details about RNS, and did not know of the existence of two files, which I mentioned as bearing notes saying they could be read only with the permission of the general manager, Stuart Underhill and Patrick Crosse. But, he said, I should certainly look at them, and see Little to establish what I could about the set-up. He would understand if some of the things I heard were so confidential I did not want to pass them on to him.

At lunch with Little on 19 July I asked what the ANA/RNS actually was. He said it was a government-subsidised news service, with no government interference in the handling of news. He would never tolerate that, and he had always had his way without argument. No world news agency could meet the cost of making a service in Arabic, which it had to be if it was to penetrate the Middle East. What the government paid for in effect was the cost of turning the news into Arabic.

The RNS relationship with Reuters was Cole's concept, as a way to get money without strings. Before Cole died, it had been arranged that Little would secure finance for Reuters to operate in Latin America, which the British government also wanted.

Little told me he was due to retire in five years. I gave Long a full report of this interview, and then got on with the trading job, dealing mostly with general news contracts, but sometimes looking at the RES (Reuters Economic Services) position. Twice a year I went to Frankfurt with Mike Nelson for meetings of VWD, the West German economic news agency in which Reuters had a one-third shareholding.

It was a joy to have Nelson on these trips; he was always so consummately well primed, courteous but tough, always realistic and stable. He was also with me in The Hague for talks with the Dutch news agency, which drew plaudits from Long for my 'tact and skill' on a delicate mission.

The next year, 1967, Long sent Underhill to the United States for three months to assess the situation created by the AP giving notice on our swap arrangement, and in September we cut loose and went over to doing all our own reporting of the US. The board was reluctant but, to his credit, Long pressed them into the calculated risk of authorising it.

The Middle East was still part of my patch and in May 1968, I reminded Long that since we had not ended the ANA/RNS agreement in 1965, as we could have done under the contract, we should give notice by the end of the year. I suggested a formula for a short-term renewal.

Long asked me how I was placed to do a two-month survey of the area to evaluate the trading prospects. I said I could do that, but in July Long said I was so well known in the area that people might draw conclusions. He was going to send in Shahe ('Gubby') Guebenlian, as a senior Reuter representative looking at things, before we decided what to do about renewing the contract. Little, meanwhile, was apparently told that Guebenlian was being sent in order not to disturb my holiday plans and 'because I might be needed for India'!

Six days later, I was told by a source quoting Guebenlian, 'It's all over. We are taking over from RNS. We are going it alone.'

In October Brian Horton, who had written the briefing letter for Guebenlian's tour, was promoted to assistant GM and editor in chief of the general news division, with David Chipp as editor responsible for general news production. Underhill was moved to New York to assume 'overall direction of the company's affairs in North America'.

In November, I saw Guebenlian's report, and told Horton I had reservations over the revenue predictions, and did not like the proposed tie-up with MENA, the Middle East News Agency, because it was a branch of the Egyptian government, and incompetent to boot.

Next day, as requested, I told Tom Little that we were studying Gubby's report and had not reached any conclusions – only to learn that evening that Long and Horton had already told the Foreign Office that Reuters might aim to take over by next 1 April. I told Horton we should not risk the appearance of misrepresentation, but should take Little into our confidence. His view was that we should leave it to the Foreign Office to tell Little.

When I remarked during a board lunch on 13 November on an item in the *UK Press Gazette* that week in which the BBC's Director-General Designate, Charles Curran, was quoted as urging the need for Reuters to remain strong and able to report from as many places as possible. Horton replied, 'Yes, that's all part of the plan. The BBC will pay us a lot more.' In other words, the government subvention towards our costs would be channelled through the BBC subscription instead of that from RNS.

Less than a week later, on 19 November, Horton phoned me to say he was seeing Little that afternoon to tell him of Reuters' decision to operate independently from 1 July. I repeated an earlier suggestion that we retain him as a consultant, but Horton refused.

That afternoon, Tom Little looked into my office to say he had had 'an upner and downer' with Horton. It was the first time anyone had told him of our intentions, and Horton had also said he was going to put Guebenlian into the area.

Then Horton phoned me and told much the same story, saying Little had 'reacted violently'. He asked me to continue liaison with RNS to ensure a smooth hand-over.

Over the next few weeks I had numerous lunches and phone conversations with Little. He said he would do nothing to oppose the hand-over to Reuters, and though Associated Press would be glad to work with him and a deputation of Lebanese editors had told him they would maintain their subscriptions if RNS continued with a regional service, he would not contemplate any successor organisation that would compete with Reuters.

He had always believed that Reuters should take over, and if Reuters had chosen to work with him everything could have been arranged smoothly, but he had learned that the Reuter document put in (presumably to the Foreign Office) before he saw Horton on 19 November specifically asked for his early removal as 'an obstacle to the implementation of the Reuter plan'.

On 2 December 1968 Long called me in to tell me he would like me to take over promotion and publicity, including helping to look after visitors to Head Office, but also to continue doing Spain and Israel. How did I feel about that?

I said I was hardly elated at the erosion of my duties, and wondered how anyone could do promotion and publicity if he was not in on all policy and other meaningful meetings. Long said he saw the point, and we should discuss it again after giving it further thought.

My exclusion from information was borne in on me powerfully on 17 December when I encountered Gubby, who told me the Reuter board, meeting five days before, had approved the Reuter plan to go it alone in the Middle East. Nobody else had told me.

The same day I ran into Gubby, Brian Stockwell (who had been responsible for staff policy since 1963 and was liked and trusted by everyone) told me he had sketched out a very rough job specification for me to see. It looked to me like a job for a section, not one man, and I again asked how I could do promotion and publicity if I was excluded from policy and other meetings.

'You would have to come to any meeting you wanted,' said Brian, and went on to suggest that I should also keep the responsibility for selected contracts, in view of my close personal relationship with the heads of several European and Middle Eastern news agencies, and newspaper executives.

In a letter to Stockwell on 4 January 1969, I suggested the promotion and publicity responsibilities be limited to: contact with the media; presentation of the Reuter image externally and internally; organising and editing a house magazine; supervising the production of brochures; and arranging the London visits of important clients. I also listed nine contracts to look after.

Five days later, Long wrote that the way I grouped the activities 'seemed a very sensible view', and he wished me success with the job. He reminded me that it was a service function, so the budgets for promotion and publicity were the responsibility of the heads of the two divisions; internal communications, including the launching of a house journal, were the primary responsibility of Brian Stockwell, and all general news contracts were Horton's responsibility. My activities would have to be in consultation with them.

That consultation aspect was also embodied in the staff notice of my new post as 'the Company's co-ordinator of publicity and promotion' starting on 1 February.

Having for years produced a fortnightly review or newsletter without guidance from anyone, on 19 February I sent senior editorial staff in London and overseas a briefing, and also wrote a letter asking the new chairman, William Barnetson of United Newspapers, if he would launch in the house magazine a regular column in which somebody would describe in each issue his normal working day.

Three days later a letter from Long told me to 'cease all activity

until you have prepared and had approved by the executive committee a detailed plan for your activities'. My briefing had said we were
planning a house journal but, Long said, there could be no such
statement until the executive committee had seen a detailed budget
and submissions on make-up and content.

He also disapproved of the fact that I had quoted from the
Company's 1969 Budget, disclosing that the growth of RES (Reuters
Economic Services) revenue was expected to be higher than that of
the General News Division (GND).

In March 1969 I launched the new *Reuters Newsletter*, which was to run
until superseded by the *Review* magazine in mid-1975. And in August,
I was plucked from Fleet Street for an exciting if brief adventure:
meeting and escorting Anthony Grey on his release after 806 days of
virtual solitary confinement in his Peking house.

I knew Tony well, having been involved in his recruitment from
Norwich's *Eastern Daily Press* through its editor, Stanley Bagshaw.
Grey was a high-calibre newsman, of attractive personality and char-
acter, and a successful correspondent in many parts of Western and
Eastern Europe before being sent to Peking in 1967. He had done
nothing to warrant his arrest, and was an innocent victim of Mao
Tse-tung's Cultural Revolution.

The usual exit from Peking to the West was via Hong Kong, but the
then Governor of Hong Kong tried to get Reuters to advise Grey not
to take this route. Horton responded that Grey's route depended on
his feelings and state of health. Reuters wanted him out as quickly as
possible, and did not want to commit him to a long flight home without a rest after his ordeal.

The Governor's view – which the Foreign Office said was supported by the British Chargé d'Affaires in Peking – was that at any press
conference in Hong Kong, Grey was likely to face 'loaded questions'.
After talking to me and Brian Stockwell, Horton rightly told the

Foreign Office we were not prepared to direct Grey to leave by any particular route.

We would make arrangements to receive him in Hong Kong. If he himself chose to leave by a Pakistan Airways flight, we would switch those arrangements to Karachi.

In late September I flew to Beirut, arranged with our bureau chief, Ian Macdowall, for him to join me later in either Hong Kong or Karachi, then flew on to Hong Kong and booked into the Mandarin Hotel. When an official from the British Chargé's Peking office came to Hong Kong a couple of days later, I had a long interview about Tony Grey's health, which was widely published, including a front-page byline in *The Times*.

We learned at very short notice that Tony would leave on a Pakistani plane bound for Dacca, in what is now Bangladesh. That meant I must fly to Karachi in West Pakistan, link up with Ian Macdowall, and cross the sub-continent to Dacca before Tony's plane got there from Peking.

I booked four first-class seats at the very front of Tony's plane, and tried to persuade the airline officials not to allow anyone else on to the aircraft in Dacca until just before we were due for take-off for the journey to Karachi. Everything went more or less according to plan.

Tony and I had the front two seats; behind were Ian and the minder, George Walden, whom the British Mission had thoughtfully attached to Tony for his flight home. Across the aisle about six British newsmen, including the *Daily Express*, *Daily Mirror* and BBC, fired questions.

I could see that Tony, though remarkably composed, coherent and articulate, was still fragile, and it was my job to ensure he was not harassed, so I crossed over and gave them a few words in choice Campbellese. However, Tony was still a newsman, and realised they had a job to do, so we worked out a compromise.

They were to nominate one person who would come and squat

between us, put the questions, and feed the answers to the others. They nominated Ian Brodie, of the *Express*, and Tony answered his questions for about an hour.

I had been worried about finding a haven in Karachi where Tony could rest before the long haul to London, but the British High Commission there offered the Residence, where he had two or three restful nights, before flying on to London to face a demanding barrage of media attention that only began to abate with the publication of his book, *Hostage in Peking*, a year or so later.

In December 1969 the bubble of Stuart Underhill's 1968 assumption of overall command in North America burst. First with the news was communications expert John Meadows, who told me, 'Complete management disarray in New York. Underhill's likely to quit.'

A few days later Underhill himself put his head round my door, to tell me he was 'quitting, retiring' after a violent disagreement with Long. This related to a former Comtelburo news editor in London, who had planned the new economic service coverage and started the expansion of Reuters Economic Services in North America.

Underhill said he had miscalculated. He had gone to New York to be in charge, but had found the RES executive was reporting direct to Mike Nelson, without even giving him a copy of his reports. He had got no backing when he tried to correct things. But the parting would be amicable; Reuters had been generous.

I was not officially told the news about Underhill until three hours before the issue of a Staff Notice announcing that he would retire on 31 March 1970, and the RES executive would be the senior company representative in North America until January 1971, when Glen Renfrew would take over as manager.

The lowest mark of my 30 years with Reuters was reached at three confrontations with Gerry Long in the spring of 1970, at all of which the treatment of Underhill and Little, as well as my own future role, were acerbically discussed. The meetings ended with no decisions on anything.

After all this, on 21 May, I had a letter from Long in which he surprised me by repeating that I was responsible for co-ordinating the Company's public relations, recognised that there had been 'deficiencies in the flow of information which you need to carry out your public relations function effectively', and said the operating divisions and service departments were responsible for making it available.

The *Newsletter*, he said, would be replaced in 1971 by a house magazine, with an editor responsible to Brian Stockwell. Creation of this post was necessary to build up the staff department to a point where it could handle all the functions for which it was responsible.

An advertising agency, responsible to the divisions, would be employed to deal with media advertising, and the contracts for which I had been responsible could be handled by the divisions involved.

The following February, I became the last survivor of the original three deputy general managers, when Patrick Crosse took early retirement. I heard about it first from Dissentshik of *Maariv*. Then Long told me, saying that Patrick's attitude was that Gerry was running Reuters the right way for Reuters, though it was not the way he himself would have run it. Long accepted this different viewpoint.

He told me he would be naming Brian Stockwell as deputy general manager, and would be issuing a detailed note setting out the Company's management and structure.

I continued to produce the *Newsletter* for the next 18 months, but it did not turn out to be a time which I remember with much pleasure. However when I finally handed over the *Newsletter* to my successor, Michael Charvet, he very kindly solicited and published in it a selection of reminiscences and tributes from some of the men with whom I had worked closely over my 30 years at Reuters. What they wrote was both moving and amusing by turns and this certainly eased the pain of parting.

16
To United with Barnetson

In November 1972, the chairman, by now Sir William Barnetson, invited me to his office nearby in Tudor Street and asked me to become manager external relations (public relations officer) for United Newspapers, and to help with the Commonwealth Press Union of which he had just become chairman.

He had checked with Long, who had agreed but suggested that for the first couple of years Reuters should retain part of my services on a consultancy basis.

United Newspapers was already one of the country's fastest-growing groups, then publishing two morning papers, seven evenings and 42 weeklies, almost wholly in Yorkshire and Lancashire, and also owning *Punch*, *The Countryman* and four popular farming journals. They had had a good half-year and better was still to come, Barnetson said, 'the big breakthrough is at hand'.

But he sometimes felt the group suffered from underexposure. It needed a PR executive and he believed I sometimes felt I did not really have enough to do at Reuters. If I took the job, I would report to him, run a small compact unit and also edit the Commonwealth Press Union's quarterly magazine. Everything I heard from him was hugely acceptable.

Gerry Long was away in Europe, so I did not see him until 14 November. He said that Reuters would still have a sizeable stake in my services for the first two years. He wanted me to go on producing Reuters' *Newsletter*, which had settled down into the right formula, excellent for morale, widely and favourably commented upon, indeed the envy of many offices. He also wanted me to handle some liaison and support work at Reuters.

So it was arranged. From 12 March 1973, I became manager external relations at United Newspapers, while remaining technically on the Reuters payroll and responsible for the Reuters *Newsletter*. I was to retire from Reuters and switch to the United Newspapers payroll on 12 March 1975. My Reuter pension was protected.

Long organised a farewell lunch for me, with my own guest list to which I added the name of Patrick Crosse. In a generous note of appreciation, Patrick later wrote, 'It was an evocative occasion and I greatly admired the way you handled it. I also admire the elegance and dignity with which you have lived through and, happily, passed by a period which must have presented many and bitter difficulties.'

Whatever the difficulties of the previous few years, I was sorry to be leaving Reuters. It had been my passion for approaching 30 years and I had belonged there, and been proud of that. But if your mistress, 'magic' or otherwise, no longer wants you, the best thing is to get out – on the best available terms. I felt no acrimony. I could see that Gerry Long had performed a tremendous service in lifting the agency out of the grinding poverty which for so long had stunted its growth potential. We exchanged parting letters of mutual praise.

The world outside Reuters turned out to be a surprise. I had never imagined that Fleet Street or, in a wider sense, journalism could offer such stimulating and satisfying experience as I enjoyed with Bill Barnetson, first as Sir William, later as Lord.

The more I got to know this soft-spoken little Scot, with a legendary capacity for work, the more I came to admire him. Regardless of pressures, he was always courteous, patient and human and never known to lose his cool, much less his temper.

Nothing was too much trouble for him. He seemed to thrive on taking on new duties and responsibilities, often unpaid. Night after night, often still in the dinner jacket in which he had just made a speech, he was there at his desk, bashing away at his old manual typewriter, drafting the address that would be acclaimed at tomorrow's or next week's dinner.

Even before I had moved into my office at United, he passed me a list of 24 questions submitted by a well known Scottish chartered accountant who was doing a piece on Reuters in *The Accountant's Magazine*. When I produced about three *Times*-length columns, Barnetson read them and, without changing a word, passed them back to me to give to the magazine. No messing about, or changing words for the sake of it. Life was going to be different.

It was also hectic. In addition to United Newspapers, Reuters, *The Observer*, Thames Television and the Commonwealth Press Union (1972–7), Barnetson was president of the Newsvendors' Benevolent Institute, the Advertising Association, the Press Club, the Periodical Publishers' Association and many other charitable and professional bodies. He was deputy chairman of British Electric Traction, master of the Guild of St Bride, appeal chairman for one year for the Newspaper Press Fund and he undertook many engagements for the Queen's Silver Jubilee Appeal, hosting lunches and dinners in London and Edinburgh.

He readily put United Newspapers resources behind me for the CPU quarterly magazine and, like Cole at Reuters, he was really the editor-in-chief, always ready to pitch in, lend a hand, always constructive, providing suggestions and plenty of morale-raising notes, especially when advertising revenue made a worthwhile profit.

He even suggested sending me to a meeting of the Commonwealth Finance Ministers in Canada as the quarterly's own correspondent, and before biennial CPU conferences he would send me ahead, across Canada, South-East Asia and India to reconnoitre the route, appraise hotels, check the quality of their food and facilities, and alert the delegates to hazards. Then I went along again to ensure full photo and news coverage.

Many thought Barnetson was one of London's most gifted public speakers. Unless dealing with a matter of some gravitas, he usually kept his speeches brief and witty. Every spring he gave two big lunches at the Savoy for 'friends of United Newspapers', each of which by the 70s included well over a hundred guests, including cabinet ministers, diplomats, business leaders, media moguls and churchmen.

An example of his skill as a speechmaker came in 1976, American Bicentennial Year, when I was able to warn him that the principal guest, the American Ambassador, Mrs Anne Armstrong, intended to deliver a special message, rather than just a few conventional remarks. With only a few hours to compose something appropriate to cementing Anglo-American relations, Barnetson offered this:

. . . for me our ties, our affiliations are symbolised by what took place in one of Glasgow's station hotels in the early months of 1941. Harry Hopkins had been sent by President Roosevelt to find out at first hand how beleaguered Britain was getting on, how morale was standing up to perpetual bombardments, and whether we really had the will to survive . . . Winston Churchill, anxious for even the slightest indication of what might be reported to the President, found him poker-faced and dumb as an oyster. And so the final dinner with still not a word, not a sign from Harry Hopkins. Then Tom Johnston, Secretary of State for Scotland . . . welcomed Hopkins 'not only for himself but specially for the sake of his old grandmother from Auchterarder.'

And then, slowly, Harry Hopkins rose ashen-faced and enigmatic. 'Mr Chairman,' he said, 'I am not making speeches over here. I am reporting what I see to the President, a very great man. But now that I am on my feet, perhaps I might say in the language of the old book to which my grandmother from Auchterarder paid so much attention (and here he looked down the table, straight at Churchill), "Wheresoever thou goest we go; and where thou lodgest we lodge,

thy people shall be my people; thy God our God, even unto the end".' Winston's
eyes welled up with tears, for this was the answer – the answer to so many things.

Anne Armstrong, moved, but keeping her composure, capped it neatly:

. . . our debt to Britain, of course, is indelible . . . My countryman Emerson trav-
elled to your land, met your forebears about 125 years ago. His conclusions were
strikingly favourable. He described Britain as America's lawgiver, instructor and
ally. Time has neither eroded nor changed that view.
* If I, too, may use the Testament to sum up my feelings on this warm occasion*
I would quote David (with some journalistic licence): 'How good and pleasant it
is for brothers to dwell together in unity. It is like the precious ointment on the head
and dew on the land.' That is how I feel about the kinship between America and
Britain today, and for years to come.

Barnetson was also skilled in other luncheon arts. We took a lot of
trouble to avoid having incompatible people seated close to each
other. I once caused a *frisson* of embarrassment when I went to check
place cards and found a senior cabinet minister switching them for
more senior and congenial names.

Sometimes an unfortunate juxtaposition would slip through our
guard. I recall interrupting Barnetson at a meeting with his board to
tell him that one of the peers invited to that day's Savoy lunch had
telephoned to say, 'Please tell Bill Barnetson that I cannot make his
lunch because I refuse to break bread with that b***** X, who is at
the same table.'

Quick as a flash, Barnetson instructed, 'Call him back, say sorry
about the slip-up but Barnetson says you're not just invited by him –
the Prince of Wales commands you to be at his table.' Prince Charles,
had, of course, no knowledge of the episode but it worked. The peer
turned up, and afterwards sought me out to offer thanks.

Barnetson never showed annoyance at being interrupted in that way. He was one of the most unpompous men in Fleet Street, always willing to enter into the spirit of the occasion – such as being photographed with a headful of snakes at a Penang temple.

Informally and unheralded, he used to pop into my office several times a week – or even a day – to show me something, invite ideas, test my reaction to a draft and so on. He was a wonderful boss, demanding yet considerate. He had rarely fewer than a dozen charitable commitments at any one time and he encouraged me to do the same. Working closely with such a man enriched the last years of my working life.

It was mainly, I imagine, my work for the newsmen's charity, the Newspaper Press Fund, the Commonwealth Press Union, the British Press Awards and other voluntary bodies that led to my being awarded the OBE.

However, whatever the pleasures and the satisfactions of working for Barnetson and United Newspapers, I was in many ways still under Reuters' magic spell. One of its most appreciated gestures – and Reuters made so many – was offering me a place, despite my septuagenarian status, in the editorial teams handling the 50th anniversaries of D-Day, in 1994, and of Indian Independence, in 1997.

Excessively complimentary though Reuters was, I felt a bit out of my time: I hadn't a clue how to operate the laptop computer and sophisticated telephone which were part of my kit. Here I was, with a nine-year-old grandson who could extract from the Internet a two-page printout of my own Gandhi assassination coverage, yet I had to stick with a notebook and pencil as I had 50 years before.

On a more personal note: Mary, an adored wife and mother, died in 1995. We had enjoyed 46 years together, first in Paris, then Coulsdon and then 40 years at Whitmore, which had been Mary's home in Merstham. We were blessed with three children: Kate, Archie and Andy, who between them gave us seven grandchildren. Thanks to Reuters and United Newspapers, we travelled extensively abroad together, mainly but not always with the Commonwealth Union, visiting Canada, Singapore, Malaysia and Hong Kong; Fiji, Hawaii, Australia, New Zealand, India, Bermuda and Jamaica.

Mary's death was a devastating blow because, besides presiding lovingly and so efficiently over the home, she had played such a supportive role in my working life. My desolation was eased by linking up again with my former fiancée, Pat Cameron, some 50 years after our parting in Edinburgh.

We had never really been together over these five decades – only for two unanticipated and fleeting meetings. Once by a freak coincidence in the early 70s we had bumped into each other on a London Underground train. With a Reuter colleague, I was returning from some assignment when Pat, in London for a short break with her husband, joined the same coach at Westminster. All three of us got off the train at Blackfriars, and enjoyed an impromptu glass of champagne at the City Golf Club.

The second occasion occurred some ten years later, in October 1984, when we found ourselves by chance among 100 guests at an *Evening Dispatch* reunion dinner at the George Hotel in Edinburgh. This again gave us a brief chance to catch up on each other's lives before another long interval of time elapsed.

I had always kept Pat's phone number, updated from time to time by my brother, a retired bank manager living in Dunbar. His home was within easy driving distance of Selkirk, where Pat, widowed for 12 years, had long lived. One day, on an impulse, I phoned her to ask if she would meet me for lunch if I routed myself through Selkirk on the way to visit my brother, who was ailing. She took a few moments to absorb the impact of my call – and agreed. We met and quickly found that our mutual enjoyment of each other's company had in no way diminished. We are above all comfortable with each other and I am pleased to record that our warm friendship continues as I write the closing lines of this memoir.

Index

INDEX

INDEX

INDEX

INDEX

Acknowledgements

The author and publishers wish to thank the following for permission to reproduce copyright material: *Daily Record*, between pp. 122 and 123; *The Observer*, pp. 236–7; Reuters, for the use of the former logo (back cover) and for the quotation on the back cover and on p. ii from a booklet about the news agency published in 1962; extract from *The Times*' obituary of Tom Little on p. 293, copyright Times Newspapers Limited 28 February 1975.

The author and publishers also wish to thank the following for permission to reproduce photographs and illustrations between pp. 122 and 123, between pp. 192 and 193 and on the cover: Reuters for a cartoon from *Reuters World* and for photos that formerly bore the Reuter-PA credit; PA News, London; Imperial War Museum, London; Photo-Jugend, Tel Aviv; cartoon from *Eagle*, copyright the Dan Dare Corporation Ltd. Every effort has been made to trace the copyright holders of other material.